AN ILLUSTRATED HISTORY

THE 23RD WAFFEN-SS

VOLUNTEER PANZERGRENADIER DIVISION

NEDERLAND

Massimiliano Afiero

Schiffer Publishing Ltd

4880 Lower Valley Road • Atglen, PA 19310

Library of Congress Control Number: 2016935493

Cover & Interior design by Matt Goodman
Type set in Minion & Antique Olive Std.
ISBN: 978-0-7643-5073-3
Printed in China

Published by Schiffer Publishing, Ltd.
4880 Lower Valley Road
Atglen, PA 19310
Phone: (610) 593-1777; Fax: (610) 593-2002
E-mail: Info@schifferbooks.com

Originally published as *23a divisione SS 'Nederland'* by Associazione Culturale Ritterkreuz
© 2014 by Associazione Culturale Ritterkreuz, Afragola, Campania, Italy.
Translated from the Italian by Ralph Riccio.

For our complete selection of fine books on this and related subjects, please visit our website at www.schifferbooks.com. You may also write for a free catalog.

Schiffer Publishing's titles are available at special discounts for bulk purchases for sales promotions or premiums. Special editions, including personalized covers, corporate imprints, and excerpts, can be created in large quantities for special needs. For more information, contact the publisher.

We are always looking for people to write books on new and related subjects. If you have an idea for a book, please contact us at proposals@schifferbooks.com.

CONTENTS

CHAPTER VII:

KAMPFGRUPPE WAGNER 68

CHAPTER VIII:

KURLAND 77

CHAPTER IX:

THE POMERANIAN FRONT 88

CHAPTER X:

THE ODER FRONT 99

CHAPTER XI

THE HALBE POCKET 103

APPENDICES 109

GLOSSARY 138

BIBLIOGRAPHY & ENDNOTES 139

INTRODUCTION

The name of the SS Division *Nederland* is linked to the main defensive battles in the northern sector of the eastern front, from Leningrad to the final desperate battles along the Oder River, continuing on to only a few miles from Berlin, capital of the Third Reich, in the final defense against the advancing Soviet troops. This is a unit that surely is one of the least studied and analyzed by most Waffen-SS historians, and which has had few editorial works devoted to it, such as that by Wilhelm Tieke dedicated to the III SS Corps and that by Perry Pierek, which was not published in English until 2001. All of this is despite the fact that the first foreign volunteer to be awarded the Knight's Cross was in fact Dutch, Gerardus Mooyman, and that Holland was among the countries that furnished the greatest number of volunteers to the Waffen-SS throughout the war, taking into account the size of its population.

Attached to the German III SS Armored Corps under *General* Felix Steiner, the unit was always employed as a quick reaction force, called on to plug gaps in the front lines or to cover the withdrawal of other units; the many decorations awarded to Dutch volunteers and numerous citations by German commands are a clear testimony to their courage and to their dedication to sense of duty. Employed exclusively on the Eastern Front, except for a brief initial period in Croatia while with the *III. SS-Pz.Korps*, the Dutch SS formation took part in all of the toughest defensive battles on the northeastern front: the Leningrad front, the bridgehead at Narva (Narwa in German), the Tannenberg line, Dorpat, Kurland, Pomerania, the Oder front, until the last desperate battle of the Halbe Pocket, where the last remnants of the division managed to avoid total annihilation, fleeing from the Soviets and turning themselves in to the American forces. In all of these battles the Dutch volunteers displayed all of their courage, showing themselves to be true Waffen-SS combatants, always on the front lines and always under constant enemy pressure.

Even though its military history was very brief, *Nederland* surely can be considered to be one of the best "foreign" volunteer military units of the Waffen-SS, and with this volume we hope to fill a void and to honor the memory of so many young Dutch and European combatants who died for Europe, fighting against Bolshevism.

ACKNOWLEDGMENTS

Production of this study was made possible by the assistance of many Italian and foreign friends and colleagues who assisted me with research concerning this Dutch unit, drawing upon the assets of the major military archives throughout the world. To list them all would be impossible, and I convey my heartfelt thanks to each and every one who assisted me and hope that this volume has resulted in a satisfactory effort.

CHAPTER I

THE DUTCH VOLUNTEERS IN THE WAFFEN-SS

Beginning in the 1930s, a large number of right-wing movements close to the Fascist and National Socialist ideology had sprung up in Holland. Among these, one that stood out prominently was the *National-Socialistische Beweging* (NSB) under Anton Adrian Mussert, an engineer who was an expert on canals and locks, as well as being in charge of the water system for the entire province of Utrecht. In addition to being a well-organized party, the NSB had its own assault militia, the *Weerbaarheidsafdeling* (literally, Defense Militia) led by ex-sergeant A.J. Zondervan, formed in November 1932. In December 1935, it was disbanded by order of the Dutch government and was not reestablished until May 1940. The uniform of *WA* members was all black, and the identifying insignia was the runic *Wolfsangel* (wolf's hook). Despite the name of his movement and his title of "*Leider*," Mussert was not a completely convinced National Socialist. He had adopted the Fascist style only so that he could follow a certain fashion of the time as well as to gain support. Up to the time of the German invasion of Holland Mussert remained very much attached to the Dutch royal family, to Christian values, and to a certain moral order, all of which were concepts very far removed from Hitlerian paganism. His deputy, Van Geelkerken, was however much more "fascist." In 1934, the NSB had 20,000 members and received fully 30,000 votes in the elections of the following year. The number of members grew dramatically until the outbreak of the war. On the eve of the war, two factions sprang up within the NSB, one which was moderate and the other which was more activist, the latter of which favored a policy of collaboration with Germany. The activists were led by Rost van Tonningen, a former Dutch commissioner of the League of Nations, who in 1936 had arranged a meeting between Mussert and Adolf Hitler. Among the other Dutch movements worthy of note was the NSNAP, led by Ridder Van Rappard, an exact copy of the German NSDAP, that had about 10,000 members.

A few days before the German invasion van Tonningen was arrested along with thousands of other Dutch citizens, accused of being part of a presumed "fifth column." Some were summarily executed by their jailers during the early hours of the war. Despite this massive presence of elements "favorable" to a policy of collaboration, the Germans wanted to deal with the legitimate government and prevent the Queen from fleeing to England, which however occurred on May 13. Two days later the Dutch armed forces capitulated and Mussert thought that his hour had come. It had been verified that during the course of military operations about a hundred NSB members had openly collaborated with the German forces, fighting against their own countrymen, but received no thanks from Mussert, who in fact expelled them from the party. It was because of this that the Germans, after their experience with the Norwegian leader Vidkun Quisling,

NSB units parading in front of Mussert.

Rost van Tonningen

did not authorize the *Leider* of the NSB to make a radio address to the Dutch populace. On May 19, Doctor Arthur Seyss-Inquart was named as Reichs Commissioner for the occupied Dutch territories. He broadcast an appeal to the Dutch population, written by Hitler himself, in which he looked forward to reintegration of the Low Countries into the Germanic community, avoiding any appeal to the local NSB politicians, a movement that the Germans felt was now too compromised. The party in fact did suffer from reduced membership in the months immediately following the German invasion, not reviving until 1941. On June 5, 1940, Mussert was finally able to meet with Seyss-Inquart, but the talks did not lead to any role for the NSB. The *Reichskommissar* judged Mussert to be too "liberal."

THE *WESTLAND* REGIMENT

In the meantime, on May 25, 1940, by Hitler's personal order, the formation of a new SS regiment, the *Westland*, was authorized in order to gather together the Dutch and Flemish volunteers. The *Westland* Regiment was placed under the command of *SS-Standartenführer* Hilmar Wäckerle. During the First World War, Wäckerle had served as a volunteer in the army, and owing to bravery shown in the field he had been promoted to officer rank. Soon after the end of the war he joined the *Freikorps*, the German Free Corps, fighting in the Baltic countries. In 1934, he joined the *SS-Verfügungstruppe*, initially becoming commander of the first *Sturmbann* of the *SS-Standarte "Germania"* and then in 1938, commander of the *I.Bataillon* of the same *Standarte*. Along with some other officers of this battalion, the *III.Bataillon* of "*Der Führer*" Regiment was formed, whose command he assumed, distinguishing himself in May 1940 during the campaign in the Low Countries. When the campaign in the west was over,

Propaganda postcard showing an officer of the *Westland* Regiment.

Wäckerle was called to lead the new *Westland* Regiment. The first Dutch volunteers were sent to *Freimann* barracks in Munich to begin their military training. In December 1940, the *Westland* Regiment was incorporated into the new SS *Wiking* Division, remaining one of its principal units until the end of the war. On June 9, 1940, SS-*Obergruppenführer* Gottlob Berger, head of the *SS-Hauptamt*, arrived personally in Holland to promote the recruitment of Dutch volunteers. Among the new volunteers was the head of Mussert's personal bodyguard, Heindrik Feldmayer. Unable to prevent his followers from joining the SS, Mussert always hoped to be recognized as their political leader by the Germans. On September 22, Mussert went to Berlin accompanied by Van Geelkerken and van Tonningen, but this meeting also met with negative results. The *Führer*, Adolf Hitler, stated simply to the three Dutchmen that, "... It is in Holland and Norway that the best representatives of the Germanic race live," almost as if to highlight his desire to definitively include Holland in the German *Reich*.

SS-Staf. Otto Reich

The *Nordwest* Regiment

Created by a *Führerbefehl* (order of the Führer) on April 3, 1941, the *Nordwest* was the third SS regiment (after *Nordland* and *Westland*) created at Himmler's behest for the purpose of accepting volunteers of Germanic origin: Flemings, Dutch and Danes. The formation of *6.Freiwilligen Standarte Nordwest* began effectively on April 10. *SS-Standartenführer* Otto Reich was designated to command the regiment. Following an intensive recruiting campaign the regiment reached a strength of about 2,500 men: 1,400 Dutch, 805 Flemings, and 108 Danes. Training the volunteers began first at Hamburg (the camp at Langerhorn), and later at Radom in Poland. There the regiment was divided into two contingents, one which was mostly Dutch was transferred to Krakow, and a Flemish contingent that remained at Radom. According to Himmler's early intentions, the *Nordwest* Regiment was to be used as a security force in northwest Europe in contrast to other SS regiments, which had been created to be employed in the front lines. As the war in the east progressed, things changed. The formations of European volunteer Legions for the fight against Bolshevism led to disbanding the units and transfer of the volunteers into their respective national contingents.

Reichsführer-SS Heinrich Himmler

Members of the Germanic SS in Holland, 1941.

The Germanic SS Units in Holland

Intending to include Holland, northeastern France and Belgium in a new province of the Reich, which was to be called *Burgundia*, *Reichsführer-SS* Heinrich Himmler ordered the establishment in those countries of structures connected directly to the *Allgemeine-SS*, the overall SS structure. In one of his speeches, while visiting Holland, he sought to explain his intentions to the Germanic volunteers:

> ... There will be only one SS Corps in Europe: the Germanic SS. You can resist it, but it makes no difference to me, because we intend to create it in any case. We do not ask you to go against your own country, nor to do anything repugnant, for anyone who is proud of his own country loves it and respects it. We do not expect you to become Germans out of a sense of opportunism. What we ask of you is to subordinate your national ideals to a higher historical and racial ideal, that of a single and all-encompassing Germanic Reich.

At the end of 1942 these national SS formations were gathered together into the new Germanic SS directly subordinate to Himmler himself. The organization of the Germanic SS was entrusted to the *SS-Hauptamt*, which was the general office of the SS. A special Germanic liaison office was also established, the *Germanische Leitstelle*, with branch offices in Oslo, The Hague, and Copenhagen to supervise propaganda and recruitment activity in Western Europe and Scandinavia. Four special camps were created for training the Germanic SS contingents, at Sennheim in Alsace, at Schooten in Belgium, at Hovelte in Denmark, and at Avegoor in Holland. In addition, the *Führerschule der Germanischen-SS*, the training school for Germanic SS officers, was established at Hildesheim, as soon as most of the volunteers had been transferred to the Waffen-SS combat units. In Holland, in November 1940, Mussert's NSB party incorporated its structure into the SS, creating an organization designated the *Nederlandsche-SS*. This initiative was the work of Johannes Hendrik Feldmeijer, the first commander of Mussert's bodyguard detachment. Its personnel wore the elegant black uniforms of the *Allgemeine SS*, imported from Germany, onto which the Dutch attached their own national insignia that consisted of a three-spoked sun wheel, and on their caps, in place of the National Socialist eagle was the runic wolf insignia. In October 1942 the Dutch SS corps was renamed as the *Germaansche-SS en Nederland*, ceasing to be a paramilitary formation of the NSB and to all effects becoming an integral part of the Germanic SS. From that moment on the Dutch volunteers were obliged to swear exclusive loyalty to Adolf Hitler. The *Germaansche-SS en Nederland* was an important reserve manpower pool for the Dutch Waffen-SS combat units.

Arthur Seyss-Inquart

Chapter II
THE DUTCH LEGION

General Seyffardt in Dutch Army full dress uniform.

July 1941: Dutch volunteers flock to the recruiting office for the Dutch Legion at Amsterdam, eager to fight on the Eastern Front.

Arnold Meijer, head of the NF.

The beginning of the campaign in the east called for the formation throughout Europe of volunteer legions to participate alongside the Germans in the crusade against Bolshevism. The idea of forming a legion of Dutch volunteers to fight on the Eastern Front was proposed on June 28, 1941, by the leader of the National Front (*Nationaal Front*), Arnold Meijer. Naturally, the Germans supported the idea and quickly authorized the project. When, however, Meijer learned of the direct involvement of the SS in the legion, he abandoned the project and left the organization in the hands of Anton Mussert's NSB. Meijer wanted an independent national legion, while the SS wanted absolute control of all of the volunteer formations of Germanic origin.[1] Mussert, in contrast to Meijer, guaranteed the Germans his complete support for the formation of the Legion and above all with respect to the recruiting campaign. The head of the NSB saw the Legion as the embryo of a new Dutch army. On July 10, 1941, the *Reichskommisar* in Holland, Arthur Seyss-Inquart, officially announced the establishment of the Dutch Legion, the *Freiwilligen Legion Niederlande* (originally designated the *Freiwilligen Verband Niederlande*). Lieutenant General H.A. Seyffardt, ex-chief-of-staff of the Dutch Army, was chosen as its first commander. The following day the recruiting campaign began throughout the country, promoted by the local chapters of the NSB party. Mussert invited all of the members of the NSB itself to join the Legion to set the example; many young people signed up, especially those who were members of the *Weerbaarheidsafdeling*, who went on to join the 1,400 Dutch volunteers of the disbanded *Nordwest* Regiment.

From nearby Flanders, some Flemish volunteers arrived who preferred to enlist in the Dutch Legion rather than in the Flemish Legion. It should be noted that some Dutch citizens of Asian origin who had emigrated to Holland from the far-off colonies of the Dutch East Indies were also accepted into the ranks. The officer cadre of the Legion was drawn from Dutch officers who were already serving with the *Westland* and *Wiking* regiments.

Departing for Training

Around mid-October 1941, the volunteers were transferred to the *Truppenübungsplatz* at Arys (in Eastern Prussia, now in Poland and known as Orzysz), where their training began under the direction of demanding German instructors. The ability of the young Dutch volunteers to adapt to the discipline and strict German training system was not easy and there were numerous incidents between the *ausbilders* (instructors) and the volunteers. There were also several defections, among those that of the

The Dutch Legion parading.

A view of Mussert from behind his shoulders at the Arys training camp.

Two images of the swearing-in ceremony for Dutch volunteers.

elderly *General* Seyffardt, who tendered his resignation when he realized that the Legion was to become a combat unit of the Waffen-SS. Command of the Legion thus passed to a German officer, *SS-Oberführer* Otto Reich, who had previously commanded the *SS-Totenkopfstandarte 4 Ostmark* and later the *SS-Totenkopfstandarte 2 Brandenburg*.

In early January 1942, the Legion completed its training and was declared officially ready to be transferred to the front. A report dated January 9, 1942, reflected the following personnel strength according to their nationality:

Nationality	Officers	NCOs	Enlisted	Total
German	40	329	331	700
Dutch	26	2	2,179	2,207
Fleming	-	-	26	26
Total	66	331	2,536	2,933

This report shows that most of the units of the Legion were commanded by German officers, while most of the troops were foreign volunteers. The presence of German NCOs, the backbone of any military unit, was particularly high. The *SS-Freiwilligen Legion Niederlande*, with a strength of about 3,000 volunteers, was organized with three infantry battalions, each with four companies, plus a thirteenth company with infantry support guns and a fourteenth anti-tank company.

The Legion Order of Battle

Commander: *SS-Oberführer* Otto Reich

Headquarters Company (*Stab Kompanie*)**:** *Legion Hauptsturmführer* Eduard Voorwinden

Engineer detachment (*Pionier*): *Legion Hauptsturmführer* Quintus De Veer

Signals detachment (*Nachrichten Zug*): *Untertsturmführer* Josef Werner

Administration (*Verwaltung*): *Obertsturmführer* Hermann Lutgerd

Arms and ammunition: *Obertsturmführer* Paul Dirk

A Dutch legionnaire.

I.Bataillon

Commander: *Sturmbannführer* Richard Pohle
1.Kompanie: *Obertsturmführer* Albert Buchner
2.Kompanie: *Hauptsturmführer* Bernhard Frank
3.Kompanie: *Legion Obersturmführer* Jacobus Bevort
4.Kompanie: *Legion Obersturmführer* Rever Clijn

II.Bataillon

Commander: *Hauptsturmführer* Alfred Reich
5.Kompanie: *Obertsturmführer* Wolfgang Vierweger
6.Kompanie: *Untertsturmführer* Josef Heinziger
7.Kompanie: *Hauptsturmführer* Wilhelm Breimaier
8.Kompanie: *Obersturmführer* Fritz Tillmann

III.Bataillon

Commander: *Hauptsturmführer* Willi Breimaier
9.Kompanie: *Hauptsturmführer* Joachim Stoige
10.Kompanie: *Legion Hauptsturmführer* Eduard Voorwinden
11.Kompanie: *Obersturmführer* Adolf Fritsche
12.Kompanie: *Obersturmführer* Friedrich Neidlinger
13.Kompanie-Infanteriegeschütze: *Ostuf.* Heinrich Nikoleit
14.Kompanie-Panzerjäger: *Hauptsturmführer* Kurt Otto

Uniforms

From the beginning, the Dutch legionnaires wore the normal Waffen-SS uniform with a special collar flash, the runic sign of

the wolf hook (*Wolfsangel*), which they wore on the uniform lapel. There were two styles of this flash: horizontal or vertical. In addition, on their Waffen-SS uniform the Dutch volunteers also wore the *Prinsevlag* (the orange, white and blue flag) that was the sleeve patch with the Dutch national colors, also produced in various styles (see the appropriate appendix to this book). In November 1941, the Dutch legion was authorized to wear a cuff title with the German inscription "*Frw.Legion Niederlande*" (Dutch Volunteer Legion).

Transfer to the Front

Once training had been completed, the Dutch volunteers were transferred by sea from Danzig to Libau, around the middle of January 1942. From there, the Legion was moved by train to the front at Volchov, north of Lake Ilmen, smack in the middle of the Soviet winter counteroffensive. The Dutch volunteers were deployed to trenches dug in the snow at Selo Gora, on the Volchov River, in front of the sacred city of Novgorod south of Leningrad, taking over the front lines from the 90th Infantry Regiment of the German 20th Motorized Infantry Division under *Generalmajor* Erich Jaschke.[2] The Dutch Legion was

Generalmajor Erich Jaschke, commander of *20.Inf.Division*.

Forward position of *1./Polizei-Artillerie-Regiment*, protected by tree trunks, in the Gusi-Selo Gora corridor, in February 1942.

Map of the areas in which the Dutch Legion was employed between 1942 and 1943.

initially subordinated to *Generalmajor* Jaschke's division, engaged in various security operations in the rear area of the 18th Army. The Dutch volunteers took up positions in a series of entrenchments between the cities of Tschudovo and Novgorod, with the mission of defending the western bank of the Volchov River. In that area, the Soviets had for days been exerting massive pressure in an attempt to establish a bridgehead on the western bank of the river. But even before dealing with the Soviets, the Dutch volunteers had to defend themselves against the terrible weather conditions, from the cold and the ice, which caused the transfer of the first casualties to the field hospitals. Covering the Legion's flanks, in addition to units of the 20th Division, there were also units from the 254th Division (commanded by *Generalleutnant* Walter Behschnitt). The Dutch, along with other German units, constituted the *Kampfgruppe Jaschke*, named after its commanding general. The 1st Battery of the *SS-Polizei* Division (*1./Polizei-Artillerie-Regiment*) commanded by *Hauptmann*[3] Hellmuth Vogel had been transferred to the Gusi–Selo Gora corridor. This unit remained in this area in support of the Dutch Legion until the middle of April. In early February 1942, the leader of the NSB, Anton Mussert, accompanied by the leader of the *Weerbaarheidsafdeling* Zondervan, made a visit to the legion bringing gift packages to the volunteers and above all a load of winter clothing to protect them better from the bitter cold of Russia. During the visit an official ceremony was also organized during which the first Iron Crosses were presented to the Dutch volunteers who had distinguished themselves in combat.

The Soviets Attack

On February 10, 1942, in the context of the great Russian counteroffensive along the Volchov, the Dutch positions were among those that were hit, first by the heavy preliminary enemy artillery shelling and then by the direct attack of infantry and tanks. The Soviet high command sent experienced Siberian units who were well suited to fighting in the cold and in the snow, in the first wave. The forward positions were overrun, but the Germans reacted promptly and carried out fierce counterattacks in which the Dutch volunteers were also engaged. The orders were clear; to hold the positions at all costs. The Dutch volunteers were able to stem the spirited enemy attack, although they paid a high price in blood. On February 11, the Legion's II Battalion was engaged along the Gora–Gusi road; the Soviets had set up a roadblock and the Dutch were called upon to eliminate it. As the Dutch column was nearing the village of Gusi it fell into an ambush and was attacked by a strong and battle-hardened Soviet unit, losing six men. The

Dutch trench position on the Leningrad front, 1942.

Soviets also suffered significant losses and also had three of their number taken prisoner. The Soviet offensive continued until the end of February, without, however, breaking through the German resistance. During the days that followed the legion was engaged in destroying pockets of Soviet resistance in the area around the villages of Pjatilipy and Gorenka; the forested nature of the area made operations more difficult, but the sweep operation was ultimately successful, with many enemy bunkers having been destroyed by the Dutchmen only after having engaged in violent close-quarter fighting. Having returned to their defensive positions and finding themselves under continuous Soviet artillery fire, the volunteers had to further fortify their own positions, building bunkers and entrenchments. Beginning in January 1942, the legionnaires were also engaged in operations against partisan units, conducting many reconnaissance patrols and several anti-partisan sweeps.

The fighting around Gorenka was especially trying, where the Dutch volunteers had to defend themselves against massive attacks by well-armed and battle-hardened partisan units. After having wrested the forest north of Selo Gora from the Soviets and having eliminated pockets of enemy resistance on both sides of the railway line, the Legion was mentioned in the official *Wehrmacht* bulletin for the first time on March 4, 1942: "... North of Lake Ilmen, the Dutch Legion distinguished itself particularly in combat."

For the entire month of March, Soviet pressure continued to be increasingly stronger; living conditions for the legionnaires accordingly continued to grow worse. The seasonal thaw had transformed the battlefield into an immense quagmire; the trenches had been filled with mud. Under these tragic conditions, the Dutchmen had to continue to defend themselves against enemy attacks. The 1220th Regiment of the 366th Division and the 1002nd of the 305th Siberian divisions attacked the Dutch positions unsuccessfully several times.

From April 1, 1942, the Dutch were temporarily put under command of *SS-Obersturmbannführer* Arved Theurermann, due to the momentary absence of *SS-Oberführer* Reich. During one frigid night in early April, about two Soviet platoons infiltrated the village of Gusi. The enemy penetration was quickly eliminated thanks to the exemplary cooperation between elements of the Dutch Legion and *1./Polizei-Artillerie-Regiment*, after furious close-quarter fighting. On April 6, the Soviets returned to attack the Dutch positions, preceding their infantry assault with a massive artillery barrage and heavy bombing by aircraft. Once the maelstrom of fire was over, a thousand Soviet infantrymen charged against the trenches defended by the Dutch; the fire from machine guns and mortars once again stopped the advance of the Soviet hordes that were finally forced to withdraw. Other attacks followed, but the Dutch managed to maintain a firm hold on their positions. At the end of April, the Soviets came back again to attack the village of Gusi, which had been abandoned a few days earlier by elements of the *Polizei*. But although by themselves, the Dutch managed to throw back the Soviets. The Volchov front, thanks in part to the actions of the Dutch volunteers, was able to hold fast. With the beginning of the German offensive, the Legion was engaged in fighting aimed at eliminating the Volchov pocket, in which the Soviet forces under General Vlasov had been surrounded. On January 13, Vlasov had crossed the Volchov River with numerically superior forces with the objective of lifting the siege of Leningrad. Ultimately, his Second Shock Army and parts of the 52nd and 59th Soviet Armies had been destroyed; the Soviets suffered the loss of more than 100,000 men dead and wounded, and tens of thousands taken prisoner. The Dutch volunteers themselves were credited with capturing 3,500 Soviet prisoners in addition to large quantities of weapons, ammunition and equipment. Fighting in the Selo Gora area continued until June 1942, after which the survivors of the Legion were pulled back from the front lines for a period of rest and reorganization. The Dutch volunteers were awarded thirty-two Iron Crosses First Class, and 158 Second Class. In a proclamation issued on June 28, 1942, by *General* Lindermann, commander of the German 18th Army, the author of Vlasov's defeat, he recognized officially the contribution made by all of the foreign volunteers to the victory on the Leningrad front:

> Soldiers of the Army. On January 13, the enemy crossed the Volchov with numerically superior forces forcing back our defensive front. His objective was the liberation of Leningrad. In five and a half months of bloody battles and unimaginably difficult conditions, our courage and our persistence have completely frustrated the enemy's intentions. The remnants of the Soviet Second Shock

Award of the first Iron Crosses to Dutch volunteers following the fighting at Selo Gora, in the presence of Zondervan, wearing the German uniform and the rank of *Untersturmführer*.

Army and large portions of the Soviet 52nd and 59th Armies have been destroyed. All units of the Army have participated in these battles. Spaniards, Dutchmen and Flemings fought side by side with units of the army and of the Waffen-SS.

Krasnoje–Selo

In June 1942, the Dutch Legion was subordinated tactically to the 2nd SS Infantry Brigade[4] commanded by *SS-Brigadeführer* Gottfried Klingemann. On July 15, 1942, *SS-Obersturmbannführer* Fitzthum[5] assumed command of the Legion, replacing the unpopular *Oberführer* Reich, who had never managed to gain the sympathy of the Dutch volunteers. Once the sweeps in the Volchov area had been completed, the Dutch volunteers were engaged in keeping watch over the Leningrad–Novgorod railway line, along with the *285 Sicherungs-Division* of *Generalleutnant* Wolfgang Edler Herr and *Freiherr* von Plotho. At the end of July the Legion, still attached to the 2nd SS Brigade, was transferred farther to the north to take part in the siege operations against Leningrad. On July 24, 1942, the Legion had about 600 men still fit for combat; specifically, sixteen officers, seventy-nine NCOs, and 478 men out of a nominal strength of more than a thousand soldiers. The difference between the nominal strength and the effective strength was attributable to the great number of personnel who were convalescing in various field hospitals. After about a month of relative calm in the trenches around Leningrad, the Legion was withdrawn from the front lines in preparation for Operation *Nordlicht* (North Light) that called for a final assault against the city. The date for the beginning of the offensive was set for August 14, 1942, but the Germans were preempted by a massive Soviet counteroffensive south of Lake Ladoga. As a consequence of postponement *sine dia* of the planned offensive the Dutch volunteers were once again transferred south of Leningrad, this time in the area of Krasnoje–Selo and were kept busy fighting off new Soviet attacks. The ensuing encounters along the front south of Leningrad passed into history as the "First Battle of Lake Ladoga."

Kampfgruppe Fitzthum

Beginning on September 2, 1942, a new independent combat group was formed within the 2nd SS Brigade, which took the name of its commander, SS-*Obersturmbannführer* Fitzthum, and which consisted of the Dutch Legion, the Norwegian Legion, and the 19th and 20th Latvian battalions. The units of the *Kampfgruppe* were engaged mainly in bitter defensive fighting until December 1942. On December 4, 1942, the Dutch volunteers were called upon to repel yet another enemy attack against their positions; a Soviet assault force of about 600 men was unleashed

A young Dutch *Untersturmführer*.

Gerardus Mooyman

against the I Battalion of the Legion and many of the Soviets were able to pass through the lines. The *Kampfgruppe* responded with a counterattack using Norwegian and Dutch units to reestablish the former defensive line. About 350 Soviet soldiers were killed and forty-two taken prisoner, while *Kampfgruppe* losses were thirty killed, sixty-six wounded and three missing in action.

The Second Battle of Lake Ladoga

In early January 1943, the Soviets launched yet another offensive south of Lake Ladoga with the intention of easing the pressure on Leningrad, known as the "Second Battle of Lake Ladoga." The Norwegians and Dutch were called upon to repel numerous Soviet armored attacks, during which the anti-tank detachments were particularly hard-pressed. During an attack by an enemy armored formation, a young nineteen-year-old volunteer, Gerardus Leonardus Mooyman of the *14.Panzerjäger Kompanie*, was able to destroy a total of thirteen Soviet tanks with his gun during a single day.

Sturmmann Mooyman was later awarded the Knight's Cross. On February 6, 1943, *General* Seyffardt, who had returned to Amsterdam to oversee a new recruitment campaign for the Legion, was assassinated by the Dutch resistance. The news upset the legionnaires, but there was not much time in which to mourn over their commander, hard pressed as they were in fighting off enemy attacks. In memory of the general, Hitler authorized the production of a cufftitle with the inscription "*General Seyffardt*," to be worn by the Legion's 1st Company. In reality the cuff title was later worn by all members of the *SS.Freiw. Pzgr. Regiment 48 General Seyffardt* of the *Nederland* Brigade. In March 1943, the Legion passed under tactical command of the 4th SS Armored Grenadier Regiment *Polizei*. Following a series of bloody engagements, attacks and withdrawals, in April 1943, the Legion was down to only 20% of its initial effective strength figure.

Johannes-Gerardus Leonardus Mooyman

Born on September 23, 1923, in Apeldoorn in the Dutch province of Gelderland, after having completed his schooling, Gerardus Mooyman took a course to become a mechanic. His first job however was as a clerk in a pharmacy. At the age of nineteen he enlisted in the Waffen-SS, and as did many of his countrymen he joined the ranks of *SS-Freiwilligen-Standarte Nordwest*, which was the regiment created by Himmler in which to gather the Flemish, Dutch, and in general all of the volunteers who were of Germanic stock. After completing training as a *Panzerjäger* (anti-tank gunner) at Hilvorsum in Holland, he was transferred to the *SS-Freiwilligen-Legion Nederland*. He began his career at the front as a message runner, despite the fact that he had been trained as an anti-tank gunner. On January 15, 1943, at the front in Leningrad, some batteries of the Dutch Legion (*14.Panzerjäger Kompanie* commanded by *Ostuf.* Walter Diener) and of the Norwegian Legion (*14.Pak Kompanie*) were temporarily detached

SS-LEGION Niederlande
AUF WACHT IM OSTEN

The terrible conditions of the Dutch Legion on the eastern front, from a page of *Wiener Illustrierte* from 1943.

German soldiers moving an anti-tank gun.

Soviet tanks attacking German positions.

from the 2nd SS Brigade, by direct order of SS-*Brigadeführer* Klingemann and assigned to reinforce *SS-Polizei Regiment 16* (*Oberstleutnant der Schutzpolizei* Kemper). On January 21, 1943, another battery consisting of two *Pak* guns of the Norwegian 14th Company, commanded by *Unterscharführer* Hans Haug, along with *Panzerjäger* from the Dutch Legion was assigned to another German unit, the *170.Infanterie Division* (*Generalleutnant* Erwin Sander), which was defending the railway hub of Mga, near Schlüsselberg. When they began their move to the front, the Norwegian and Dutch volunteers knew only that their destination was the village of Mga.

They also knew that south of the Neva River a battle was raging. When they reached Mga they found the village overflowing with German reinforcements. The news that "foreigners" had arrived spread swiftly and they were given a very warm welcome. Soon after, orders came to begin the march. Guide personnel accompanied the soldiers outside the village along the road called the *Burma Road*, only because it led to a Soviet station called *Rangun* (*Rangoon*)! Under the light of the moon, the Norwegian and Dutch volunteers passed in front of the German artillery positions under incessant shelling by Soviet batteries. The capable German gunners, all of whom had been killed, were still next to their guns. The march continued until dawn, at which time the fire of mortars and heavy artillery began, soon followed by fire from the terrible *Katyusha* rocket launchers. For four times the volunteers were forced to seek shelter to escape from the storm of Soviet fire. The Norwegians were the first to occupy forward positions. At the same moment in which the enemy tried to break through a gap that had been created in the German defensive line, the first Soviet tanks made their appearance. Soviet artillery began to shell the Norwegian positions, but to no effect. Other Soviet tanks were knocked out by Norwegian anti-tank fire, completely halting any attempt by the enemy to break through in the Rangun sector. The Dutch message runner Gerardus Mooyman was not, however, happy with his job assignment within the Legion. He was furious that he was still a simple runner rather than an anti-tank gunner. His repeated requests to his commander had fallen on deaf ears. Nevertheless, he decided to try yet again. But once again his commander was laconic, saying: "You are beginning to get on my nerves." Mooyman remained calm and a few days later his wish was granted. In fact, following the heavy losses suffered by the anti-tank company, replacements were requested from all units of the Legion. Mooyman, with his training as an anti-tank gunner, was thus one of the first to be transferred to the company, with the position of gun commander (*Geschutzführer*). During the night of January 30, the Dutch *Panzerjägers* Närger and Mooyman took up positions east of Mga. They were only 800 meters apart from each other. The main aid station and the regimental command post were located between the two positions.

It was not until dawn that they were able to have a clear view of the battlefield in front of their guns. On one side there was a thick forest while on the other side was a sort of passage about

An anti-tank crew in action on the Leningrad front.

thirty meters wide through which the Soviets would certainly attempt to pass. From early morning, enemy machine gun fire hit the German positions incessantly. Suddenly, Mooyman spotted movement from the forest. He took his scope, slowly scanned the terrain, and saw about a dozen Soviet tanks with infantry following behind them advancing towards his position. There wasn't a moment to lose! The Soviets intended to pass right in front of his *Pak*. Mooyman had the gun loaded, continuing in the meantime to carefully monitor the enemy's movements. When the first Soviet tank entered into his field of vision, he gave the order to fire. The first round quickly hit its target, raising an infernal racket. Another round was fired while the first tank was in flames. Another tank turned and backtracked to escape the Dutch fire. The Soviet infantry then began to fire on the *Pak* crew, who continued to fire against the Soviet tanks, heedless of the bullets whistling past them. After having hit another tank, the gun jammed unexpectedly, as a round had become stuck in the breech.

Gunner Ruiter came up with an idea, even though it may have seemed stupid as well as dangerous. He jumped from his position and grabbed a heavy branch. He very calmly began to bang violently on the *Pak* with the branch, knowing full well that the banging could blow up the gun and himself along with it. However, his efforts finally paid off and the gun was able to resume firing. The Dutch anti-tank gunners stopped only after they had destroyed another four tanks and having damaged yet a further four. In the face of such determination the Soviet infantry also opted to pull back. Only two Soviet tanks managed to break through the Dutch positions, but they were quickly knocked out with hand grenades. That day the Soviets had had enough. The next day, however, they resumed the attack, preceded by a massive barrage by their artillery. At six in the morning of January 31, 1943, First Gunner Närger was alert at his position. The Soviets were approaching him rapidly. Närger opened fire with high explosive shells in order to eliminate the massed Soviet infantry. Two hours of close-quarter combat action between the German and Soviet infantry ensued. The Germans, who were heavily outnumbered, were finally forced to withdraw. Närger was now by himself, thirty meters from the forward line of combat! His anti-tank position became a center of resistance by default. The Soviets tried to avoid his fire, advancing on his flank under cover of the forest. Two light anti-tank guns belonging to the same Dutch company, situated to the right and left of Närger, were destroyed. There were, however, five mortars in action to his left. When they had run out of ammunition, the mortar crews reached the Dutch anti-tank positions and continued to fight with their rifles. In the meantime Second Gunner Kortenbach had been wounded. Närger assigned one of the ex-mortar men to replace him, but his new gunner was also hit by Soviet fire shortly afterwards, and the same fate was suffered by the next replacement as well. The machine gun covering the anti-tank gun was alone in firing against the Soviets. There was an urgent need for men. Between nine and ten in the morning ammunition also ran out. The last two rounds were held back in order to destroy the anti-tank gun itself. *Panzerjägers* and grenadiers gathered together around the guns with their rifles in their hands. A German assault gun arrived from the rear as reinforcement, but after having fired a couple of rounds, quickly pulled back.

Dutch volunteers on the eve of an action in enemy territory.

Mooyman seated in the left rear, on his way to receive the citation for the Knight's Cross.

Kortenbach, wounded in one arm but still able to walk, went to look for ammunition. *SS-Sturmmann* Schaufeli accompanied him. Despite the heavy enemy fire, the pair, after having found a small cart, managed to go back and forth three times, each time carrying nine rounds. During the second trip, Schaufeli was wounded in the legs. *SS-Sturmmann* Eklenz saw to the resupply of ammunition for Mooyman's gun. This enabled the two Dutch anti-tank guns to resume their fire. The Dutch battery commander, *SS-Oberscharführer* Weide, was wounded while attempting to conduct a visual reconnaissance near Närger's position. Närger remained alone with his gunner Stevelmanns to man his *Pak*. Ammunition ran out once again, and there were only about a dozen hand grenades left for their final defense. The Soviets emerged from the forest barely forty meters from their position. "Whichever of us is the last left standing will destroy the gun, understood?" shouted Närger. When all seemed lost, in the midst of the din of battle, he suddenly heard the roar of an engine at his shoulders. He raised his head and carefully looked behind: "Why, it's Bochy!" Bochy was the Dutch motorcycle courier. His sidecar was full of ammunition and he had come through at full speed in the midst of explosions and under fire from the Soviets. Now the Dutch *Panzerjägers* could resume their fire once again. Around noontime another motorcycle appeared. This time it was the commander who was shuttling between the two anti-tank guns commanded by Närger and Mooyman. He had his pockets full of chocolate bars for his men. Because of a round that exploded nearby, Närger had temporarily lost his hearing, which meant that he was unable to understand anything that his company commander said to him. Around evening, several platoons of German infantry reached the gun positions, managing to reestablish a defensive line. *SS-Obersturmführer* Diener had to appoint a new commander, as *Oberscharführer* Weide had deserted, and his choice fell upon *SS-Sturmmann* Feldt, who had already led a combat group from the same company. Feldt was only nineteen years old, but he was a strong and resolute young man, and it seemed that nothing ever caused him to lose his calm demeanor.

Awards and Decorations

Owing to the success achieved against the Soviet tanks, both the Dutch and the Norwegians began to be considered as heroes by the German soldiers. When the men of the other units passed by their positions they greeted them in a friendly manner and while food was being served, the cook arrived to say, "... Ah, it's you. Help yourselves to whatever you want!" Naturally, after the verbal comments, awards also were given. *SS-Sturmmann* Närger was the first to receive the Iron Cross First Class. A dozen other Dutch volunteers were awarded the Second Class; among them were Mooyman, Ruiter, Stevelmanns, Feldt, Schaufeli, Kortenbach, Bruinsvel and Erklenz. No one had expected that it would end like this. In the depths of their hearts they felt very proud of themselves.

The words of a German *Panzerjäger* were emblematic, who while smiling, said to them: "You, a handful of men, come here and in three days knock out more enemy tanks than we did throughout the entire campaign!"

New Attacks

On February 10, 1943, the Soviets launched a surprise attack without any preparatory artillery fire. Mooyman quickly opened fire, while the German infantry, exhausted after days of uninterrupted combat, retreated in great disorder. The Dutch volunteers ran to their aid, convincing them to return to their positions. Meanwhile, Mooyman had continued to do his duty; First Gunner Buttinger had by himself managed to destroy a Soviet anti-tank gun in an intrepid action. After having been able to get close to the Soviet position without being detected, at about twenty meters from the enemy position he cut down all of the gunners. The Bolshevik attack was finally stopped just a few meters short of the main defensive line. That evening, Mooyman was presented with the Iron Cross First Class while the hero of the day, Buttinger, was awarded the Second Class. During the night it began to snow heavily. The countryside became covered completely in white. Mooyman remained at his post, heedless of the snow that was falling. When the relief squad appeared, he was found covered with snow up to his nose. Two hours later, some cannon fire was heard. Kooper, a Dutch medical aide, fired a white flare into the air to illuminate the area, thus revealing that the Soviets had emplaced an anti-tank gun along the railway line. Mooyman quickly got it in his sights

An anti-tank gun ready to fire.

and gave the order to fire. The resulting shot managed only to drive off the crew, as the gun itself was in a defilade position and was impossible to hit with direct fire. What could be done? At about thirty or forty meters from the gun the Soviets had placed some lookouts in the hulk of one of their knocked out tanks. Those enemy observers had to be eliminated at all costs. From the other side of the railroad embankment the Soviets could be heard yelling and screaming. Could this be the beginning of a new attack, asked Erklenz. "Don't be foolish, they're only drunk, let's move," replied Mooyman.

At that moment the young Dutch volunteer showed his wits and his ability to make a quick decision. His sole intention was to eliminate the dangerous enemy anti-tank gun. Volunteers Kooper and Hissink followed him. The three of them advanced with the greatest caution towards the enemy position. Then Mooyman left the other two behind to cover him. He then reached the enemy gun and placed a 3 kg explosive charge under the gun. When the explosion blew the Soviet gun to bits, the trio had already returned to their position without incurring any wounds. On the morning of February 13, the Soviets resumed their attack with tanks. The Dutch anti-tank guns, however, were still in place. Four Soviet tanks were destroyed and another two were damaged. But Mooyman was once again left without any ammunition; the platoon leader arrived just as five Soviet tanks were drawing perilously close. He gave the order to fire the last armor piercing round against the lead enemy tank and to fire high explosive rounds[6] against the others. But Mooyman didn't want to admit to being beaten, and with Feldt's assistance, was able to get some fresh ammunition. Gunner Bouts, farther to the north with his gun, still had a good supply on hand as his sector had been quiet. *SS-Sturmmann* Fekter, a young Hungarian volunteer who was an excellent harmonica player, carried the ammunition while under Soviet fire. Mooyman's gun resumed firing and two Soviet tanks were knocked out. Meanwhile, the gap that had been opened in the main defensive line had been plugged, and without tank support the Soviet infantry chose to withdraw. Around 1100, about twenty Soviet tanks returned to attack, heading towards the position occupied by Bouts. About 800 meters from his position, however, the tanks abruptly changed direction, once again heading for Mooyman's position.

German defensive position with an *MG-34*.

Luckily the Dutch *Sturmmann* had been resupplied well, which enabled him to fire against the enemy at a furious rate. Six of the twenty Soviet tanks went up in flames, one after another. Still other tanks were hit and damaged, and the rest opted to turn around. Mooyman had won once again. It was then Bouts' turn to suffer a new tank attack; the untiring Fekter managed to get a few rounds to him in time. Bouts destroyed three tanks, but could have done more if he had had more ammunition. He was in somewhat of a rage because he had given up his own ammunition to supply the other guns. Mooyman had been firing for the whole day and he had to let several enemy tanks get away without being able to do anything about it. Närger no longer had any enemy tanks within sight, as Mooyman had already dispatched all of them. The last rounds fired by Bouts fell at the moment that the German counterattack began. The reserves had arrived; they were grenadiers from a German division to the north.

Stupefied, the Dutchmen watched this marvelous battalion advance, in close ranks, with their major leading them. The *Wehrmachtsbericht* of February 13, 1943, emphasized the heroism of the Dutch volunteers: "... The Dutch volunteers played an important role in stopping the Bolshevik attack south of Lake Ladoga, protecting the flank with their anti-tank guns. The most courageous Dutch gunner, who destroyed thirteen enemy armored vehicles, was SS-Mann Gerardus Mooyman."

Citation for the Knight's Cross

At the end of the day the accounts were tallied: the Dutch *Panzerjägers* had destroyed fifteen tanks, thirteen for Mooyman and two for Bouts. That night *Generalleutnant* Erwin Sander,

Mooyman receiving congratulations and the award of the Knight's Cross by *SS-Brigadeführer* Fritz von Scholz, commander of the *2.SS. Infanterie Brigade*. Von Scholz came from the *Wiking* Division.

A Dutch sniper on the Leningrad front.

commander of *170.Infanterie Division*, wrote up a citation for Mooyman for the award of the Knight's Cross. The young Dutch *Sturmmann* had fired against the Soviet tanks as though he had been in a shooting gallery, with odds of 1 to 10. The proposal was also warmly endorsed by *SS-Brigadeführer* Fritz von Scholz, commander of the 2nd SS Infantry Brigade. The next day the Soviets attacked again, and Mooyman destroyed another three enemy tanks. He painted the twentieth white ring on the barrel of his gun, signifying twenty enemy tank kills. Stories of Mooyman's success began to make the rounds at the front and the brigade received a message of congratulations from the *OKW*. There was also talk of the Dutch *Panzerjäger* on German radio.

Quite suddenly the presence of Dutch volunteers on the Leningrad front was noticed by everyone. Mooyman himself would later say: "... Our jaws dropped when all of a sudden we saw a large group of officials who came to visit our positions and our anti-tank gun." But not all of the Dutch anti-tank guns were as lucky as was Mooyman's. On February 15, 1943, the *Pak* commanded by *SS-Rottenführe*r Kosbau was hit by Soviet artillery fire after having fired only a few rounds. *SS-Sturmmannn* Wituschek, Diner and de Wit were killed outright. The sense of comradeship was, however, stronger than death itself and that night *SS-Sturmmann* Närger received orders to retrieve the bodies of his fallen comrades. Närger left soon thereafter; it was a difficult task, and many preferred to face death rather than to touch a corpse. But a sentiment of indissoluble solidarity prevailed at the front, based upon a shared sacrifice. During his difficult trip along the trace of the old main defensive line, Närger met many German units that were pulling back. The German infantrymen asked Närger where he was headed, but he limited his answer to saluting them. After a while he finally reached the destroyed gun and luckily for him, just at that moment a German truck happened to be passing by, which was ideal for towing the anti-tank gun and the bodies of his comrades. Legionnaire

A decorated Dutch legionnaire.

Mooyman with the Knight's Cross around his neck.

de Wit, who had been seventeen years old, was so light that Närger needed no effort to take him in his arms and place him on the vehicle. The lifeless bodies of Dinter and Wituschek turned out to be somewhat heavier.

The Dutch anti-tank company was able to deploy only four anti-tank guns along the new front line. During the three days that followed the Soviets sent out only reconnaissance patrols and limited themselves to shelling German positions with their artillery. During one attack, *Sturmmannn* Buttinger and Ruiter were seriously wounded; they both died shortly after in a hospital from the wounds they had sustained. Bouts and Mooyman took advantage of a brief respite in the fighting to arrange for a "Russian style" resupply effort, looting the knocked out Soviet tanks; although the Soviet infantry may have had nothing more than a few kernels of corn and some raw fish in their knapsacks, the tankers were much better supplied. More decorations arrived for the Dutch anti-tank gunners in those days; the Iron Cross First Class for Feldt and for the tireless aid man Kooper, while the Iron Cross Second Class was awarded to Bouts, Fekter, van der Wey, Benzinger, Wolferen, Waardenburg and Hissing. Almost all of the crews of Bouts and Mooyman received decorations.

Men Against Tanks

The Soviets needed four days to reorganize and to return on the attack in the Schlüsselburg corridor. On the morning of February 22, a tempest of fire fell upon the German positions. The crews of the *Paks* of Bouts and Mooyman stayed in their bunkers to listen to the "concert." It was a veritable hell. The lookout suddenly gave the alarm: "... Three tanks, back there, in the forest!" This time it looked like the end was at hand. The enemy tanks had come very close to the Dutch positions. Fortunately, the anti-tank guns had been well revetted and camouflaged. Mooyman ran between his men and the tanks, galloping along towards his gun that was about 150 meters away. Once he reached the position, he realized that there were five tanks advancing towards him. He gave a quick glance to Bouts, who had also joined his men, and he swung into action. The *Pak* with the twenty white kill rings on its barrel was swung around 180°, which certainly was not child's play given the weight of the gun and the frigid temperature. Then he began like a madman to fire against the enemy tanks; two were hit immediately, but a third was missed. Bouts was luckier this time, managing to knock out three tanks. Once again the Dutch *Panzerjägers* had repulsed a Soviet armored attack; enthusiastic over their success, the Dutch volunteers began to inspect the destroyed tanks, oblivious of the danger of ambush. Soviet artillery had in fact begun to shell their positions, which had been spotted during their duel against the tanks, with violent fire. The *Pak* belonging to Bouts was the first to take a direct hit; a cloud of smoke wreathed the position. Mooyman was the

Another photo of Mooyman with the *Ritterkreuz*.

Mooyman in front of his anti-tank gun.

first to run to the scene to see what had happened to his mates. Bouts fell in his arms, his uniform full of blood. "Everyone else is dead, the gun is done for," he said with a trembling voice. Van der Wey, Arts and Fekter had fallen on the field of honor. Moorman turned to Bouts: "Your wound isn't serious, let's go look at the gun."

The sights were ruined and one wheel was sheared off cleanly; for the time being the gun was out of action. Mooyman and Bouts then went to Mooyman's gun. When they got there all of the crew were gathered around Hissink, who had been wounded in the arm. After having been patched up as best as conditions would allow, Hissink was sent to the aid station, while Bouts wanted to stay where he was, requesting to take the place of Hissink in Mooyman's anti-tank gun crew. This was the last combat action for the Dutch on the Neva front. Two days later the order came to withdraw towards the Mga River. Bouts was awarded the Iron Cross First Class.

The Knight's Cross

When the Dutch volunteers reached the railway station at Mga, as they were waiting for the train, a motorcycle messenger arrived at full speed. "*Where is Mooyman,*" he shouted. The young Dutch *Sturmmannn* stepped forward. "Tomorrow you have to report to the *28.Jäger-Division* command post, understood?" "Yes, but what do they want with me?," replied Mooyman, horrified. The courier departed without another word. On February 26, 1943, *SS-Sturmmannn* Gerardus Mooyman, nineteen-years-old, mechanic's apprentice, stood at attention in front of a guard of honor that saluted him. *General der Artillerie* Johann Sinhuber, commanding the German *28.Jäger-Division*, drew close and awarded him the Knight's Cross. The scene was filmed by operators from the newsreel "*Die Deutsche Wochenschau*," and was shown in movie theaters throughout half of Europe. Mooyman was the very first non-German European volunteer to be awarded the Knight's Cross. From that moment on his comrades took to jokingly calling him "*der Panzerjäger*" (the Tank Destroyer). His epic story was published in many newspapers and magazines. Himmler personally congratulated him, inviting him to participate in many ceremonies and parades held in his honor. When he returned to Holland, after having been given a period of leave as a reward, he was welcomed with all honors by his countrymen. Mooyman continued his military career first in the *Nederland* Brigade and then in the *Nederland* Division. In early 1944, after having been promoted to the ranks of *Rottenführer* and then *Unterscharführer*, he attended an officer's course, graduating in June of that year with the rank of *Untersturmführer*. His activity as an anti-tank officer continued until the end of the war in *SS-Panzerjäger Abteilung 23* of the *SS Nederland* Division.

Withdrawal of the Legion

On April 27, 1943, the surviving members of the Dutch Legion were withdrawn from the front line and transferred to the Grafenwöhr training area for a period of rest. With the Legion officially disbanded, Himmler convinced the Dutch volunteers to stay to fight alongside the German armed forces. After having seen with how much passion and courage the European volunteers had fought on the Eastern Front, both Himmler and *SS-Obergruppenführer* Gottlob Berger, head of the *SS-Hauptamt* (the SS Central Office), decided to transform the Legions into larger independent units, include them officially in the Waffen-SS, and upgrade them to new brigades or divisions. Formation of the *SS Panzergrenadier Nederland* Brigade was initiated using the Dutch volunteers.

Mooyman at a meeting with the head of the NSB, Mussert.

Dutch volunteers.

Return of Dutch legionnaires to Holland, welcomed with full honors.

FORMATION OF THE SS NEDERLAND BRIGADE

Recruiting officer for volunteers for the Waffen-SS in Amsterdam.

The birth of the *SS Nederland* Brigade is closely tied to the formation of another SS division, the *Nordland*. The order authorizing formation of this unit was issued in February 1943, with the intent to incorporate it in the new *III.(Germanische) SS-Panzerkorps* commanded by Felix Steiner[1]; the new Waffen-SS armored Corps was also to include the *SS Wiking* Division and was to be ready by March 30, 1943. This was an original idea of Himmler's, who wanted to form new SS divisions with the veterans of the national Legions (Flemish, Dutch, Danish and Norwegian) that had fought on the Eastern Front between 1941 and 1943. After having seen how bravely and valorously the European volunteers had fought, the German military authorities decided to transform the legions into larger independent units and to include them officially in the Waffen-SS.

On February 10, 1943, *SS-Obergruppenführer* Gottlob Berger, head of the *SS-Hauptamt*, issued the order to withdraw the four national legions from the front and to give them a period to rest and reorganize. Decimated by combat on the Eastern Front, the European volunteer units had to be disbanded in order to transform them into new SS brigades or divisions. Small units such as the Legions could not be effective now that the Germans were forced to fight purely on the defensive, thus it would be better if they were reorganized as larger units, which was why on February 11, 1943 the *Reichsführer-SS*, in a note to his staff, decided that the first new European SS division was to be formed by three new SS regiments, the *Nederland*, the *Danmark*, and the *Norge*, based naturally on the remnants of the national legions. The Flemish volunteers were to be transferred into a new independent brigade, the *SS Langemarck*. The new division

Training of new recruits at a training camp.

SS-Oberführer Jürgen Wagner.

SS-Gruppenführer Felix Steiner.

was to be called the *Nordland*; the Dutch nationalist leader Anton Mussert, head of the NSB, strongly supported creation of the new SS division, but quickly opposed the use of the name *Nordland*, which referred only to the Scandinavian origin of the volunteers, to the exclusion of the Dutch. In the end Mussert and Himmler agreed to create an exclusively Dutch SS division, the *Nederland*. On July 19, 1943, Adolf Hitler personally authorized the formation of a new Waffen-SS armored grenadier unit, designated as the *Nederland*.

To make up for the shortfall of Dutch volunteers, Himmler was forced to use the *Nordland* Regiment of the *SS Wiking* Division as the nucleus of the other new volunteer unit. This decision was dictated in part also by the impossibility of withdrawing the *Wiking* Division from the Eastern Front in its entirety because it was engaged in fierce fighting along the Dnieper, so accordingly the formation of the new *SS-Panzerkorps* was postponed.

Formation

In April 1943, the remnants of the Dutch Legion were withdrawn from the Leningrad front and in early May were transferred to the camp at Thüringen, near Sonneberg. There the Legion was officially redesignated as *the SS-Freiwilligen-Panzer-Grenadier-Brigade Nederland*. During the next two months, the formation of all of the new units was begun. In the meantime, the recruiting campaign began in Holland; many volunteers reported in to the recruiting centers, of whom, however, only 3,000 passed the medical exam. With some 2,000 veterans of the Dutch Legion and of other German military and paramilitary formations, a total of 5,000 men was reached for the new unit; this was not enough to fill out the required manning levels for a division (from 16,000 to 18,000 men), but enough for formation of an SS brigade. A special field hospital was also created to treat all of the Dutch volunteers still convalescing from the fighting on the Leningrad front, designated the *SS-Lazarett Freiwillige Legion Nederland*, which in February 1944, became redesignated as the *SS-Lazarett Niederlandische Ambulanz*, headed by Doctors Heinz Schlegel and Paul Stefany. During the months of July and August, formation of the two regiments of the brigade got under way, each consisting of three battalions, initially designated as *SS-Frw.Pz.Grenadier-Rgt.1 "Nederland"* and *SS-Frw.Pz. Grenadier-Rgt.2 "Nederland."*

Most of the volunteers from the disbanded Legion were merged into the 1st SS Dutch Regiment. In October the two regiments were redesignated respectively as the *SS-Frw.Pz.Gren. Rgt.1 "General Seyffardt"* and the *SS-Frw.Pz.Gren.Rgt.2 "de Ruyter."* The first was named in honor of *General* Seyffardt, the

III.SS-Pz.-Korps units during operations on the Croatian front, autumn 1943.

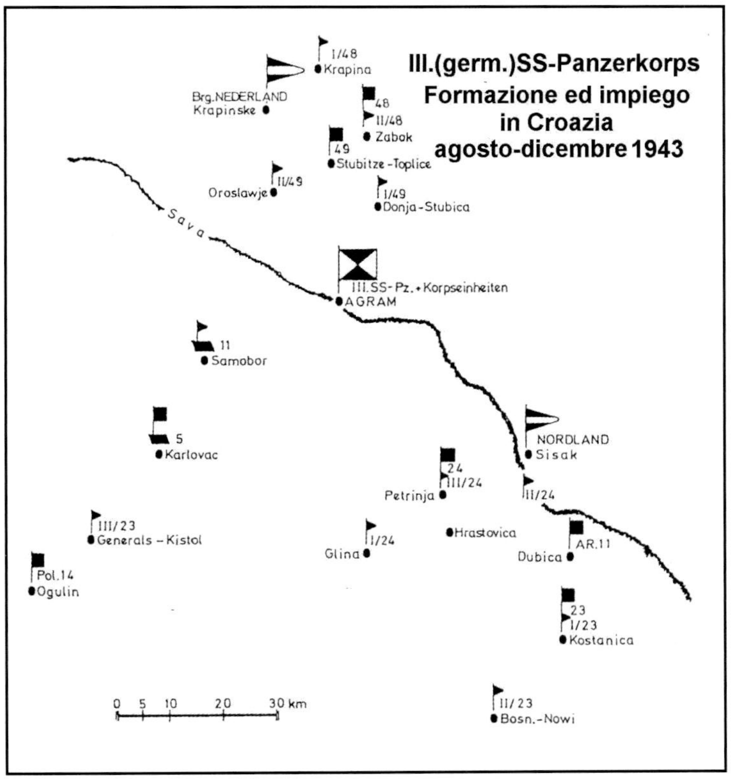

III (German) SS-Panzerkorps formation and employment in Croatia, August–December 1943

ex-head of the Dutch general staff and a great recruiter of volunteers for the Dutch Legion in 1941, who was assassinated by the Dutch resistance movement. The second regiment was named in honor of Dutch Admiral de Ruyter, who had defeated the British fleet in the seventeenth century. The Dutch volunteers were assembled for training at the Sonneberg training area in Thuringia. The volunteers were authorized to continue to wear the distinctive NSB insignia and the special *Wolfsangel* collar flash, although most of the Dutch volunteers opted to adopt the official Waffen-SS flash with the double runes. The brigade was organized with two armored grenadier regiments and an artillery regiment. The organizational structure also included reconnaissance elements, an engineer company (whose formation was undertaken at the camp at Hradischko under the supervision of Danish *SS-Stubaf.* Ernst Viffert) and an anti-tank company equipped with *Sturmgeschütz III* self-propelled assault guns. The artillery and some service units were, however, still lacking. Command of the brigade was assumed by *SS-Oberführer* Jürgen Wagner,[2] former commander of the *Germania* Regiment and of the *Wiking* Division, and decorated with the Knight's Cross on July 24, 1943. Designated as his adjutant was *SS-Stubaf.* Christian Steenholt-Schütt (born January 2, 1911, SS Number 291 206), who later held the position of Staff Officer (*IIa*). *SS-Stubaf.* Dietrich Ziemssen (born August 26, 1911, SS Number 232 940) was designated as Brigade Chief of Staff (*Ia*), Supply Officer (*Ib*) was *SS-Stubaf.* Gerhard Noatzke (born August 21, 1905, SS Number 289 224), and as Intelligence Officer (*Ic*) was *SS-Ostuf.* Paul Koopmann (born December 19, 1911, SS Number 413 727). As aides Wagner selected *SS-Ostuf.* Georg Kormann (01) and *SS-Ustuf.* Alfons Graf (02). The medical company was entrusted to *SS-Stubaf.* Dr. Van Heutsz (born October 1, 1882, SS Number 393 343). The war correspondent platoon (*Kriegsberichter Zug*) was under the command of *SS-Ostuf.* Hendrik van Deventer. *SS-Feldersatz Bataillon 54*, which was the brigade's training and replacement battalion, was commanded by *SS-Stubaf.* Kurt Pachur (born November 14, 1908, SS Number 53 748).

Transfer to Croatia

Nederland was assigned to Steiner's III SS Armored Corps. Before departing for the Eastern Front, the units of *Nordland* and *Nederland* were transferred to Croatia in early September, to the area around Zagreb, where the Dutch volunteers continued their training. In particular, the Dutch units were deployed north of Agram (Zagreb). The brigade staff was located at Krapinske, and the 48th Regiment in the area of Zabok, with its staff and *II.Bataillon* also at Zabok, while *I.Bataillon* took up quarters at Krapina. The headquarters of the 49th Regiment was set up at Stubitze–Toplice, the *I.Bataillon* at Donja–Stubica, and the *II.Bataillon* at Oroslawje. During the same period the Dutch brigade was assigned about 1,500 new personnel, most of who were Dutch volunteers who had already seen combat with *Wiking*, and *Volksdeutschen* from Romania. Assigned to the *Armeegruppe von Weichs* directly subordinate to the 2nd Panzer Army under General Lothar Rendulic, the units of *III. SS-Panzerkorps* were initially employed to disarm Italian units (Operation *Achse*) which had been left by the Badoglio government without any guidance following the signing of the armistice by the Italians with the Allies on September 8, 1943. Above all, the Germans wanted to prevent the weapons and equipment of the disbanded Italian units from falling into the hands of the communist partisan bands led by Tito.[3]

It was in fact due to the availability of huge amounts of arms and ammunition taken from the Italian units that the communist partisans were able to intensify their activity in all of the territory occupied by the German forces, thus involving the participation of units of Steiner's SS Corps. The Dutch volunteers were accordingly committed to anti-partisan sweep operations in the area around the cities of Oroslavje and Donja Stubica, honing their skills in combat tactics. At the same time they were also tasked to provide security for roads and railway lines, engaging in sporadic encounters with local partisan formations. In contrast to their comrades from *Nordland*, who were caught up in bitter fighting with rebel forces in the area of Glina, south of Zagreb, the Dutch volunteers suffered only a few lightly wounded casualties during the Croat "campaign."

SS-Mann Heinz Slegtenhorst

A Dutch SS volunteer.

SS-Ostubaf. Hans Collani

SS-Oberführer Kurt Brasack

Helmut Breymann

SS-Ostubaf Hans Collani

New Reorganization of Units

On November 30, 1943, the *SS-FHA* assigned new numbers to both of the regiments: *SS-Frei.Pz.Gren.Rgt.1 "General Seyffardt"* was numbered as "45," and *SS-Frei.Pz.Gren.Rgt.2 "de Ruyter"* was numbered "*46*." In addition the Brigade was assigned the identification number *4*, becoming the *4.SS-Freiwilligen-Panzer Grenadier Brigade Nederland*. The two armored grenadier regiments later underwent another change in numeric designation, becoming the *48th* and *49th*. The total strength figure for the Dutch SS Brigade on the eve of its departure to the Eastern Front was 9,342 men.

Order of Battle

SS-Freiwilligen-Panzer-Grenadier Brigade 4 "Nederland"

Brigadestab

SS-Frei.Pz.Gren.Rgt.48 "General Seyffardt"

Stab und Stabskompanie
I.Bataillon (1.-4. Kompanie)
II.Bataillon (5.-8. Kompanie)

Dutch units training on the Croatian front, autumn 1943.

SS-Frei.Pz.Gren.Rgt.49 "de Ruyter"

Stab und Stabskompanie
I.Bataillon (1.-4. Kompanie)
II.Bataillon (5.-8. Kompanie)

SS-Freiw.Artillerie Rgt. 54

Stab
I.Abteilung
II.Abteilung
- *SS-Panzer-Aufklärungs-Kompanie 54*
- *SS-Panzerjäger-Abteilung 54*
- *SS-Pionier-Bataillon 54*
- *SS-Nachrichten-Kompanie. 54*
- *SS-Feldersatz Btl. 54 (Stab, 1-5 Kp.)*
- *SS-Sanitätskp. 54*
- *SS-Wirtschafts-Kp. 54*
- *SS-Nachschub-Truppen. 54*

Christmas in Croatia for the Dutch volunteers.

It should be noted that because of a shortage of soldiers each *Panzergrenadier Regiment* had only two battalions. The *Seyffardt* Regiment was initially commanded by *SS-Obersturmbannführer* Josef Fitzthum, who, on November 3, 1943, was transferred to the SS headquarters in Albania. Command of the regiment thus remained "unfilled" until the brigade reached the front at Leningrad in January 1944. Command of the I Battalion was assigned to *SS-Hstuf.* Hans Joachim Rühle von Lilienstern,[4] command of the II Battalion went to *SS-Stubaf.* Helmut Breymann.[5] Command of the *de Ruyter* Regiment was assigned to *SS-Obersturmbannführer* Hans Collani.[6] Command of the I Battalion was assigned to *SS-Hstuf.* Eduard Voorwinden, a post he held until December 1944, when he was replaced by *SS-Hstuf.* Werner

A bridge over a river in Croatia destroyed by communist partisans; in the foreground a Waffen-SS amphibious vehicle, a *Schwimmwagen*, is attempting to cross the river.

Mosenthin (born March 28, 1911, SS Number 367 762). Command of II Battalion was initially assigned to *SS-Stubaf.* Karl Götttsche (born February 25, 1903, SS Number 33 537); in January 1944, he was transferred to the 10th *SS Frundsberg* Division and was replaced by *SS-Hstuf.* Hans Bürmeister (born February 25, 1915, SS Number 124 163), a former officer of the *SS Wiking* Division.

Command of the artillery regiment (which would not be actually formed until March 1944) was initially assigned to *SS-Standartenführer* Karl Diebitsch[7] who had been a staff officer with *III.SS-Panzer-Korps (IIa)*. During the month of November Diebitsch received orders reassigning him to the staff of the *Reichsführer*, so that command of the *Nederland* artillery regiment was passed on to *SS-Oberführer* Kurt Brasack.[8] The engineer battalion was commanded by *SS-Stubaf.* Ernst Wendland, the former engineer officer of the *Wiking*. The reconnaissance company was led by *SS-Ostuf.* Erich Kuhne.[9] The signal company was commanded by *SS-Hstuf.* Wilhelm Thissen who also came from *Wiking*, and the *Flak Kompanie* commander was *SS-Ustuf.* Nieuwendijk-Hoek, likewise coming from *Wiking*.

Chapter IV
THE ORANIENBAUM FRONT

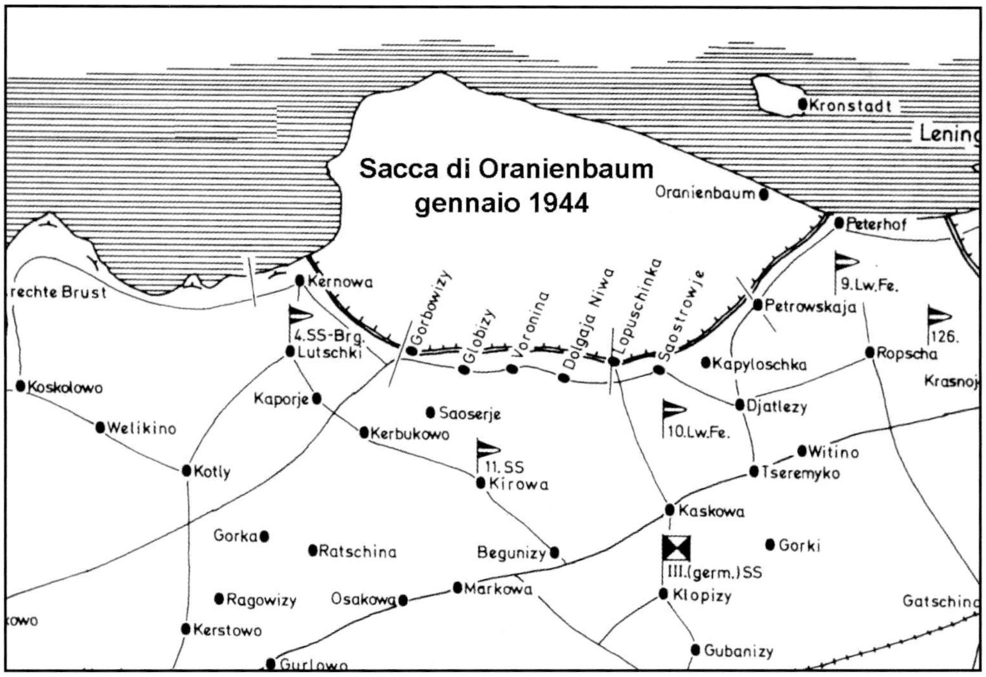

Unit deployments on the Leningrad Front, January 1944.

Generaloberst Lindemann

Beginning on November 25, 1943, units of III SS Panzer Corps began to deploy to the Eastern Front; the transfer of units was not completed until December of that year. The units of the *Nederland* Brigade were the last to leave, as they still had to complete their training and also still had to form some additional units. When it began its move to the front, the brigade still lacked its heavy armaments and its artillery component; a first artillery battalion was being formed at Beneschau, but was not yet ready for deployment to the front line. The *Flak* company had not yet been issued its anti-aircraft guns, and the reconnaissance company had practically no motor vehicles.

A German defensive position on the Leningrad front.

Unit Deployments

The *III.SS-Panzerkorps* was subordinated to the German 18th Army under *Generaloberst* Lindemann, whose operational sector ran from Lake Ilmen in the south, to the Gulf of Finland in the north. The units were deployed west of Leningrad, in forward positions along the Soviet salient at Oranienbaum, which from the north dominated the German 18th Army positions. After the rapid advance against Leningrad in 1941, this patch of ground on the Gulf of Finland had remained firmly in Soviet hands, representing a veritable thorn in the side of the German offensive positions, and later of their defensive positions. The German high command had for some time been expecting a Soviet offensive to be launched from the Oranienbaum salient, and *III.SS-Panzerkorps* was tasked with holding against the attack. A variety of units were positioned along the German defensive line, belonging to almost all of the armed forces; these included the *SS-Polizei Division*, coast artillery gunners, Estonian border guard battalions, Luftwaffe infantry, and Germanic Waffen-SS volunteers. The *Norge* and *Danmark* regiments of the *Nordland* Division were by themselves charged with defending twenty-four kilometers of the front, equating to about 250 men per kilometer; the Danes were located to the west and the Norwegians to the east. To their left, as far as to the sea, were units of the *SS-Polizei Division*, while to their right, also as far as to the sea, were two infantry divisions, the 176th and 126th, and two Luftwaffe field divisions, the 9th and 10th *Luftfelddivisionen*. On their side, the Soviets had fielded two army corps in the Oranienbaum salient, with nine Guards divisions, three tank

SS-Ostubaf. Wilhelm Bock

An *SS-Polizei* unit on the Leningrad front.

Members of a Luftwaffe field division.

SS-Ostubaf. Wolfgang Jörchel

brigades, and a coastal brigade. The commander of the SS corps, Felix Steiner, decided to reinforce his positions with a strong concentration of artillery, entrusted to the Danish *SS-Obersturmbannführer* Kryssing, formerly a lieutenant colonel in the Royal Danish Army.

The Dutch Arrive

It was not until close to the end of 1943 that deployment of the III SS Germanic Panzer Corps was definitively completed, with the arrival of the two Dutch regiments of the *Nederland* Brigade; the staff under Wagner, the commander, was posted at Lutschki. Considering the fact that the formation had not yet officially completed its training cycle, the unit was temporarily designated as the "*Aufstellungsverband Nederland*" (Training Unit "Holland"). Steiner decided to employ the Dutch in the sector of the *Kampfgruppe* of the *SS-Polizei*, which was being reorganized, on the left flank of the deployment. Beginning on December 28, 1943, the first elements of *Nederland* began to arrive. Wagner and his chief-of-staff, *SS-Stubaf.* Ziemssen, reported in for a discussion with *SS-Stubaf.* Wilhelm Bock, commander of the *Polizei Kampfgruppe*. The first Dutch unit to be committed to the front line was the reconnaissance company under *SS-Ostuf.* Kuhne, which relieved the Polizei Second Engineer Company southwest of Mustovo. Soon after, it was the turn of *I./General Seyffardt*. At the beginning of the new year, the Dutch took over the entire *SS-Polizei Kampfgruppe* sector. Only the *Polizei* artillery battalion remained on the line, as the Dutch Brigade was still awaiting arrival of its own artillery assets. The *SS-Frw.-Pz. Gr.Rgt.49* took up positions to the east and the *48* to the west. *SS-Panzer-Jäger-Abteilung 54*, under command *of SS-Stubaf.* Knud Schock,[1] located in the area south of Kotly, finally received

A German machine gunner repelling an enemy attack.

its assault guns and its *Pak* issue. The battalion, along with other *III.SS-Pz.Korps* units, was immediately employed against Soviet partisan forces that were operating in the Kotly area. Following transfer to the front at Oranienbaum, command of the 48th *General Seyffardt* Regiment was assumed by *SS-Ostubaf.* Wolfgang Jörchel,[2] who had previously commanded the *Norge* Regiment of the *Nordland* Division. On January 5, 1944, the first wartime conference between Steiner, Wagner and Bock was held to prepare a defensive plan to cope with the imminent Soviet attack. The massing of Soviet troops along the Leningrad front and the Volchov front left no room for interpretation. Among the problems that Wagner had to deal with on an immediate basis was that of communications, which were essential for the correct execution of orders. *SS-Hstuf.* Thissen had only a signal company under his command, rather than the complete *Abteilung* that was needed for the communications requirements of the whole brigade. The lack of radio sets made it difficult for Wagner to communicate properly with his unit commanders. At Steiner's behest, all of the engineer units in the Corps were ordered to lay minefields along the length of the front, in front of the Oranienbaum salient, and to the east along the course of the Volchov. The *Nederland* engineer battalion, whose command had in the meantime been assumed by SS-Stubaf. Günhter Wanhöfer (born November 18, 1916 in Berlin, SS Number 277 917), busied itself with building even more defensive works. Two army engineer companies and a construction battalion with Eastern volunteers, the Turkmen *156.Bau-Bataillon*, were also attached to the *Nederland* engineer battalion.

An MG-34 being manned by several members of the Luftwaffe.

The Soviets Go on the Attack

On January 4, 1944, Soviet forces of the 2nd Baltic Front launched an offensive from the east and from the Oranienbaum salient, overrunning the German defensive positions assigned to the Luftwaffe field divisions. The choice by the Soviets to attack that sector was not by chance, but was dictated by the Soviet conviction that those units were qualitatively inferior to German Army

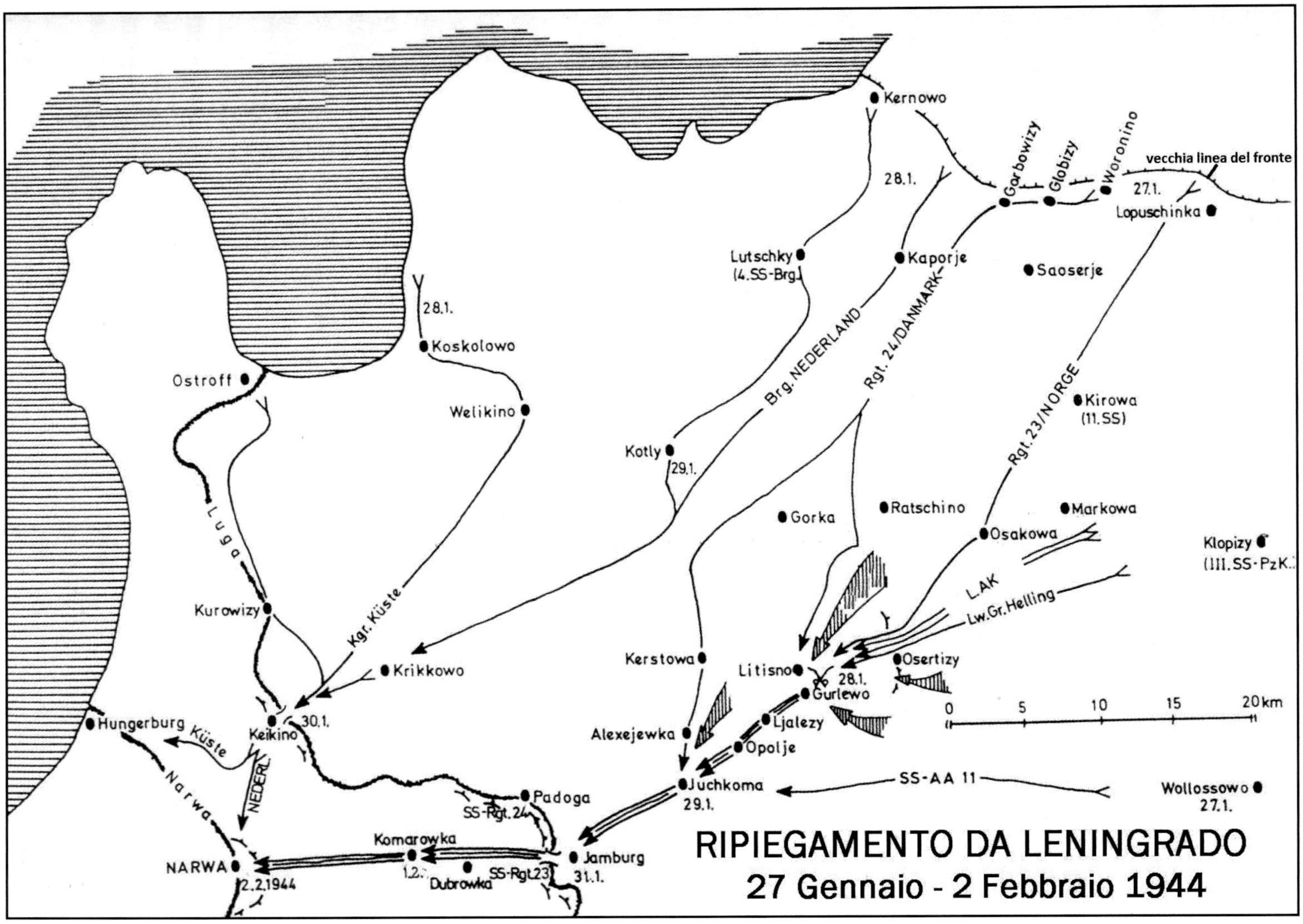

Withdrawal from Leningrad, January 27 – February 2, 1944

and Waffen-SS units. The unfortunate Luftwaffe infantrymen, badly armed and even more badly equipped, could do little against the deluge of fire and steel that fell upon them, and ended up being literally demolished. When the Soviet infantry attack began, the situation became even more critical. All of the defensive line pulled back under the enemy pressure, despite the desperate counterattacks by units of *Nordland* and the *Nederland* Brigade. The two pincers of the Soviet offensive, which had emanated from Oranienbaum and from Leningrad, had closed in a terrible grip when they linked up at Ropscha, not far from Krasnoje Selo.

From there, once they had united their forces, the Soviets thrust towards the west in the direction of Jamburg (Kingisepp) on the Luga River; this maneuver threatened to put all of the German forces along the Oranienbaum front at risk of being attacked from the rear. The German command, realizing the seriousness of the situation, committed all available forces to the battle in an attempt to put a halt to the enemy's advance. When the Soviet infantrymen of the 43rd and 122nd Rifle Corps broke through the third German defensive line, Steiner decided to organize a counterattack and intervene with the units under his command, at the same time ordering a massive blocking barrage by his artillery. Considering the fact that the Dutch were deployed in a sector that was not yet involved in the fighting, Wagner's headquarters received the order to provide troops for the planned counterattack. The Brigade headquarters sent *Kampfgruppe Rühle* (led by *SS-Hstuf.* Hans Joachim Rühle von Lilienstern) consisting of three companies of I Battalion of the 48th SS Regiment. The combat group was moved to the position at Koproje. On January 20, it was subordinated to the *10.Luftwaffe-Feld-Division*. Meanwhile, other units of the Dutch 48th SS Regiment were temporarily transferred to the *Nordland* Division. On 21 January, during a counterattack carried out by units *of SS-Panzer-Jäger-Abteilung 54, SS-Ostuf.* Theo Hickfang (born 15 October 1913, SS Number 343 236), commanding the 1st Company, was killed. Command of the company was then assumed by *SS-Ostuf.* Gerhard Schnurre (born January 21, 1920, SS Number 378 289). On January 22, the Soviets shifted their axis of attack to the area around Witino, where the men of *Kampfgruppe Rühle* had settled in, occupying new defensive positions on both sides of the village. Two companies of *SS-Pionier-Bataillon 54* had also been attached to the combat group at the last moment. This Dutch *Kampfgruppe* was able to throw back repeated attacks during the night between January 22–23. Its commander, Rühle von Lilienstern, personally led numerous counterattacks to ease the enemy pressure and to negate the dangerous Soviet penetrations. On January 25, the companies of *I./Danemark* that were engaged in the same sector were overrun by the Soviet attack. The battalion commander, *SS-Hstuf* Karl Wichmann and two company commanders, *SS-Hstuf.* Heinz Henneke and *SS-Ostuf.* Eduard Hein, were killed in the fighting.

Hans Joachim Rühle von Lilienstern

A Dutch unit on the move, January 1944.

A dangerous gap was thus opened with the Soviets attacking the German positions from three sides. Danish *SS-Hstuf.* Per Sörensen assumed command of the battalion and gave the order to pull back in the direction of Witino, where the Dutch were still located. Sörensen placed himself in the lead and *SS-Ostuf.* Sidon, commander of the *9./Danmark*, provided cover for the withdrawal. After fierce and bloody fighting, the remnants of *I./Danemark* reached the Dutch *Kampfgruppe* positions at Witino. *SS-Hstuf.* Rühle von Lilienstern deployed the Danish grenadiers south of the village. These positions were held until January 27, to cover the retreat of other III SS Corps units to the west. On January 26, *Brigadeführer* von Scholz had in fact received the official order to withdraw his units to the west, toward Jamburg on the Luga River. Despite the fact that he had been wounded, *SS-Hstuf.* Rühle von Lilienstern remained in command of his battalion until he himself was given the order to pull back towards Jamburg. The Danish volunteers, led by *SS-Ostuf.* Fritz Sidon, covered the withdrawal of the Dutch *Kampfgruppe*. For his exemplary conduct on the battlefield *SS-Hstuf.* Rühle von Lilienstern, after having been awarded the Iron Cross First Class on January 22, 1944, was awarded the Knight's Cross on February 12, 1944. The valor of the Dutch volunteers was also cited in the *III.SS-Panzer-Korps* order of the day, signed by its commander Felix Steiner:

> … I wish to express my special appreciation for the excellent work done by *Kampfgruppe Rühle*, of the *SS Nederland Brigade*. I feel honored to have these men under my command, in the *III.SS-Germanischen Panzer-Korps*.

The adjutant of the 48th SS Regiment "*General Seyffardt*," *SS-Hstuf.* Albert Faass (born September 18, 1912, SS Number 284 442) also particularly distinguished himself during the withdrawal operation, as is clear from the citation for the awarding of the German Cross in Gold written on March 19, 1944, by *SS-Ostubaf.*

A German assault gun and grenadiers on the Leningrad front.

Wolfgang Jörchel, commander of the 48th SS Regiment:

1). During the morning of January 31, 1944, the village of Keikono on the Luga River fell into the hands of the enemy, who by now was everywhere. The situation was very serious, given the strong pressure exerted on the Regiment that consisted mostly of young soldiers who were under fire for the first time and because of the high losses of officers and NCOs. There was danger that the enemy might advance along the road that led through the swampy forest to Narva and that it might bypass the positions covered by heavy weapons and artillery. In this way the enemy would have not only attacked the other units of the *Nederland* Brigade from the rear, but also those of the *Nordland* Division, putting our ability to hold our bridgehead in serious jeopardy. During this serious situation, *SS-Hstuf.* Faass received orders from the commander of the Regiment to launch an attack against the enemy forces coming from Keikino by collecting all available personnel and to reestablish the former defensive line.

SS-Unterscharführer Kaspar Sporck's *Stummel*.

SS-Hstuf. Karl Heinz Ertel

SS-Ostuf. Günther Steffen

SS-Hstuf. Faass was able to gather together the last remaining NCOs, the personnel of the regimental headquarters, and a reserve company. With these forces as well as with new units that had meantime arrived as reinforcements, in the dead of night he launched an attack against Keikino, breaking into the village. He himself, fighting with a machine pistol and hand grenades, led his men to where the enemy was offering the most resistance, inflicting heavy losses on the Soviets and occupying a large part of the village. When the Soviets counterattacked with vastly superior numbers, in danger of running out of ammunition, *SS-Hstuf.* Faass along with his command group gathered together all of the wounded and set his men up in defensive positions. He himself, with several grenadiers, covered the withdrawal and prevented the enemy from reaching the new position.

2). On February 1, 1944, the enemy attacked, supported by fire from heavy weapons and artillery, attempting to break through in the direction of Narva. Once again with his determined action Faass personally led the defense of the positions, holding them at all costs. When the order later came to pull back to a new line, Faass protected the withdrawal of all of the units of the Regiment, which were able to reach the new positions by the only road that was open. He continued to remain in his position with his command group, continuing to inflict great losses to the enemy.

3). On February 2, 1944, the enemy renewed its attacks, again supported by massive artillery covering fire, against the position held by Faass' command group (along the Narva–Keikino road). Numerous attacks were repulsed with heavy losses, when the enemy attacked from both sides of the road from the swampy forest. In view of the strong enemy pressure and the shortage of ammunition, Faass took action, continuing to fight in the most forward position using his machine pistol and grenades, and carrying wounded soldiers to a collection point two kilometers to the south. The reason that this withdrawal was able to be carried out, was due only to Faass!

4). As soon as the new rally point was reached, Faass quickly organized a new counterattack, which because of the swampy forest could only be carried out along the road. Faass therefore split his men into four assault groups and with them he threw himself against the enemy's blocking fire. Despite the tenacious enemy resistance, still at the head of his men, he led them in the attack against the most heavily defended point, annihilating the Soviet forces."

Kaspar Sporck

The units of *SS-Panzer-Aufklärungs Abteilung 11* of *Nordland* were heavily engaged during this period in covering the retreat of their comrades; the armored vehicles of *SS-Stubaf.* Rodolf Saalbach[3] had concentrated near the village of Gubanizy, a few kilometers south of Klopizy, where the corps commander Felix Steiner had set up his headquarters. The leading Soviet tank elements, followed by numerous infantry units, attacked at dawn on January 26, right in the area of Gubanizy; the *5.Kompanie* of *SS-Ostuf.* Georg Langendorf was the only unit of the *Nordland* reconnaissance detachment that still had operational anti-tank weapons, including a heavy anti-tank platoon with three 75 mm guns and eight *SdKfz 251/9* half-tracks equipped with a short-barrelled 75 mm gun. The large Soviet tank formation consisted of about sixty tanks and Langendorf recognized T-34 and older type tanks. The anti-tank gun layers began to get the leading tanks in their sights. The first group, consisting of seven vehicles, ended up being taken under fire by the German *Pak* guns; six tanks were knocked out within a few seconds. With the arrival of the second wave of tanks, the *Stummel* (*Stummel* is the German word for "stub" or "stubby," an apt reference to the short barrel of the 75 mm gun which it mounted), which were the company's half-tracks, joined the action; Dutch *SS-Rottenführer* Kaspar Sporck[4] with his half-track armed with a 75 mm gun, flung himself against the enemy without a moment's hesitation. Along his destructive path, a total of eleven tanks were destroyed and anther four seriously damaged. The Soviet offensive thrust against Gubanizy was thus transformed into a veritable slaughter of enemy tankers; fully forty-eight tanks were destroyed by *5./SS-Aufkl.11* alone. *SS-Ostuf.* Langendorf was one of the first officers from *Nederland* to be awarded the Knight's Cross (March 12, 1944). Within the space of a few days *SS-Rttf.* Sporck was presented both classes of the Iron Cross (January 30 and February 7, 1944), while awaiting the award of the Knight's Cross. On May 1, 1944, he was promoted to the rank of *SS-Unterscharführer.*

Beginning the Withdrawal

The withdrawal by the Dutch SS units began on January 28, 1944. The Dutch volunteers had to march in the cold and in the snow, moving through thick forests, incessantly hounded by Soviet artillery fire. Their weapons and equipment were loaded on *Akjas*, the boat-like sleds used by Nordic people to transport loads over the snow. The engineers were kept busy mining the roads to slow the advance of Soviet units that were never far behind. *SS-Panzer-Jäger-Abteilung 54* under *SS-Stubaf.* Knud Shock reinforced the rear-guard forces before pulling back to the south with its assault guns, crossing the Luga River at Jamburg. *SS-Ostuf.* Kuhne's reconnaissance company assumed responsibility for covering the flanks and for maintaining contact among the various units. When they reached the area near Kotly, the Dutch were attacked by the Soviets.

SS-Ustuf. Karl Heinz Ertel,[5] Collani's aide-de-camp, was seriously wounded while he was attempting to lead the withdrawal of the last units of the "*de Ruyter*" Regiment. A lone *Flak* gun from the regiment's *14.Kompanie* managed to keep the Soviets at a distance, freeing the road to the west. The Dutch volunteers continued to fight a rear-guard action against units of the Soviet 47th Army. As soon as the last units of *Kampfgruppe "Küste"* (the *III.SS-Panzer Korps* unit defending the coastal sector) crossed the Luga River at Keikino, the Dutch took up new

Eugen Deck (on the left) and *SS-Stubaf.* Collani in the Ukraine in 1942, when they were assigned to *Wiking*.

German grenadiers retreating, February 1944.

A German unit while withdrawing. In the foreground is an enemy tank that has been knocked out.

German soldiers in bivouac in the snow, February 1944.

An *SdKfz 250* half-track belonging to the *Nordland* reconnaissance battalion.

defensive positions in a semi-circle around the city. *SS-Hstuf.* Günther Wanhöfer, who took command of an engineer squad, took action to destroy the bridge north of Padoga, thus denying the Krikkowo–Jamburg road to heavy vehicles. During the whole withdrawal and establishment of a new defensive line along the river, the *Nederland* Brigade held the bridgehead at Keikino. On January 30, the last units of the "*General Seyffardt*" Regiment, led by *SS-Ostubaf.* Jörchel, crossed the Luga. That same day, in the final actions against the Soviet forces, *SS-Hstuf.* Günther Steffen, commander of *6.Kompanie* of the 48th Dutch SS Regiment and a veteran of the Flemish Volunteer Legion, was killed in combat. In order to continue to keep the Soviets at bay, *SS-Stubaf.* Engelhardt, chief of staff of *Kampfgruppe "Küste,"* detached a company of the group (an NCO training company) to the Dutch regiment. *SS-Ostubaf.* Jörchel placed this company north of Keikino. Meanwhile, the *Nederland* engineers had blown the bridge at Keikino.

The Luga Front

By the end of January all of the III SS Panzer Corps was established along the new defensive line that followed the course of the Luga River. *General* Walter Model, commanding the northern front, ordered Steiner to hold the positions along the river for as long as possible so that other German units could pull back to the west. The commander of *Heeresgruppe Nord* intended to form a new defensive front along the banks of the Luga. His attention was focused on the Leningrad–Jamburg railway line and the main supply route. Model thus ordered the *III.SS-Panzer Korps* to hold this new line and the bridgehead northwest of Jamburg, at Keikino. Steiner was not happy with that order, knowing that the "*Luga Linie*" could not be held for long, as the Soviets had already crossed the river farther to the south with their 8th Army and were about to reach the shores of Lake Peipus. But orders were orders. Beginning on January 31, the Soviets had infiltrated between Kurowizy and the coast at Hungerburg. The training company attached to the "*General Seyffardt*" Regiment was given the impossible mission off defending about twenty kilometers of the sector and to cover the northern flank of the defensive line. Swamps and wild forests, with no roads or railway lines, characterized the company's operational area. No one had foreseen that it would be in this sector that the Soviets, at first in small groups, then employing large forces, would have been able to reach the point of threatening the banks of the Narva River. The NCO cadets fought strenuously, inflicting heavy losses on the Soviets, and it was only after tough and bloody fighting that they were forced to give ground; two

SS-Hstuf. Günther Wanhöfer

SS-Stubaf. Rudolf Saalbach

Kaspar Antoine Sporck

of the company's officers were killed and half of the unit was wiped out. The few survivors barely managed to withdraw, bringing numerous wounded along with them. Another dangerous Soviet penetration at Pulkowo was halted by grenadiers of the *6.Kompanie* of the *de Ruyter* Regiment, commanded by *SS-Obersturmführer* Eugen Deck.

For this action and for the bravery that had been demonstrated within the ranks of *SS-Panzer-Aufklärungs-Abteilung Wiking* and with the *Finnisches Freiwilligen Bataillon*, the officer was presented with the German Cross in Gold on March 12, 1944, based on the recommendation of the brigade commander, *SS-Brigdf.* Wagner and the corps commander himself, *Ogruf.* Felix Steiner, with the following citation (with respect to his action with *Nederland*):

> ... while fighting a rear-guard action in February 1944, *II./SS-Panzergrenadier-Regiment 49 "de Ruyter"* prevented crossing of the Luga River at SSala and Pulkowo–Keikino. During the night between January 31 and February 1 the enemy was able to cross the Luga River with a battalion and broke into Pulkowo, defended by *6. de Ruyter*. Faced with inexperience and with exhausted troops involved in difficult nighttime fighting, the full weight of responsibility fell upon the company commander, *SS-Obersturmführer* Deck. He rallied all of the scattered elements of the company, deployed them properly among the houses, and checked the Soviet penetration into the village. Following the arrival of the regiment's motorcycle platoon, he carried out an immediate counterattack, leading it personally. Leading his men, he ejected the enemy from the village after five hours of house-to-house fighting. Despite the fact that he had been wounded during the fighting, he stayed with his company until the end. When the order to pull back was received, he covered the company's disengagement with a machine gun. *SS-Obersturmführer* Deck demonstrated extraordinary courage in this action and by his personal example inspired the demoralized troops with renewed vigor and leading them himself in an immediate counterattack. It was due entirely to his courage that *6./de Ruyter* was able to disengage in good order.

Farther to the south, also on January 31, the Soviets attacked the Jamburg bridgehead, defended by grenadiers of the *Norge* Regiment and by *Nordland*. The pressure point subsequently shifted against the positions held by *Danmark* in the area of Padoga. Jamburg was abandoned on February 1. The *III.SS-Pz. Korps* artillery pulled its guns back across the Narva River. Its commander, Felix Steiner, gave the following orders to *SS-Stubaf.* Poul Ransow Engelhardt: "... Assemble all of the survivors of *Kampfgruppe Küste* and all of the other units located in the area of Hungerburg and with them organize a defensive line along the Narva River from its mouth as far south as possible. *Nederland* and *Nordland* are still holding the Luga–Linie, but I do not know for how long they will still be able to hold out." Soon afterwards the official order to withdraw was issued by headquarters: "... Soviet units have pushed through the positions on the Luga River. The new main line of resistance must be established along the course of the Narva River."

The German command had thus decided to attempt to stop the Soviet offensive more to the west, along the Narva, which was the river that had always, both historically and geographically, marked the boundary between Estonia and Russia. The new defensive line, designated the *Panther* line, was based on natural defensive barriers represented by the Narva and Velikaya rivers and Lakes Peipus and Pskov. Work on constructing fortifications had begun as early as September 1943, but were far from having been completed. The *Nordland* and *Nederland* units thus began their new withdrawal. Once again it was the reconnaissance elements of the SS Corps to provide cover for the German withdrawal, and more specifically, that the Dutch *SS-Rottenführer* Kaspar Sporck was yet again able to distinguish himself in the combat engagements, destroying numerous enemy vehicles.

CHAPTER V
THE BRIDGEHEAD AT NARVA

A panoramic view of Narva, from a postcard dating back to 1939.

General Johannes Friessner

In early February 1944, after having abandoned the bridgehead at Jamburg, the German forces took up positions at Narva; founded in the thirteenth century by the Danes and built up as a fortress by the Teutonic Knights against the Russians, the city was only about ten kilometers from the Baltic Sea. To the south, the area between the city and Lake Peipus was covered by dense forests and swamps that were not easy to cross. At Narva, on the western bank of the river bearing the same name as the city, rose the fortress of Hermannsburg, built by the Teutonic Knights, while on the eastern bank, directly opposite it, was the fortress of Ivangorod which was built by Russian Grand Duke Ivan III. For centuries the Germanic and Slavic peoples had fought over these places and once again in 1944 Narva returned to represent the bulwark of European civilization against the barbarians coming from the East. Defending the city this time were military units of all types: Estonian volunteers, German soldiers of the Wehrmacht, infantrymen of the Luftwaffe and Kriegsmarine, but above all were the Germanic volunteers of the Waffen-SS coming from throughout Europe; German propaganda was happy to portray the defense of Narva as the Battle of the European SS Volunteers.

FORMATION OF *ARMEE-ABTEILUNG NARVA*

Initially the *III.SS-Panzer-Korps* was subordinated to *LIV.Armee-Korps* of *General der Infanterie* Otto Sponheimer. On February 4, the corps was detached from the *18.Armee* and subordinated

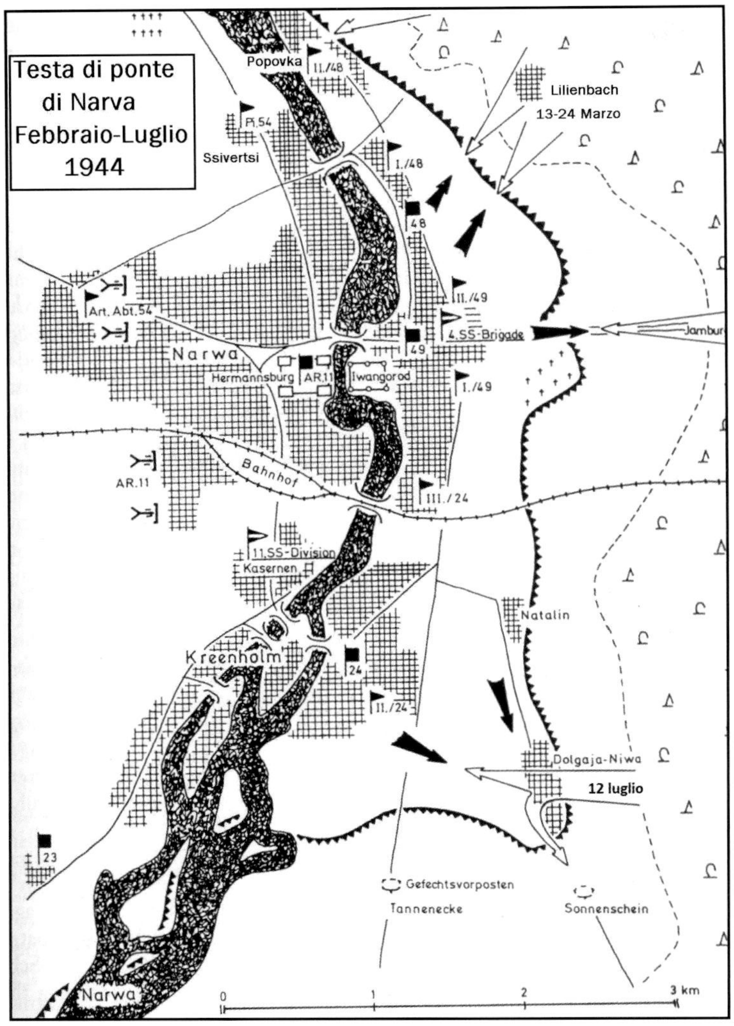

Bridgehead at Narva, February–July 1944

Trucks towing guns over the Narva River, with the fortress of Ivangorod in the background.

directly to Army Group North (*Heeresgruppe Nord*). To reinforce the bridgehead at Narva, Hitler ordered the dispatch of all available forces; accordingly, units from every corner of Europe arrived. On February 15, *General* Sponheimer was replaced by *General* Johannes Friessner, and on February 23, the "*Sponheimer Gruppe*" was renamed as *Armee-Abteilung Narva* with the mission of controlling all units north of Lake Peipus. On February 22, the headquarters of Army Group North ordered deployment of *Armee-Abteilung Narva* along the following positions: *III./SS-Panzer-Korps* (*SS-Obergruppenführer* Felix Steiner) north of Narva and on the bridgehead on the eastern bank of the Narva River, *XXXXII.Armee-Korps* (*General der Infanterie* Karl von Oven) at the bridgehead of Auvere south of the city, and *XXVI. Armee-Korps* (*General der Infanterie* Anton Grasser) in the sector between the Auvere bridgehead and Lake Peipus.

Composition of *Armee-Abteilung Narva*[1]

XXVI.Armee-Korps

11.Infanterie-Division
58.Infanterie-Division
214.Infanterie-Division
225.Infanterie-Division
3rd Estonian Border Guard Regiment

XXXXIII.Armee-Korps

61.Infanterie-Division
170.Infanterie-Division
227.Infanterie-Division
Panzergrenadier Division "Feldherrnhalle"
"Gnesen" Grenadier Regiment

III.SS-Panzer-Korps

11.SS-Panzergrenadier Division "Nordland"
4.SS-Panzergrenadier Brigade "Nederland"
20 Waffen-Gren.Div. der SS (etnische Nr.1)

Corps Units

Eastern sector, coastal defense
Estonian "Reval" Regiment
29th Estonian Police Battalion
31st Estonian Police Battalion
32nd Estonian Police Battalion
658. Ostbataillon (Estonian)
659. Ostbataillon (Estonian)
113th Artillery Command
32nd Engineer Command
502.Schwere Panzer Abteilung
752.Panzerjäger Bataillon

Unit Deployments

As soon as they had arrived at their new positions, commanders von Scholz and Wagner quickly had to see to the deployment of their units. The Soviets were making haste to besiege the new German defensive positions with a total of three armies: the 47th Army to the north, the 2nd Shock Army to the east and the 8th to the south. In particular, the *Nordland* and *Nederland* units were deployed as follows: *I./Danmark* took positions along the Narva–Jamburg road, to the north were the Dutchmen of

Waffen-SS grenadiers at Narva.

Dutch grenadiers at Narva, 1944.

Anti-tank gun position in the northeastern sector of the bridgehead.

Nederland and to the south other units of *Norge* and *Danmark*. Supporting them were *Tiger* tanks of *2./Schwere-Panzer-Abteilung 502* and of the *1./SS-Panzer-Abteilung 11 "Hermann von Salza,"* in addition to the remaining assault guns of *Nordland* and *Nederland*. The Dutch SS Brigade thus occupied the area north of the city; the Dutch volunteers occupied positions at the bridgehead on the eastern bank of the river, between the fortress of Ivangorod and Lilienbach. The "*General Seyffardt*" Regiment was deployed around and to the south of Popovka, while "*de Ruyter*" was deployed from Lilienbach to the main road for Jamburg. During the night of February 2–3, the Soviets initiated a series of offensive actions against the German positions on the eastern bank of the river; the Dutch volunteers were also caught up in the attacks but were able to repulse all of the enemy thrusts and maintain a firm hold on their new positions. Two days later the Soviets attacked again with greater forces, first subjecting the German lines to artillery fire, then employing air attacks, and finally committing infantry and tank units along the entire Narva front. It was a veritable storm of iron and fire that, however, was shattered against the strenuous resistance put up by the European volunteers. *SS-Artillerie-Regiment 11* and the *Polizei* artillery battalion, both of which were now permanently assigned to the Dutch Brigade (and officially redesignated as *I./SS-Art.Rgt. 54*, commanded by *SS-Stubaf.* Josef Rüschoff), played a pivotal role during the defensive battles of the early days on the Narva bridgehead.

A brief lull in the fighting allowed the commands to quickly reorganize the units that had reached Narva after many days of wearying marches. Following the decision to definitively disband the two Luftwaffe field divisions (9th and 10th *Luftwaffen-Feld-Divisionen*) which had been decimated and were without leaders, the survivors were sent as replacement personnel to reinforce units of *Nederland* and *Nordland*, which was a forced integration but one which was dictated by the seriousness of the military situation in the field. Of the 1,336 survivors, 710 went to *Nordland* and 482 to *Nederland*. The Luftwaffe infantrymen, after having been tempered by the fighting of the preceding days, were able to adapt very well and very quickly to the fighting spirit and iron discipline of the Waffen-SS. The brief pause in the fighting enabled to Germans to transform Narva into a veritable fortress; night after night the engineers *of SS-Pionier-Bataillon 11* and *SS-Pionier-Bataillon 54* were busy erecting palisades, stringing barbed-wire barricades, digging trenches, and laying kilometers of telephone wire.

Clashes at Ssivertsi

On February 11, the Soviets resumed the attack north of the bridgehead, between Riigi and Ssivertsi, managing to break through the defensive positions of two German units; about 3,000 Soviet infantry crossed the Narva, establishing a bridgehead of their own on the western bank of the river in the woods southeast of Riigi. The German units, *Kampfgruppe Wengler* of *227.Infanterie-Division* were somehow able to limit the expansion of the bridgehead at the cost of great sacrifice. Between the German and Soviet positions, which were separated by 600 to 2,000 meters, there was swampy terrain; on the two flanks, to the northeast of Riigi and Ssivertsi, the positions were much closer. The hamlet of Paklamae, situated on a small hill, was organized as a support area for the successive counterattacks. Around it, the forward artillery observers from *Nederland*, whose batteries had been emplaced about a kilometer to the south, took up positions. While the *Wehrmacht* grenadiers continued to stoutly defend their positions at Riigi, the *Nederland*

SS-Stubaf. Albrecht Krügel

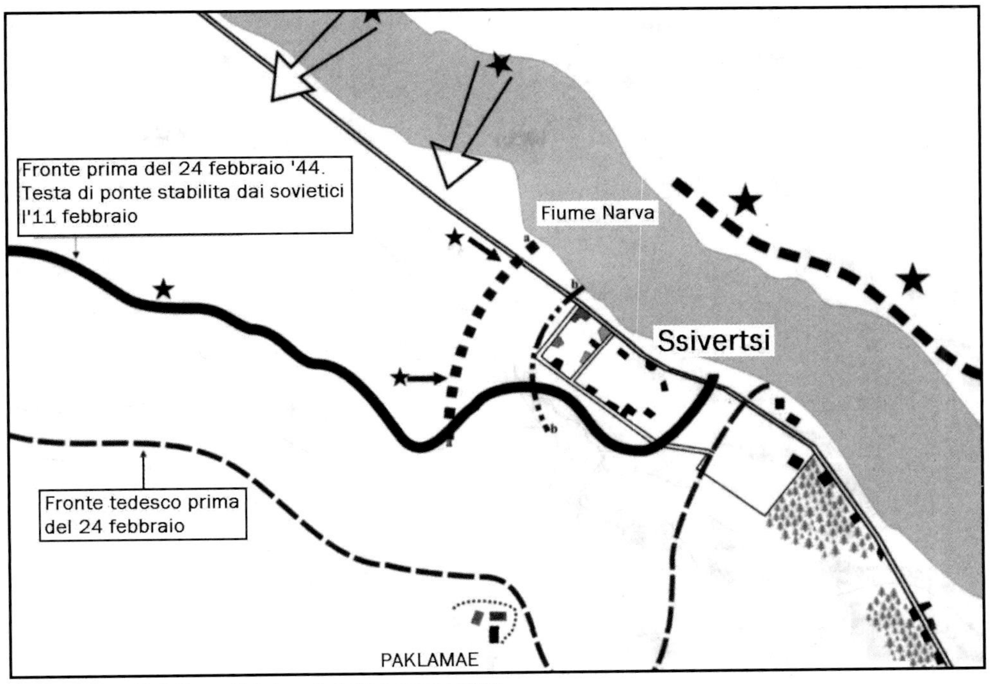

Map of the fighting at Ssivertsi, February 1944

A *Panther* tank of *Nordland* at Narva, February 1944.

engineers, led by *SS-Hstuf.* Günther Wanhöfer, were sent to seal the gap at Ssivertsi. The Dutch engineers were soon engaged in brutal close-quarter fighting in the cemetery at Ssivertsi, which was repeatedly attacked by Soviet infantry. *SS-Hstuf.* Wanhöfer, after having rallied as many men as possible from his engineer battalion, personally led a fierce counterattack that managed to wrest several positions from the enemy. However, the Dutchmen were not able to eliminate the dangerous Soviet bridgehead, which was of vital strategic importance; if the Soviets were able to enlarge it further, Narva would fall soon after and all of the German forces in the bridgehead would be surrounded. The commander of *III.SS-Panzer-Korps*, Steiner, ordered all available forces to be sent to the area in which the enemy penetrations had occurred; accordingly a *Kampfgruppe* began to be formed, under command of *SS-Stubaf.* Albrecht Krügel, commander of *II./Norge*. There were only two engineer companies from the *Norge* and *Danmark* regiments available. The unfortunate engineers had spent the whole night stringing barbed wire, reinforcing bunkers, and above all laying hundreds of mines. Weary from lack of sleep and paralyzed by the cold, they were quickly called back into the front lines after a cup of lukewarm coffee and a half-frozen chunk of bread. In addition to them, at the last minute, the grenadiers of *11.Kompanie* of *Norge* and a motorcycle platoon were scraped up.

As soon as they had reached Ssivertsi the reinforcements found themselves under violent fire of Soviet artillery, which was well emplaced on the eastern bank of the river, and which was able to hit almost anything that moved on the opposite bank. The massive artillery bombardment was followed quickly by an infantry attack; the Soviet infantrymen, in a compact mass, crossed over the frozen surface of the river, again throwing themselves into an attack against the cemetery of Ssivertsi. Norwegian, Danish and Dutch engineers engaged in hand-to-hand combat with their enemies, fighting like devils amongst the tombstones. There was fighting with hand grenades, bayonets and knives, but some of the engineers found that they were more comfortable using their pick mattocks, which were formidable tools for digging, but which were also able to split enemy skulls with great ease. The cemetery of Ssivertsi changed hands several times in a series of fierce attacks and counterattacks; wherever one looked, there were bodies and wounded groaning amidst the ruined tombstones.

Throughout the day of February 12, Soviet artillery continued to heavily shell the German positions along the Narva River, and in particular, the cemetery of Ssivertsi which continued to be defended by the *Nederland* and *Nordland* engineers. In an attempt to dislodge the Soviets permanently from the bridgehead at Ssivertsi, it was decided to launch yet another counterattack, committing the assault guns of *SS-Pz.-Jg.-Abt.54* under *SS-Stubaf.* Schock, supporting *Kampfgruppe Krügel*, an entire company of assault guns with fourteen *Sturmgeschütz III*. The attack was also to be supported by *Nederland's* artillery assets. In addition, a platoon of 120 mm heavy mortars, emplaced in the hamlet of Paklamae, was to use its fire to impede the arrival of any enemy reinforcements. The attack was to be led by *SS-Stubaf.* Schock. After discussing the attack plan with the commanders of the *Nederland* artillery batteries, the idea of using direct supporting

February 1944: a defensive positon in the Narva bridgehead. The unfortunate German grenadiers had to fight first against the cold as well as against the enemy.

German soldiers carrying a wounded comrade to the rear.

fire against the Soviet positions in Ssivertsi was abandoned because it was felt that the fourteen assault guns would have already provided enough fire support. It was a serious error in judgment, because it was of absolute importance that the Soviet firing positions northeast of the river be neutralized beforehand, which was a mission that had to be carried out by the *Nederland* gunners. Some thought was given to using smoke shells to "blind" the enemy observers, but at the last minute the order was cancelled because of a sudden shift in wind direction.

During the night the European grenadiers and engineers marched toward the cemetery of Ssivertsi, about a kilometer north-west of Narva, while the assault guns kept to the outskirts of Narva. In an attempt to evade the fire of the Soviet heavy weapons that were emplaced on the opposite bank of the river, a route of march was selected that ran about three hundred meters away from the river, concealed by vegetation and by houses. The column was led by two grenadier companies, one on either side of the path. A flamethrower detachment accompanied each company. The first elements to attack the Soviet positions were the assault guns belonging to *Nederland*, which soon found themselves under a massive barrage of fire from the Soviet heavy weapons. After a few of the assault guns had been hit and knocked out, Schock jumped from his vehicle to organize the resistance and to try to get his men to renew the attack. Unfortunately a stray Soviet round struck him a deathblow just as he was issuing orders to his unit commanders. With the death of Schock almost all hope of continuing the attack was lost. Accordingly, the remaining Dutch assault guns pulled back in order to escape the fire of the Soviet anti-tank guns. Other German units engaged in the attack against Ssivertsi were somewhat luckier, managing to advance and to wrest several positions from the Soviets.

The Germanic grenadiers and engineers continued to attack the enemy bridgehead and to shift the fighting even into the village of Ssivertsi. By now the men were exhausted, but their unit commanders continued to throw them into battle in the vain hope of ejecting the enemy from the positions they had occupied. It was not until late in the evening that the fighting ceased, giving both parties a moment of rest. Reinforcements arrived from the rear area; cases of ammunition and shells were quickly distributed, along with a ration of soup. The wounded were loaded aboard vehicles, hoping that they would not die from the cold before they reached Narva. *SS-Brigadeführer* von Scholz also reached the position at Ssivertsi, and who after having personally taken stock of the state to which his men and those of the *Nederland* had been reduced, ordered the cessation of all offensive action; they were to be relieved by a Wehrmacht company. A new Soviet attack the following morning led to a series of new bloody encounters, during which Albrecht Krügel was seriously wounded and evacuated to the rear. Command of the *Kampfgruppe* fell to his adjutant, *SS-Hstuf.* Michael Thöny. With a final desperate assault, Ssivertsi was wrested completely from the Soviets. There remained only to eliminate another island of enemy resistance, that of Vepsküla. An initial attack by the grenadiers of *11./Norge* was not, however, successful. The 150 mm howitzers of *13./Norge* then joined in to support, as later the artillery from *Nederland* as well. Even though they were subjected to a deluge of fire, the Soviets held their positons at Vepsküla. In the end, the German command decided to have the Germanic volunteers be relieved by Estonian Waffen-SS volunteers. On February 29, 1944, the Soviets still held a small bridgehead on the western bank of the Narva. It was a simple twenty-two-year-old Estonian sergeant, *Unterscharführer* Haralt Nugiseks (*Zugführer* of the 1st Company of the 1st Battalion of the 46th Estonian SS Regiment) who with a small assault group of his countrymen was able to close the gap and to surround the Soviets on the western bank after brutal close-quarter fighting. He was one of the first Baltic volunteers to be presented the Knight's Cross. The 20th Estonian SS Division, commanded

Estonian unit of the *20.SS* on the front at Narva.

Estonian *SS-Unterscharführer* Haralt Nugiseks.

Dutch grenadiers in the Lilienbach position.

by *SS-Brigadeführer* Franz Augsberger, was also assigned to the *III.SS-Panzer-Korps*. On February 29, *SS-Gruppenührer* Matthias Kleinheisterkamp, former commander of the *SS-Division Nord*, and now an aide-de-camp to Steiner, arrived to visit the Dutch positions. The officer, who was a veteran of the Finnish front, had a long meeting with the brigade commander, Wagner, to examine the military-strategic situation of the bridgehead. The positions assigned to the Dutch were of vital strategic importance for the defense of the entire area around Narva.

A Hurricane of Fire Against Narva

As all of the attacks by their infantry had failed, the Soviets tried to break German resistance at Narva with heavy air bombing. The Soviet bombs caused high losses to units of III SS Corps, not only in terms of human lives, but also with respect to equipment, vehicles and heavy weapons. Once the air attacks were over, the Soviets continued with their artillery; hundreds of medium and large caliber guns concentrated their fire on the city. Over the course of two nights and one day Narva was transformed into a heap of rubble. Only the two medieval citadels were left standing, almost as a sign of challenge to the Soviet attackers. Following the massive shelling of the southern suburbs, where units of the *Danmark* Regiment were deployed, the Soviets once again turned their attention to the area to the north of the city, renewing the attack with infantry. The Dutch volunteers were the first to be hit; every enemy attack was followed by a counterattack by the defenders, resulting in bitter close-quarter fighting. The grenadiers of the *Nederland* Brigade were determined to hold their positions at all costs. It was only at Lilienbach, the large hamlet northeast of Narva on the eastern bank of the river, that the Soviets were able to open a gap. The Dutch units defending the sector, lacking adequate anti-tank weapons, were forced to withdraw in the face of an attack by Soviet tanks. The SS Corps headquarters was again forced to send reinforcements to the position, constituting a new *Kampfgruppe* with Germanic volunteers from the two *Nordland* regiments, still under the command of *SS-Hstuf.* Thöny. The *Nordland* grenadiers moved in all haste towards Lilienbach in an attempt to eliminate the new Soviet breakthrough. Brutal close-quarter fighting ensued, with heavy losses on both sides. One of the first to be seriously wounded by enemy fire was *SS-Ostuf.* Fritz Sidon, commander of *9./Danmark*. His comrade Thöny was able to expel the Soviets from the hamlet and manage after a fashion to establish a new line of resistance. Throughout the night the Dutch engineers dug new holes and trenches to reinforce their defensive positions, which soon were almost completely surrounded by enemy units. This forward position defended by the Dutch volunteers covered all of the northeastern part of the bridgehead and thus represented an important strategic objective.

A Dutch unit awaiting an attack at Lilienbach.

The *Nederland* command post at Narva. From the left: Wagner, commander of the Dutch Brigade, *Stubaf.* Ziemssen (Ia) and *General* Kleinheisterkamp, aide de camp to Felix Steiner.

During the night of March 6–7, Soviet aircraft returned to heavily bomb the bridgehead at Narva, causing further death and destruction. At dawn on March 7, the Soviets renewed their attack with infantry and tanks. The greatest weight of this new attack fell on units of the 48th Dutch SS Regiment that was conducting the defense of the northern part of the bridgehead at Popowka. *SS-Stubaf.* Jörchel threw all of his reserves into the fight in order to fend off the blow. The Soviet infantry flung itself fearlessly against the fire coming from the positions of the European volunteers, breaking through at Povka, Telliskivi and Lilienbach, where fierce hand-to-hand combat occurred. The Soviets were, however, stopped by the fire of the heavy machine guns and mortars deployed along the second defensive line, while artillery and 88 mm *Flak* guns using direct fire destroyed all of the tanks supporting the infantry. The fighting was terrible; mountains of enemy corpses were piled on the ground between the first and second defensive lines. But it wasn't over yet; the Soviets attacked again soon, using fresh forces. The two battalions of *General Seyffardt* were able to hold their positions, throwing back the new enemy assault and counterattacking ferociously.

A number of *Panzers* came to their aid. The *Nordland* tank battalion *Hermann von Salza* was able to gather together a company of *Panther*[2] tanks commanded by *SS-Ostuf.* Rott. His tanks went head-to-head against the T-34s that the Soviets sent unceasingly against Lilienbach. One of his platoon leaders, *SS-Oberscharführer* Philipp Wild, managed to stem an enemy tank attack near the cemetery. For this action he was subsequently awarded the Knight's Cross on March 21, 1944, on the personal recommendation of the commander of the Dutch SS Brigade, Wagner, with the following citation:

> ... Numerous enemy aircraft incessantly bombed the bridgehead and city of Narva during the nights of March 6/7 and 7/8, with attacks that lasted from ten to eleven hours. On March 8, 1944, at 0700, following a heavy shelling by Soviet artillery that lasted two and a half hours, an attack by the 63rd Guards Rifle Division followed. The attack was supported by fourteen tanks and was conducted on a narrow front, in the northeastern area of the bridgehead. Twelve tanks broke through the main line of resistance pausing towards the positions defended by the heavy weapons of the *SS-Freiwilligen-Panzer-Grenadier-Regiment 48 "General Seyffardt."* At the most critical moment of the battle, *SS-Oberscharführer* Wild, of *1./SS-Panzer-Abteilung 11,* joined combat with his Panther, and in a very brief time destroyed all of the T-34 tanks that had overrun our defensive line. His action was decisive in blocking the Soviet attempt to break through the Narva bridgehead. The destruction of these tanks was likewise decisive, as the enemy infantry, after having lost its tank support, was easily repulsed.

The Soviets renewed their attack against the position at Lilienbach, where the Dutch engineers had in the meantime been relieved by the comrades from "*de Ruyter*." Yet again the Soviet infantry and tanks were able to achieve a penetration. *9./Danmark* and the remnants of *Kampfgruppe Thöny* were again sent to reinforce the position. After bitter close-quarter fighting the main line of resistance was reestablished. Stalemated north of the bridgehead, the Soviets shifted their attack axis farther to the south, north of the main supply line, right in front of the command post of the *Nederland* Brigade. Close by was the 1st Company of *SS-Panzer-Abteilung 11 "Hermann von Salza."* It was in fact the *Panther* tanks of *SS-Ostuf.* Rott that, following repeated and furious attacks, halted the attack of the Soviet tanks, which as a consequence also removed the immediate threat posed by the enemy infantry. Wagner, the commander, was keeping a particularly close watch on the unfolding combat activity from his command post. Using telephone and radio communications he was keeping track of the movements of his units and directing the movement of reserves, munitions and rations. The fighting for Lilienbach continued for another two days during which the Dutch regiment "*de Ruyter*" suffered serious losses. Among the dead was the commander of II Battalion, *SS-Hstuf.* Burmester. Enemy penetrations, defensive actions and counterattacks followed in rapid succession, completely tiring out the already exhausted Dutch volunteers. Commander Hans Collani wondered just how much longer his valorous grenadiers would be able to hold out under those trying conditions.

Dutch trench in the bridgehead. Note the jury-rigged periscope used to scan the enemy positions while keeping safe from enemy fire.

Dutch soldiers in movement within the bridgehead.

The Devil's Meadow

The enemy artillery continued to savagely punish the positions of the Dutch volunteers in the bridgehead. In the end, it was decided to abandon the Lilienbach position, which was judged to be too exposed to enemy fire and attacks. The Dutch units withdrew to a new positon known as "the Devil's Meadow" (*Teufelwiese* in German). During the night of March 13–14, the Soviets lost no time in attacking the new position, catching the Dutch units, who were still setting up their new positions, by surprise. The new commander of *II./de Ruyter, SS-Hstuf.* Walter Diener (born May 26, 1917, SS Number 367 337) was killed during the defensive fighting. Another company commander was wounded while leading a counterattack. The commander of a nearby company, the 7th, *SS-Ostuf.* Helmut Scholz,[3] seeing the seriousness of the situation, immediately organized a counterattack with a few courageous volunteers, and with the force born of desperation was able to throw the enemy from their positions. The next day the regimental adjutant, *SS-Ustuf.* Karl-Heinz Ertel, assumed temporary command of *II./de Ruyter*, before handing it over a few days later to *SS-Hstuf.* Karl-Heinz Frühauf.[4] The valor and efforts of the Dutch volunteers were mentioned in the *Oberkommando der Wehrmacht* report of March 15, 1944: "... During the final days of combat in the northern sector of the eastern front, the Dutch regiment *"General Seyffardt"* of the *SS "Nederland" Brigade* distinguished itself particularly under the command of *SS-Ostubaf.* Jörchel."

After further local attacks, a new extraordinary Soviet artillery barrage was unleashed on the hill at Lilienbach and on the "Devil's Meadow" during the day of March 22. The positions of the 5th Company of *SS-Ostuf.* Helmut Hirt (born October 29, 1916, SS Number 357 778) were literally pulverized. The Soviets attacked soon after with infantry. *SS-Hstuf.* Frühauf, having collected all of the men that were available, including grenadiers, messengers and radiomen, led a desperate counterattack against enemy units that had been able to penetrate the forward positions. The action came close to failing several times because of the enemy's superior numbers, but Frühauf knew how to courageously lead his men in the attack and in the end was able to retake all of the positions that had been lost. Scholz and Frühauf played a decisive role in the defense of the bridgehead during the month of March. *SS-Hstuf* Frühauf was cited for the Knight's Cross on March 31, 1944, by request of the regimental commander Collani and approved by the brigade commander, Wagner:

Brief Citation and Declarations by Superiors

"On 3/22/1944, the enemy broke into the sector held by *5./de Ruyter* following a heavy concentration of artillery fire. The commander of *II./de Ruyter, SS-Hauptsturmführer* Frühauf, reported to the 5th Company command post at the first sign of the enemy attack. There he joined the remnants of the unit that were withdrawing. The enemy continued to exert heavy pressure on the Battalion's positions, with the aim of reaching the outskirts of Narva. The remnants of the 5th Company again found themselves under heavy fire of the advancing enemy, and continued to suffer heavy losses, with no reserve available. Even though he had set up a defense perimeter for the company command post, while awaiting the divisional reserve that was present in that sector, *SS-Hauptsturmführer* Frühauf made the

German grenadiers moving in the trenches in the north-eastern sector of Narva.

SS-Hstuf. Karl-Heinz Frühauf

decision to stop the enemy's frontal assault with all the forces still available. He then rallied the remnants of the 5th Company and all other personnel he was able to gather together, including personnel of the signal detachment and went on the attack against the enemy that by this time had reached the edge of the Dutch positions. On more than one occasion the enemy attack threatened to overwhelm the defenders, but each time *SS-Hauptsturmführer* Frühauf was able to get his men up again and throw them into a counterattack. Thanks to his exceptional work all of the positions that had been lost were retaken after heavy close-quarter fighting that lasted about half an hour. During the fighting that followed throughout the entire afternoon of March 22, *SS-Hauptsturmführer* Frühauf continued to be the heart of the resistance, always under enemy fire and always at the most dangerous point of the position in order to keep track of the fighting. His personal decision to gather together the remnants of his Battalion coupled with his personal valor, were the decisive factors that allowed that sector of the bridgehead at Narva to be held."

The Knight's Cross for *SS-Hauptsturmführer* Frühauf arrived officially on June 4, 1944. The *Nederland* artillery pieces commanded by *SS-Stubaf.* Schlüter, which remained emplaced north of the main supply line, continued to be hard pressed to hold back the attacks of Soviet units during this period.

SS-Kriegberichter Reisberg of the Dutch SS Brigade, in his observation balloon on the Narva front, February 1944.

Another photo of the observation balloon on the Narva front, 1944.

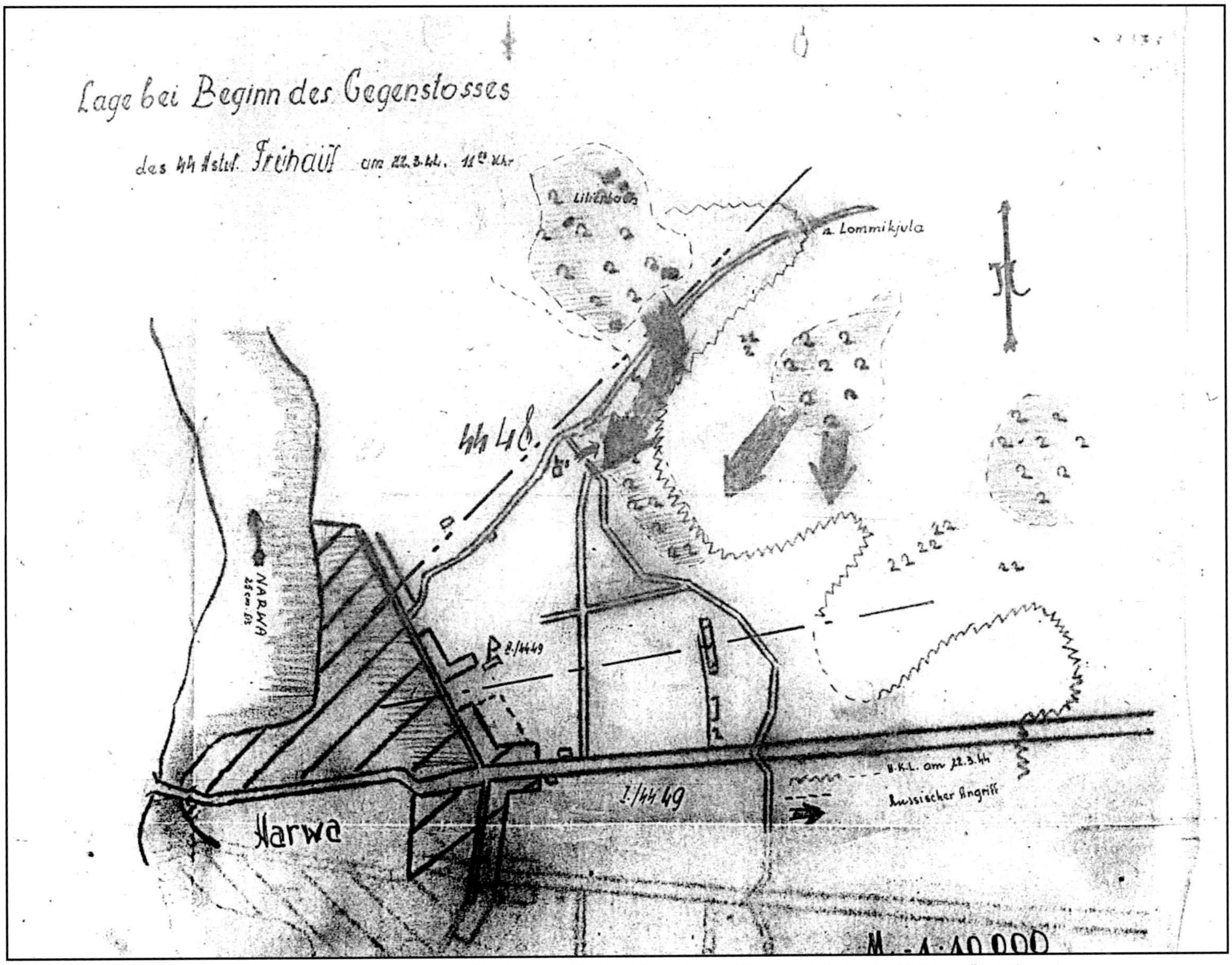

Map of Frühauf's action. Document attached to the citation for the Knight's Cross (*Personalakte Karl-Heinz Frühauf*).

Propaganda Activity

On the Narva front, the group of war correspondents attached to the *Nederland* Brigade managed to capture a Soviet observation balloon. With this balloon, the photographers from the *Kriegsberichter Zug* were able to photograph the enemy positions on the eastern bank of the Narva from high in the air, providing important information to all of the artillery units of the SS Corps. Among the photographers assigned to *Nederland* were *SS-Ustuf.* Reisberg, formerly an official photographer attached to the Dutch Legion, Helmut Moebius, a photographer first

A defensive position, a Dutch bunker on the Narva front, made entirely of logs.

March 1944: The commander of the *Nederland* Brigade, Wagner, during the presentation of several Iron Crosses.

SS-Hstuf. Karl Heinz Ertel

SS-Ostuf. Helmut Scholz

SS-Stubaf. Wilhelm Schlüter

Members of *SS-Pz.Jäg.Abt.54*, taken during a rare moment of rest.

with the *SS Wiking* Division, and later with the *Nederland* Brigade who had been awarded the Iron Cross First Class, and Bruno Wisniewski, formerly a photographer with the *SS Nord* Division, who had been awarded the Iron Cross Second Class.

The photos of the *SS-Kriegsberichter* were generally reproduced in the official Waffen-SS newspaper, *Das Schwarze Korps*, and in many other German magazines, such as *Signal* magazine and the *Illustrierte Beobachter*. On the Narva front, the Dutch Brigade printed its own wartime newspaper, titled *Het Bruggehoofd* (The Bridgehead) that was printed until July 1944, distributed to all of the Dutch volunteers, and which was a propaganda publication aimed at maintaining the morale of the soldiers on the front line. Naturally, among the newspapers most widely read by the Dutch volunteers was also the *SS-Storm*, the official publication of the Dutch SS, printed in Holland, but distributed for free to all soldiers serving on the front lines.

Festung Narwa

On March 23, 1944, Hitler officially proclaimed *Festung Narwa*, or Fortress Narva. Because Narva had been designated as a fortress city it therefore had to be defended at all costs. For the defenders this meant that while everyone else was able to abandon their positions, they had to remain at their posts and risk ending

Nederland Brigade officer corps at Narva, springtime 1944: from the left, *SS-Ustuf.* Hofer, commander of *II./SS.Art.Rgt.54; SS-Hstuf.* Frühauf, commander of *II./de Ruyter, SS-Stubaf.* Ziemssen, chief-of-staff; Wagner; *SS-Hstuf.* Steenholt-Schütt, Wagner's aide; *SS-Hstuf. Meyer*, commander of *I./de Ruyter; SS-Ostubaf.* Collani, commander of the *de Ruyter* Regimet; *SS-Hstuf.* Schlüter, commander of *I./SS.Art.Rgt.54* and *SS-Ustuf.* Wanhöfer, commander of *SS-Pionier-Bataillon 54.*

Grenadiers on the Narva front, 1944.

up as prisoners of the Soviets or, at worst, to be killed. *Nordland* and *Nederland* had already contributed to the defense of the city, paying a high price in blood, suffering overall losses of about 7,500 men, calculated beginning in December 1943. During the same period, the *SS Nederland* Brigade had received only 1,336 replacements, which were the previously cited survivors of the two Luftwaffe field divisions that had been disbanded after the terrible fighting at Oranienbaum.

Losses

Unit	Killed	Wounded	Missing
Nordland	24/788(*)	58/2,708	9/516
Nederland	25/626	33/2,244	5/473

* Officers/NCO and troops

Details of Nederland Losses by Unit (*Ia/151/44 g.Kdos*)

Losses from January 1 to April 13, 1944

Unit	Officers	NCOs	Troops
Stabs Kompanie	4	7	47
SS-Freiw.Pz.Gren.Rgt. 48	32	252	1,410
SS-Freiw.Pz.Gren.Rgt. 49	30	161	1,257
SS-Aufklärungs-Kp. 54	3	18	93
SS-Pz.Jg.Abt. 54	5	15	73
I./SS-Art.Rgt. 54	3	35	54
SS-Pionier-Btl. 54	9	10	75
SS-Sanitäts-Kp. 54	1	-	6
SS-Feldgendamiertrupp 54	-	3	2
SS-Nachrichten-Kp. 54	-	1	19
SS-Wirtschafts-Kp. 54	-	-	3
Total	87	502	3,139

With the arrival of the spring season and the beginning of the thaw, the front stabilized during the months of April and May, except for long-distance artillery duels, aircraft encounters, and clashes between reconnaissance patrols. As of April 13, the overall losses of the *Nederland* Brigade amounted to eighty-seven officers (dead, wounded and missing), 502 NCOs and 3,139 soldiers. Effective strength of the Brigade had thus fallen to 6,305 from an initial strength figure of 9,342. On April 20, the commander of the Dutch SS Brigade as well as of "*Festung Narwa*," Jürgen Wagner, was promoted to the rank of *SS-Brigadeführer und Generalmajor der* Waffen-SS. Wagner also chose a new Chief of Staff (Ia), as on May 6, *SS-Stubaf.* Ziemssen had been temporarily removed from his position by order of Himmler, in order to attend a training course. *SS-Hauptsturmführer* Helmut Kordts (born August 7, 1914, at Bendsburg, SS Number 174 902) took his place. On April 21, 1944, the commander of *SS-Freiw.Pz.Gr.Rgt. 48 "General Seyffardt,"* Wolfgang Jörchel, was awarded the Knight's Cross for the exemplary performance by his men during the defensive battles at the Narva bridgehead. On April 24, several officers of the Dutch Brigade were presented with the German Cross in Gold: the recipients were *SS-Ostubaf.* Collani, commander of the 49th SS Regiment, *SS-Hstuf.* Walter Diener (posthumously), commander of *II./de Ruyter, SS-Ostuf.* Hans Robert Jauss (*4./General Seyffardt*) and *SS-Ustuf.* Hermann Schoofs, adjutant of *Pionier-Bataillon 54.* In early May, *SS-Ostubaf.* Jörchel was designated as the new commander of the *SS-Junkerschule* at Prague, which resulted in command of the *General Seyffardt* Regiment being assumed at first by *SS-Sturmbannführer* Herbert Garthe (born October 3, 1907, SS Number 12 327) and later, at the beginning of July, by *SS-Ostubaf.* Richard Benner,[5] coming from the *SS-Division Nord.* In the following weeks, the defensive battles along the entire length of the front continued and increased in intensity, although the Soviets were unable to make any gains worthy of note. The Germanic volunteers of the Waffen-SS continued to stubbornly defend their positions without giving up an inch of ground to the enemy. During the months of April and May the commander of the III SS Armored Corps, Steiner, and the commander of

III./SS-Pz.Korps defensive position in the Narva sector, April 1944.

A Waffen-SS soldier armed with a *Panzerschreck* at Narva.

the *Heeresgruppe Nord*, *General* Friessner, often visited the Dutch positions, complimenting Wagner on the exemplary conduct of his men. During this period the Dutch volunteers were trained in the use of new individual anti-tank weapons, the *Panzerfaust* and *Panzerschreck*. The first of these proved to be a formidable anti-tank weapon especially when fighting in urban areas, and was capable of penetrating the thick armor of the Soviet tanks.

The *Panzerschreck* was instead the German version of the American bazooka and in contrast to the *Panzerfaust* needed a team of two men in order to be employed properly in the field: one soldier manned the weapon and another soldier loaded it from behind. Large numbers of these anti-tank weapons were delivered to the Dutch SS Brigade. On May 20, 1944, *SS-Oberführer* Kurt Brasack left command of the *Nederland* Brigade's artillery regiment because he was reassigned to *IV.SS-Panzerkorps*, with command of the artillery unit passing to *SS-Sturmbannführer* Wilhelm Schlüter,[6] former commander of *III./Art.Rgt.4* of the *SS Polizei* Division.

A New Soviet Offensive

During the month of June, *Festung Narwa* continued to hold up against enemy attacks. On June 12, 1944, the Soviets launched a new massive offensive all along the *Panther* line. In the afternoon of that same day the area of Narva found itself once again under a hurricane of fire. The Dutch volunteers, who were deployed in the northeastern sector of the bridgehead, burrowed into their bunkers to escape the hail of fire and steel. From his command post in the *Hermannfeste*, Wagner apprehensively followed the unfolding situation. The first assault by the Soviet infantry was unleashed around 1615, north of the Dolgaja–Niva railway line, in the southern sector of the bridgehead. The shelling against the northern sector had only been a diversion. When all communications with the *Danmark* Regiment broke down, there was complete chaos. Around 1720, word was received that the Soviets had passed at Dolgaja–Niva. The reserves of the Dutch Brigade, which had already been put on alert, were committed immediately. Support was provided by artillery fire from *Nordland* and *Nederland*, as well as by a

SS-Oscha. Philipp Wild, awarded the Knight's Cross.

A toast to celebrate the destruction of more enemy tanks. In the photo are *SS-Hstuf.* Scholz, first from the left, and *SS-Rottenführer* Stefan Strapatin, third from the left.

SS-Stubaf. Rühle von Lilienstern, in the center of the photo, conferring with other officers of the Dutch SS Brigade, 1944.

handful of *Sturmgeschützen*. At 1756, the positions at Dolgaja–Niva and Sonnenschein were once again in German hands. The Soviets renewed the attack about an hour later. At 1906, Wagner received word that the position at Sonnenschein, which was the southernmost outpost of the bridgehead, had been captured by the Soviets. A new counterattack was planned for 1935. At 2135, *SS-Stubaf.* Krügel reported that the counterattack was under way. Meanwhile, north of Sonnenschein other Soviet units were attempting to break through the *HKL* (*HauptKampfLinie*), the main combat line. The Waffen-SS soldiers were able to stop this new attack with the fire from machine guns, while *Panzerfaust* teams took care of the tanks.

At 2335, Sonnenschein was returned to German hands. On June 19, *SS-Stubaf.* Wolfgang Grosch, a special envoy of Himmler's, reached the bridgehead. The *Reichsführer* wanted Narva to serve as an example to all of the German Army. Grosch presented Wagner with a plan of Himmler's to continue to defend the bridgehead to the last and to push back the Soviets. But on that very same day a number of assault guns were transferred from *Nederland* to *Nordland*. Only two *Panther* tanks and ten *Sturmgeschützen* remained under command of the *Nederland* Brigade. Following the death of Shock, *SS-Panzerjäger-Abteilung 54* had come under the command of *SS-Hstuf.* Paul Krauss (born September 16, 1913, SS Number 14 945). To compensate to some extent for the loss of the assault guns, the initial elements of *II./SS-Art.Rgt. 4* finally arrived from Beneschau, consisting of a few guns (*leichte Feldhaubitze 18*, which were light field howitzers) and three quad-barrel *Flakvierling* anti-aircraft guns. The guns and the *Flakvierling* were unloaded at Suur–Soldino and from there were transferred to the front at Narva. The new artillery group was commanded by *SS-Ustuf.* Fritz Topeters (born October 30, 1914, SS Number 393 303), while the *Flakzug* (the platoon with the "quad" guns), which was subordinate to the artillery regiment, was commanded by *SS-Ustuf.* Willi Krämer (born April 16, 1921, SS Number 451 097). The *Flak* guns were quickly employed against the Soviet air attacks that were concentrated against the main bridge over the Narva River, near the textile factory west of Natalin. On June 20, Soviet artillery resumed its shelling of the Dutch positions for the entire day. However, there were no attacks by the enemy infantry.

Operation *Urlaubsperre*

Encouraged by the continuing defensive successes by his men, in an attempt to ease the enemy pressure and to somehow raise the morale of the troops who had for months been engaged in a wearying passive defense posture, *SS-Brigdf.* Wagner conceived a limited offensive action with the objective of shifting the defensive line more to the east, along the line that ran from Narva to the area east of Lilienbach. The operation was assigned the code name *Urlaubsperre* (end of the vacation). However, before launching the attack, Wagner sent out many reconnaissance patrols in order to determine the precise locations of enemy

SS grenadiers on a sweep, hidden amongst branches, to observe enemy positions on the Narva front.

firing positions and the strength of the forces that were facing him. To that end, on June 23, a platoon of Dutch volunteers entered no-man's land with the aim of taking prisoners in order to obtain intelligence from them. However, before they could complete their mission the SS grenadiers realized, too late, that they had strayed into an enemy minefield. As soon as the first volunteer triggered a mine, all hell broke loose. The Soviets quickly opened fire with their mortars. A group of Dutchmen managed to take cover in several enemy trenches that had been abandoned and stayed there until dusk fell. When it became dark, the group was able to return safe and sound to friendly lines. This reconnaissance operation thus closed with nothing to show for it, and as Wagner wrote in the Brigade diary, with "*Erhebliche Verlust*," that is, with significant losses. On June 25, Wagner reported for a conference with von Scholz, commanding *Nordland*, to discuss operational plans. Both agreed that a mixed combat group should be employed, consisting of units from *Nederland* and from *Nordland*.

It was therefore decided that Dutch 48th SS Regiment *General Seyffardt* would form the leading element, supported by *III./Norge* along with *SS-Pionier-Bataillon 11* (the *Nordland* engineer battalion). Supporting fire would be provided by the artillery of both units. On Wagner's orders, small groups of soldiers began a series of "instigating" actions along the entire Narva front in order to deceive the Soviets as to where the counterattack would actually take place. Despite all of these preparations, in the end the operation was cancelled, mainly due to the lack of information on the true strength of the enemy forces. It should also be noted that only a few days earlier, on June 22, the Soviets had begun a large offensive against the German Army Group Center (Operation Bagration) in order to separate it from Army Group North. Once the central front fell, the German forces in the Baltics risked being completely isolated. Contemporaneous Soviet attacks in Karelia on the Finnish front were about to cause Finland to capitulate, posing an even greater threat to the entire Estonian front. Isolated at the tip of the northern front, Narva was by now indefensible. Within the German high command, plans were being made for its abandonment, despite the fact that by now the city had become the symbol of resistance by the European volunteers against the Soviet forces.

Abandoning the Bridgehead

In early July the units of *Nederland* and *Nordland* were again engaged in the area of Dolgaja–Niva, repelling new enemy attacks. On July 8, grenadiers from *General Seyffardt* and *Danmark* were caught up in a furious defensive battle that did not end until late at night, with heavy losses on both sides. On July 11, 1944, the southern wing of the German 18th Army was attacked by Soviet forces of the Second Baltic Front; this caused a general retreat of German forces to the west. Consequently, *III.SS-Panzer-Korps* also received the order to pull back about

Wagner surrounded by some of his courageous volunteers, May 1944.

The final German resistance in the western part of Narva. Note the destroyed bridge over the river and the fortress of Ivangorod.

twenty kilometers from Narva along a new defensive line designated *Tannenbergstellung*, along the Narva–Riga road; the name Tannenberg commemorated the great German victory in 1914 against the Czarist army. Naturally, the withdrawal movement required time to execute and above all required the sacrifice by several units that had to remain as a rear guard to cover the withdrawal in good order by all of the other units. The Dutch units were committed to that mission and while the "*de Ruyter*" Regiment commanded by *SS-Obersturmbannführer* Collani was able to disengage following some tough fighting, the *General Seyffardt* Regiment under Benner was not able to break off contact and was surrounded by the enemy. On July 19, 1944, in an official communique addressed to the brigade, *General* Steiner again complimented the Dutch volunteers for their combat successes in the defense around Narva: "... The exceptional behavior of the troops and the strong leadership of the *Nederland Brigade* commanders deserve limitless recognition. I thank both for their valorous courage that they have demonstrated until now."

Steiner and Kleinheisterkamp.

The Soviets returned to attack the bridgehead on July 24, as always preceded by the usual preparatory artillery fire. That same day, by order of Hitler, *General* Friessner was replaced as commander of *Heeresgruppe Nord* by *General* Schörner, who arrived in Narva while it was under enemy attack. The *Nederland* units that were engaged in covering the withdrawal of the other German units towards the *Tannenbergstellung* had been reinforced by other units including the II Battalion of the 47th Estonian SS Regiment commanded by *SS-Stubaf.* Alfons Rebane, a coast artillery detachment from Hungerburg, and a *Pak* platoon from the 20th Estonian SS Division. Their mission remained defense of the far northern sector of the bridgehead, from the center of Narva to Hungerburg on the Baltic coast. To the south were units from *Nordland* reinforced by part of *Panzer Abteilung 11 Hermann von Salza*, the *Gruppe Riipalu* (the staff of the 45th Estonian Regiment), the reinforced 5th Company of the 48th Dutch SS Regiment, known as the "*Seyffardt*," and a section of *SS-Panzer Jäger Abteilung 20*. The *III.SS-Panzer Korps* units that comprised the rearguard remained in the city. *SS-Hstuf.* Wanhöfer, commander of *SS-Pionier Bataillon 54*, arranged to blow all of the bridges over the Narva River. Only one of the bridges was left still standing because the charges did not ignite. Luckily Wanhöfer was still on the scene: "... Damn it all! The bridge must not remain intact. The enemy's forward elements can pass without a problem!" he shouted to his men. New charges had to be placed, so Wanhöfer ordered his driver to: "go immediately

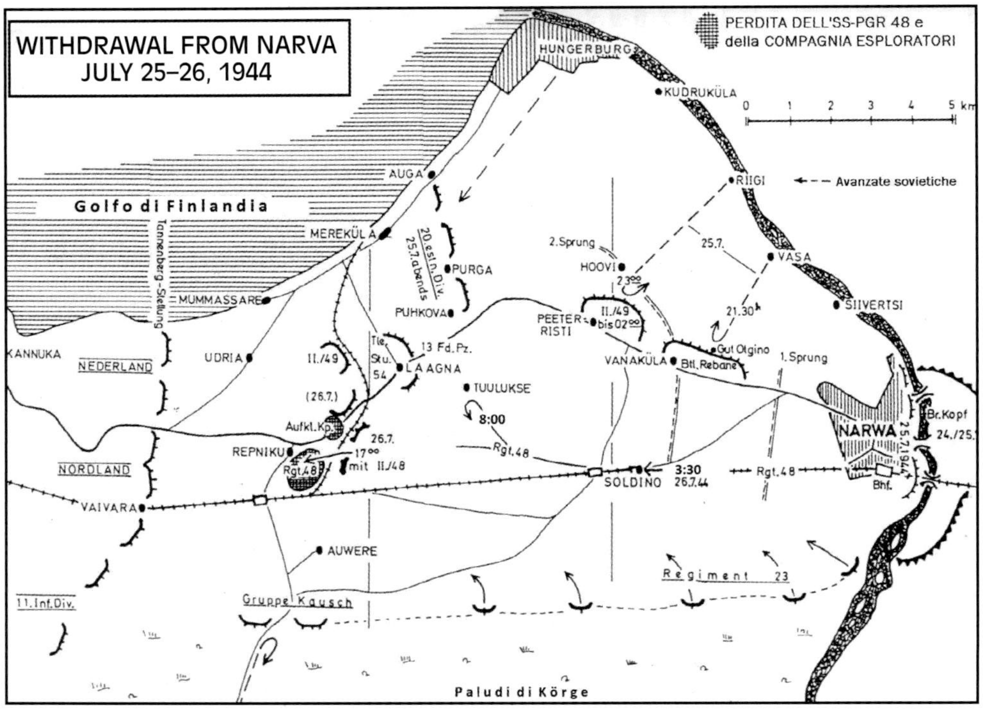

Map relating to the withdrawal of units of *III.SS-Panzer Korps* from Narva, between July 25–26, 1944, to the *Tannenbergstellung*.

Günther Wanhöfer, here pictured with the ranks of *SS-Obersturmführer*.

Crew of an assault gun ready to enter into action.

to Petri Square! Get as much explosives as you can carry and get back here as quickly as possible!" While awaiting the return of the little *Kübelwagen* with its new load of explosives, a squad of Dutch engineers took up the defense of the bridge itself, which was already under fire from Soviet mortars. The *Kübelwagen* returned shortly thereafter and the engineers placed the explosive charges, all the while under enemy fire. Their other comrades provided covering fire, and the new charges were soon set in place. After all of the men had taken cover, the bridge was blown up with a tremendous roar. When the Soviets reached the bank of the river they found not a single intact bridge. That same day of July 25, the "*General Seyffardt*," the *II./de Ruyter*, and the *7./Danmark* were still in Narva. The artillery forward observers were still in place, while new emplacements for the batteries of *III.SS-Pz.Korps* were being established farther to the west. Soviet aircraft again bombed the city, destroying the few ruins that had still been left standing.

The diary of a forward observer from *4./SS-Art.Rgt. 54,* dated July 25, reported that: "… 0600 hours: Heavy artillery fire on the main supply line. Waves of air attacks. Observation position in the tower of the cotton mill in the northern part of Narva. I directed the fire of my battery on several enemy mortars that were getting ready for action. Visibility is very limited because of the flames and smoke coming from the buildings that are on fire."

Testimony of *Ustuf.* Nieuwendijk-Hoek[7]

"I was one of the last to abandon our position, running with my men across the streets that were in flames. There was one violent explosion, soon followed by another [*Author's note*: the bridge over the Narva had been blown]. The fortress of Ivangorod will not triumph over the fortress of Hermannsburg, the two ancient fortresses facing each other from opposite banks of the river, the symbol of our struggle: Asia against Europe, symbols of two worlds, which had always loomed over us like an encouraging omen … Narva, the small welcoming city that so much resembled Haarlem. I feel guilty to abandon it like this, as though I were leaving something precious behind, it pains me very much!"

In the early afternoon, *SS-Hstuf.* Wanhöfer and his engineers moved to the west aboard three vehicles to reach the new positions established for the assembly of the units. The Soviets were by now very close. For his excellent actions during the fighting for Narva, Wanhöfer was awarded the Knight's Cross on August 27, 1944. On July 25, the second day of the Soviet offensive, in the area around Vasa, north of Narva where the Estonian SS units were deployed, the enemy was able to achieve a dangerous breakthrough. Around 1050, Wagner, who was still firmly entrenched in his command post, received news that units of the 20th Estonian SS Division had begun to pull back, thereby leaving the northern sector undefended. Because of this, units from *Nederland* had to hurry to close the dangerous

A *Tiger* tank of *s.Pz.Abt. 502* employed on the Narva front.

Waffen-SS soldiers on the Baltic Front, 1944.

A gunner of the Dutch SS brigade standing by his gun.

gap at Hungerburg; the units included grenadiers of the 48th SS Regiment and I Battalion of the 49th, along with other Army units. This meant a new defensive battle calling for extreme sacrifice to protect the withdrawal of other German units. These continual rear-guard covering actions in the end proved to be fatal to the Dutch SS detachments.

The Dutch Retreat

In fact, when *II./de Ruyter* and units of "*General Seyffardt*" finally began to withdraw to the west, they soon found their route blocked by Soviet units that had already come from Vanaküla. The Dutch volunteers prepared to fight their last battle during that tragic retreat. Along with Benner's regiment were other units: the *7./Danmark*, the *II./de Ruyter*, the *Bataillon Rebane* of the *20.SS-Division*, the *Nederland* disciplinary platoon,[8] and *SS-Pz.Jg.Abt. 54* (minus one battery). The withdrawal of the units had been planned by phases, after having established several intermediate positions to be occupied as the maneuver was being carried out. On the regiment's left was the *Bataillon Rebane*, and on the right was *II./de Ruyter*. *SS-Ostubaf.* Benner had assumed command of the regiment only a few days earlier, and coming from the Finnish front from the *SS Nord* Division, was not accustomed to facing such a difficult situation. The most serious shortcoming was a lack of coordination between the various units and higher headquarters. The regiment was supposed to receive fire support from the divisional artillery regiment. *SS-Nachrichten Kompanie 54* maintained telephone and radio communications up until the last minute. However, after 1700, telephonic contact with the regiment was cut due to enemy artillery fire. *SS-Ostubaf.* Benner delayed transferring the artillery and heavy weapons units, but above all he wasted precious time in deciding whether to proceed along the Narva-Reval road or along the railway line. The order to fall back to the *Tannenbergstellung* arrived from the brigade headquarters via radio. However, the movement could not begin until the artillery regiment first began its move. *SS-Stubaf.* Schlüter received a separate order that directed that all of his guns were to be pulled back to the west. Several batteries of the *Nederland* artillery regiment were delayed owing to a shortage of vehicles.

At 2000, *SS-Ostubaf.* Benner called his commanders to a meeting at his command post in Narva; these included the commanders of *I./General Seyffardt*, *SS-Stubaf.* Karl Betzwieser (born July 3, 1912, SS Number 244 028), of *II./General Seyffardt*, *SS-Stubaf.* Helmut Breymann (born February 9, 1911, SS Number 292 791), of *II./de Ruyter* (*SS-Hstuf.* Frühauf), of *SS-Art.Rgt. 54* (*SS-Stubaf.* Schlüter), and *SS-Ustuf.* Philipp Römmelt (born August 20, 1921, SS Number 362 287) platoon leader of *1./SS-Pz.Jg.Abt. 54*. He discussed the withdrawal to the *Tannenbergstellung* with them. Around 2100, *SS-Ustuf.* Gustav Seinfeldt (born October 15, 1920, SS Number 379 056), a brigade staff officer, brought a written order authorizing the withdrawal. At 2130, from headquarters of the 20th SS Division, the news came that the Soviets had already reached the main supply route at Olgino. At that point, *SS-Hstuf.* Frühauf received the order to protect and if possible take the Narva–Tallin highway from the enemy forces, with the support of the two assault guns under *SS-Ustuf.* Römmelt. The *Bataillon Rebane*, which was already in the area of Olgino, was to have participated in the action. The men under *SS-Hstuf.* Frühauf thus began to move to the west along the highway, establishing contact with Estonian units of the *Bataillon Rebane* (*II.47th SS Regiment*) at Vanaküla. Following a quick counterattack the enemy units were pushed back north of Olgino.

Römmelt's two assault guns played an active role in the action. While *Bataillon Rebane* remained in place to defend the road, *II./de Ruyter* continued its march to the west. Frühauf's battalion clashed with several enemy units along the main road, managing to destroy several Soviet tanks. After having deployed his men in a ditch that ran along the road, he awaited the arrival of units

SS-Ostubaf. Benner, here shown on the Finnish Karelian front in 1943.

Dutch grenadiers during the retreat from Narva.

from *General Seyffardt*. From that time on, however, communications with Benner had broken down. Around 2300, other Soviet forces cut the highway to Peeterristi, but were quickly thrown back by Frühauf's men. In the meantime, at 2150, *SS-Ostubaf.* Benner had received a new radio message from brigade headquarters that informed him that the time of the beginning of the withdrawal had been moved to 2200. A subsequent message reported a further delay until 2315, a delay that proved to be fatal for the regiment. Once he had received the news that the highway had been cut in several places by Soviet units, Benner decided along with his two battalion commanders to pull back along the railway line. This was a tragic choice.

A Tragic Withdrawal

At the hour set for the withdrawal to begin, all of the component elements of *General Seyffardt* assembled at the railway station of Narva/Kreenholm, following which they began their march following the railroad tracks. At 0330 on July 26, the leading elements reached Soldino, with the last arriving at 0500. According to the testimony of several veterans, once they had reached Soldino, Benner received additional bad news: the Soviets had reached the railway line and had blocked the highway at Peeterristi. The commander then decided to return to the highway and to attack the "Reds" at Peeterristi, where he expected to find other friendly forces. However, he changed his mind again when some of his scouts told him that they had found an alternate route that led from Soldino to Laagna. Frühauf waited in vain at Peeterristi until 0800 for the arrival of Benner's regiment. Around 0530 the remnants of the *General Seyffardt* Regiment began its march towards Laagna, through a wooded and swampy area, that soon made movement of the heavy vehicles difficult.

By now it was no longer possible to turn back and the march proceeded slowly and inexorably. From the air, Soviet planes bombed the Dutch columns, bogged down in the Estonian swamps and forests, many times. Soviet artillery also began to harass Benner's column, thanks to an observation balloon that was hovering over the swamp at Körge farther to the south. Around 0800, the leading elements of the regiment reached the area south of Tuulukse. Frühauf's battalion (*II./de Ruyter*), after having waited in vain for Benner to arrive at Peeterristi, sought to find the *General Seyffardt*, but was forced to retire from the area to the west of Laagna because of strong enemy pressure. When the I Battalion of *SS-Stubaf.* Betzwieser emerged from the forest and attempted to attack Tuulukse, it found itself facing the fire of an entire Soviet infantry battalion supported by a tank unit. The regiment's anti-tank guns, which were quickly emplaced at the edge of the forest, quickly opened fire on the enemy armor, firing until the last round. During the hellish encounter four enemy tanks were knocked out, but this did not save the Dutch battalion from total annihilation, which fought doggedly to the last man, yielding only because of the strong enemy superiority. When news was received of the action at Laagna, the last of the assault guns of the *Nederland* Brigade were sent to the area to try to open an escape route for the *Seyffardt* Regiment. During this attack, *SS-Rottenführer* Derk Elsko Bruins,[9] a *Geschützführer* in the *1./SS-Panzerjäger-Abteilung 54*, knocked out eight enemy tanks with his *Sturmgeschütz*. On August 23, 1944, he would be awarded the Knight's Cross and would be promoted to *Oberscharführer* for having destroyed a total of twelve enemy tanks. The attack by the *Nederland* assault guns was, however, easily overcome by the numerical advantage held by the Soviet tanks; two vehicles, those commanded by Kuyl and Pempelt, were lost during the engagements.

Estonian SS grenadiers gathered in a village while awaiting orders.

Estonian SS volunteers with a *Panzerschreck*, August 1944.

Testimony by Derk Elsko Bruins

"... On the morning of July 27, 1944, we received the order, employing three assault guns, to move to the Rollbahn and open the road to the west for *Pz.Gren.Rgt. 48*, which was halted ten kilometers further back from our positions. The Regiment still consisted of two strong battalions and two heavy companies

A *StuG.III* attacking enemy positions, July 1944.

Estonian *SS-Ostubaf.* Alfons Rebane, with the Knight's Cross.

SS-Uscha. Derk Elsko Bruins

equipped with anti-tank guns, therefore capable of being able to repel an enemy armored attack. Our commander did not like the order, seeing that none of the three *Sturmgeschützen* was in perfect operational condition and needed repairs … During the night most of the units of *Nordland*, of *Nederland* and of the Estonian SS division had been able to withdraw in good order to the west and I was not able to believe that one of our best regiment had instead been cut off. To my great surprise,

Steiner with Knight's Cross recipient Derk Elsko Bruins.

after having covered a few kilometers along the Rollbahn, I spotted a column of Soviet tanks moving to the west ... I then found a good position for my assault gun, where I was to await the arrival of the 48th Regiment. From that excellent position I began to fire on the enemy tanks, destroying several in a few minutes. Having run out of ammunition, I had to turn back to the rear to resupply and continued my battle against the enemy tanks ... however, our mission could be considered a failure because we had not been able to make contact with units of the 48th Regiment."

II./de Ruyter was again forced to pull back from its positions between Laagna and Repniku under the threat of a renewed enemy attack. *SS-Aufklärungs-Kompanie 54* under *SS-Ostuf.* Erich Kuhne, which remained in place until 0900, as a rear guard, ended up being surrounded by the Soviets on a farm near Repniku and was completely wiped out. A few survivors were taken prisoner, but nothing else was heard about them. In the same area the tragedy of the *General Seyffardt* played itself out. After having used up all of the ammunition for the heavy weapons, *SS-Ostubaf.* Benner ordered his men to destroy them to prevent the enemy from using them. At 0907, the regiment sent his final radio message to the brigade headquarters: "...We are fighting to try to open a gap through the forest south of Laagna to the west!" Around 1000, the *Nederland* headquarters once again tried to establish radio contact with the regiment: "...Where are you? There are still German units in Repniku, but also enemy units, be careful!" Having probably received this final message, *SS-Ostubaf.* Benner decided to proceed with the survivors in the direction of Repniku. As soon as he reached the vicinity of the position, after another exhausting march through the swampy forest, Benner discussed the plan of attack with Betzwieser and Breymann. *II./General Seyffardt* was to lead the attack. Its mission was to open a gap through the enemy positions to allow the rest of the units to pass through. It was a bold plan, but it did not take into account the fact that there were no longer any German forces in Repniku. The attack was kicked off at 1730; after only a few minutes *SS-Ostubaf.* Benner was killed while leading his men in a desperate attack against the Soviet positions. Confusion and panic took hold over most of the Dutch volunteers, who ended up under a massive enemy artillery barrage, and who found themselves completely scattered.

In small groups they tried to reach friendly lines farther to the west, but only a few dozen survivors were able to succeed in that desperate attempt. Among the survivors was *SS-Ustuf.* Cornelius Nieuwendijk-Hoek, commander of *5.Kompanie*, who was able to confirm the death of the commander, Benner, in the field. Those that did not die in the fighting ended up in the hands of the Soviets. Many of the Dutch volunteers preferred to fight to the last bullet and let themselves be killed rather than surrender to the hated Bolsheviks. According to reports by German radio intercept units, a Soviet artillery unit captured twelve German soldiers on July 26; at 0820 near the railway station of Auwere. Another unit reported the capture of four men of the *Seyffardt*, following a firefight that day. On July 30, another Soviet unit captured four members of *SS-Panzer-Aufklärungs-Kompanie 54* and *SS-Pionier-Bataillon 54* who had been wandering about in the forest since July 27. Soviet radio carried a message announcing that officers Betzwieser and Breymann had committed suicide rather than be taken prisoner. Breymannn assuredly fell in combat, but with respect to Betzweiser several sources state that he was kept in a Soviet concentration camp until 1955, when he was released. At Chanelo, *SS-Hstuf.* Frühauf was able to gather together other survivors of the Dutch 48th Regiment. *SS-Hstuf.* Friedrich Tröger (born January 25, 1913, SS Number 319 929), formerly the commander of the *General Seyfardt Stabskompanie*, assumed command of the *Kampfgruppe* that bore his name, in which the few survivors of the regiment were gathered along with other German personnel that had belonged to Kriegsmarine infantry units.

July 26 Report on the Loss of the SS-Freiwilligen-Panzergrenadier-*Regiment 48 "General Seyffardt"*

"The combat actions by *SS-Freiwilligen-Panzergrenadier-Regiment 48 'General Seyffardt'* made it possible to withdraw all of the Brigade's artillery and of other attached artillery units on the right (*11.SS-Freiwilligen-Panzergrenadier-Division Nordland*). The artillery had been placed in serious danger because of the situation of the division on the right (*20.Waffen-Grenadier-*

SS-Ustuf. Karl-Heinz Frühauf.

An *SS-Ustuf.* of *SS-Pz.Jg.Abt.54.*

Two Dutch volunteers at the Narva bridgehead.

Division der SS). In addition, numerous enemy forces had been stopped by the regiment causing heavy losses to the enemy. The positions along the Tannenberg line were held thanks also to the heroic battle waged by the *SS-Freiwilligen-Pangergrenadier-Regiment 48 'General Seyffardt'...*"

When *Reichsführer-SS* Himmler was informed of the total annihilation of the Dutch regiment, in a vain attempt not to demoralize his trusted European volunteers he ordered that in official reports it be reported that only one combat group from the regiment had been destroyed, sacrificing itself heroically to the end. In any case, the *General Seyffardt* Regiment was to be reconstituted at the camp at Schlochau in Pomerania (today's Cluzchow in Poland), an area within the *Truppenübungsplatz* of Hammerstein. The I Battalion of the regiment, under the command of *SS-Hstuf.* Wolfgang Vieweger (born September 14, 1918, SS Number 367 837) was reconstituted in part with 400 volunteers coming from the *Kriegsmarine.*

Secret Message Dated August 25, 1944

"The *Reichsführer-SS* has ordered, regarding the heroic combat by *SS-Freiwilligen-Panzergrenadier-Regiment 48 'General Seyffardt,'* considering the fact that elements of the Regiment still exist, to report that only one *Kampfgruppe* of the Regiment sacrificed itself in heroic battle until the end."

Chapter VI
THE TANNENBERGSTELLUNG

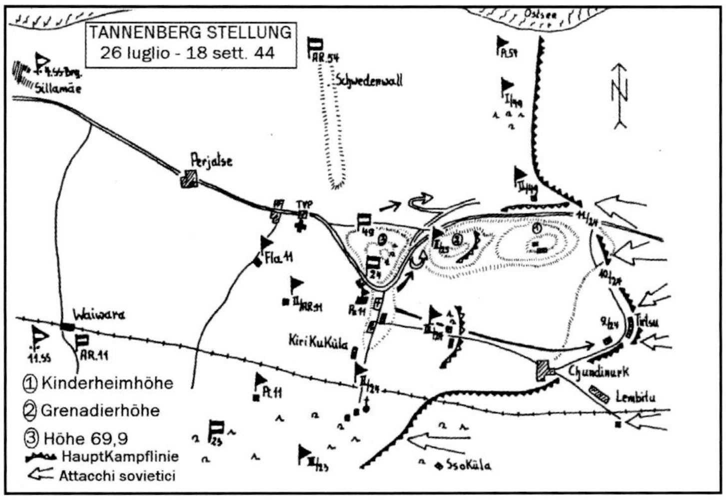

Tannenbergstellung, July 26 – September 18, 1944

SS grenadiers under enemy fire on the Blue Mountains.

The German defensive line along the *Tannenbergstellung* was concentrated on the Blue Mountains (*Blauberg*, or in Estonian the Sinimäed Hills), which was a series of three hills called *Kinderheim* (Orphanage), *Grenadier* (Grenadier) and *69.9* (*Liebhöhe*, or Love Hill), which dominated all of the surrounding terrain as far as to the coast. The position was situated near the coastal city of Sillmäe. The new line extended for about three kilometers in a flat area through which the Narva-Reval road ran. *4.SS-Pz.Gren.Brigade*, which was now down to only one regiment, was sent to occupy the northern area of the *Tannenbergstellung*. Commander of the "*de Ruyter*" Regiment, SS-*Obersturmbannführer* Collani, established his command post on the western side of Hill 69.9, where the *Danmark* Regiment of *Nordland* also established its command post. *Kampfgruppe Tröger*, consisting of the few remaining survivors of the *General Seyffardt* Regiment and some naval infantry units, took up positions along the Narva–Reval highway (the *Rollbahn*). From north to south in the *Tannenbergstellung* were: Estonian units of the *20.SS.Division*, *SS-Pionier-Bataillon 54*, and the I and II Battalions of "*de Ruyter*." The "*de Ruyter*" was in contact with *Nordland* units up to the *Rollbahn*. From that point, going south, were the II and II Battalions of *Danmark*, the latter of which was in contact with the *11.Inf.Div. II./Norge* had been temporarily placed in reserve. "Orphanage Hill" was held by Flemish volunteers of *Kampfgruppe "Langemarck,"*[1] whose anti-tank guns had been emplaced at the foot of the hill. On "Grenadier Hill" and Hill 69.9 were other elements of the Estonian SS Division and two companies of *SS-Pionier-Battaillon 11*. The most forward positions on both sides of the *Rollbahn* were defended by *II./de Ruyter* under *SS-Hstuf.* Karl-Heinz Frühauf on the northern side, and by *II./Danmark* under *SS-Stubaf.* Hans Kappus on the southern side.

Under Enemy Fire

On the afternoon of July 26, 1944, the Soviets unleashed a tempest of fire on the positions occupied by the European volunteers and more particularly against the *Kinderheimhöhe* and along the main supply route. The Flemish *Kampfgruppe* lost almost all of its officers during the terrible shelling. *SS-Hstuf.* Karl Meggl (born November 15, 1917, SS Number 274 938), former commander of *13./de Ruyter* and commander of an *Alarm Einheiten* (an alarm unit) of *de Ruyter* was killed on the *Kinderheimhöhe* while he was trying to find cover from the enemy fire. As soon as it became dark, the Soviets attacked south of the *Rollbahn* with infantry and tanks, overwhelming the positions held by a naval infantry company. The enemy tanks parked themselves facing the *Kinderheimhöhe*, while the Soviet infantry entrenched itself firmly on the eastern side of the hill. With his anti-tank squad, *SS-Uscha.* Mellenthin of *Danmark*, however, managed to knock out all of the enemy tanks, one by one, at close range. That same day *Kampfgruppe Tröger*, in position along the Narva-Reval road, had to face at least four enemy attacks during which numerous Soviet tanks were destroyed. Distinguishing himself during that fighting was, *SS-Standarten-Oberjunker* Georg Schluifelder (born April 14, 1918), a former member of a *Luftwaffe Feld Division*, ex-commander of the motorcycle rifle platoon of the staff of the *General Seyffardt* Regiment, and now adjutant of *Kampfgruppe Tröger*. As all of the radio and telephone communications had broken down between the various front-line units, having been cut by the devastating enemy artillery fire, *SS-Std.Obj.* Schluifelder took it upon himself to maintain contact with the brigade command post.

At the same time he continued to direct the defensive operations and to lead the men of the *Kampfgruppe*, most of who were undergoing their first taste of combat. Thanks to his

Defensive position on the *Tannenbergstellung*.

A *Kampfruppe Langemarck* anti-tank gun, summer 1944.

Remy Schrijnen with the *Ritterkreuz*.

unshakeable will, all of the positions were held and all of the enemy attacks repulsed. On July 27, the Soviets resumed shelling the *Tannenbergstellung* with their artillery; shells of all calibers fell in the area between the *Rollbahn* and the railway line. Around nine in the morning the enemy launched a new attack with infantry supported by tanks, and once again the *Nordland* and *Nederland* anti-tank detachments were sorely tested, destroying numerous enemy tanks at close range and with *Panzerfaust* weapons. Soon after, the Soviet attack was concentrated against the area of Chundinurk and the sectors defended by *II./Danmark* and *III./Norge*. At the same time the enemy attack against the *Kinderheimhöhe* was renewed; the Flemings, now commanded

Command post of the Dutch SS Brigade at Sillamäe: seated on the left is *SS-Stubaf.* von Bock, Chief of Staff of the unit (*Ia*).

Flemish SS grenadiers during an attack, on the Estonian front, summer 1944.

An observer from "*de Ruyter*," summer 1944.

The "*de Ruyter*" command post on the *Tannenbergstellung*.

by *SS-Ustuf.* Georg D'Haese, the last officer of the unit that was still alive, were the first to be hit. Because of the strong enemy pressure, the Flemish volunteers were forced to abandon their positions and to pull back in small groups towards Grenadier Hill. At the base of the hill only one 75 mm anti-tank gun was left, manned by the Flemish *Sturmmannn* Remy Schrijnen.

Partially hidden by the smoke from the ongoing combat, Schrijnen was left by himself, as all of the other gun crewmembers had been killed or wounded shortly before. From his position the Flemish corporal saw the Soviet tanks passing by him only a short distance away; it was an opportunity not to be passed up. Before being completely bypassed by the enemy column, he decided to act. Despite the fact that he was alone, Schrijnen loaded his gun and fired, loaded again and fired again, continuing to fire until he ran out of ammunition, after having knocked out three *Josef Stalin* tanks and four T-34 tanks, and having damaged at least another pair. For this exemplary action, *Sturmmannn* Remy Schrijnen was awarded the Knight's Cross on September 21, 1944.

While the survivors of *Kampfgruppe Langemarck* were pulling back, *II./de Ruyter* continued to hold its positions north of the *Kinderheimhöhe*. *SS-Hstuf.* Frühauf was wounded during the fighting. *SS-Ostuf.* Scholz replaced him as commander of the battalion. The Dutch *Panzerjägers* continued to take a horrific toll of enemy tanks.

During that same day of July 27, the *Tiger* tanks of *502. Schwere Panzer Abteilung* and the remaining tanks of the *Nordland Panzer Abteilung* were able to stave off numerous enemy tank attacks, destroying 113 Soviet vehicles, among which were many T-34 tanks and assault guns. Throughout the day of July 28, the

SS-Ostuf. Helmut Scholz. In the summer of 1944, on the *Tannenbergstellung* front, he replaced *SS-Ustuf.* Frühauf as commander of *II./49 "de Ruyter."*

A short 75mm anti-tank gun mounted on an *SdKfz 251/9*. The white rings around the barrel indicate the number of enemy tanks killed.

fighting continued to focus mainly around the *Kinderheimhöhe*, but later also extended to Grenadier Hill. At dawn on July 29, the third day of the battle along the *Tannenbergstellung*, Soviet artillery began to shell the German positions heavily; the two main targets were Grenadier Hill and the village of Chundinurk. The enemy attacks soon encompassed all of the area of the Blue Mountains, including the positions held by the Dutch. More than a hundred Soviet tanks of all types were thrown into the attack.

German artillery quickly responded, firing upon the mass of armor and the throngs of infantry. However, it seemed that nothing and no one was able to stop that flood of flesh and steel. *SS-Ostuf.* Helmut Scholz somehow managed desperately to hang on to his positions. The Soviets assailed the rear of the southern flank of the Dutch battalion. Attacking tanks were knocked out by *Panzerfaust* weapons and the Soviet infantry was cut down with machine gun fire. Despite heavy losses, the Soviets continued their advance towards the west. Grenadier Hill was on the verge of falling into enemy hands. At the same time other enemy units began to draw dangerously close to Hill 69.9. The Soviet tanks that were in close support of the infantry made shambles of the German bunkers. The "*de Ruyter*" regimental command post itself was hit. *SS-Ostubaf.* Collani was seriously wounded. When the Soviets drew close to his command post, after having fired the last rounds from his pistol at the enemy, he used the very last round against himself, preferring to commit suicide rather than to become a prisoner of the Bolsheviks. Following Collani's death, command of the Dutch regiment passed temporarily to *SS-Hstuf.* Karl-Heinz Ertel. Thanks to his determination and nerves of steel, the Dutch regiment continued to repel all of the enemy attacks with great tenaciousness.

The Attack Continues

Yet another tank attack swamped the *II./de Ruyter* positions. *SS-Ostuf.* Scholz continued to stubbornly defend his positions, setting the example for his grenadiers. When Soviet tanks appeared unexpectedly to the right of his command post, he picked up a *Panzerfaust* and knocked out the leading tank. He hurriedly found another *Panzerfaust* and destroyed a second enemy tank. None of the Soviet tanks managed to get through. Fighting continued on into July 30–31.

On July 30, 1944, Steiner issued a new order of the day, addressed to the Dutch Brigade: "Comrades, today you have won a decisive defensive battle. During this past day you have destroyed more than 110 tanks, inflicted severe losses on the enemy and blocked his intention to advance on Reval. Your courage and your heroism have been exemplary. With your excellent performance you have demonstrated your profound loyalty to our *Führer* Adolf Hitler."

The *Wehrmachtbericht* of August 1, 1944 reported: "... On the isthmus of Narva the enemy has ceased his offensive because of the heavy losses he sustained. The following formations played a significant role in the defense against the Soviet offensive: *III. (germanische) SS-Panzer Korps*, commanded by *General der Waffen-SS* Steiner, with the *11.SS-Freiwilligen Panzer Grenadier Division Nordland* and the *4.SS-Panzer Grenadier Brigade Nederland*, the *20.Waffen-Grenadier Division der SS*, the *11 Infanterie Division*, along with other units of the Army, the Kriegsmarine, and the Luftwaffe."

During the first two weeks of August, fighting continued with increased intensity. During this same period, the brigade's artillery regiment was reorganized: *I.Artillerie-Abteilung* became *III.Artillerie-Abteilung* (*7., 8. and 9. Batterie*), under the command of *SS-Stubaf.* Lothar Hofer.[2] A new *I.Artillerie-Abteilung* was created by transferring the *III.Artillerie-Abteilung* of the *SS-Polizei Division* to *Nederland*. *II.Artillerie-Abteilung*, that, meanwhile, had been put under the command of *SS-Ustuf.* Quintus de Veer (following the death of Topeters on August 4, 1944), remained unchanged. In the meantime (from August 5), command of the *de Ruyter* Regiment had been assumed by *SS-*

SS-Usuf. Edmont le Roux of *Flak Kompanie 54.*

Interior of the "*de Ruyter*" command post, where its commander, *SS-Ostubaf.* Collani, met his death.

A German soldier armed with a *Panzerfaust*, 1944.

Ostubaf. Fritz Bunse,[3] former commander of the *Nordland* engineer battalion. On August 19, *SS-Ostuf.* Otto Scholz was transferred to the rear to be treated for several wounds he received in the fighting, and command of *II./de Ruyter* passed to *SS-Hstuf.* Ertel. The battalion was assigned to defend several trench lines northeast of the *Kinderheimhöhe*. It was precisely there that at the end of August, the Soviets attacked with a penal battalion following a heavy artillery bombardment. German artillery in turn joined the action, as did the Dutch heavy weapons, repelling the enemy attack. *SS-Oberscharführer* Walther, recently assigned to *II./de Ruyter* from a *Luftwaffe Feld Division*, led a counterattack to eliminate a dangerous enemy penetration. He also was able to establish contact with several friendly companies that had been cut off during the enemy attack. On August 29, *SS-Hstuf.* Ertel turned over command of *II./de Ruyter* to *SS-Hstuf.* Otto Petersen (born September 2, 1919, SS Number 115 809).

CHAPTER VII
KAMPFGRUPPE WAGNER

Commander Wagner, second from the right, along with his adjutant, *SS-Stubaf.* von Bock, during a reconnaissance in the Dorpat area, summer 1944.

Soviet offensives in the Baltics between summer and autumn of 1944.

While fighting continued in the Blue Mountains, the Soviets launched a contemporaneous flanking attack from the south, in the direction of Latvia and Lithuania. The Soviet offensive had Riga, the capital of Latvia, as its objective, with the aim of cutting the German defensive deployment in the Baltic region in two. After having crossed the Narva River south of Lake Peipus and the city of Pleskau, the Soviets turned to the north to take the German forces still in northern Estonia from behind. In order to prevent the *III.(germ) SS-Panzer Korps* from being trapped, the German high command planned a withdrawal from the *Tannenberg* line and to set up a new defensive line along the Pleskau–Jacobstadt railway line, with the city of Tartu (Dorpat in German). It was in the area of Tartu that the German command decided to launch a counteroffensive to cover the withdrawal of the German troops towards Latvia and to contain the Soviet attack that had been launched south of Lake Peipus. General Steiner was ordered to send troops to the south to block the Soviet advance. Accordingly, a *Kampfgruppe* commanded by *SS-Brigadeführer* Jürgen Wagner was formed, consisting of the last remaining vehicles of the *Nordland* reconnaissance battalion (most of the unit had been transferred to the south days before), the Dutch volunteers, the Flemings and the Estonians of *I./Waffen Grenadier Regiment der SS 47 (etnische Nr.3)*. The other elements of the *Nordland* Brigade that remained on the *Tannenbergstellung* were placed temporarily under the command of *Oberst* Friedrich, aide-de-camp of *Armee Abteilung "Narwa,"* and later by *Oberst* Paul Kresin, *Arko* (commander of all artillery units) of *III./SS-Pz.Korps*.

During the night between August 15–16, the units of the newly constituted *Kampfgruppe Wagner* were pulled back from their positions on the *Tannenbergstellung* and from the *III.(germ) SS-Panzer Korps* rear area. The last remaining assault guns from *Nordland* and *Nederland* were also assigned to the *Kampfgruppe*.

To reinforce the combat group, three hundred volunteers from the *SS Wallonien* Assault Brigade were taken directly from the training camp at Debica where the unit was undergoing reorganization, and would be led in the field by their commander, Léon Degrelle.[1] On August 16, *II./SS-Art.Rgt. 54*, commanded by *SS-Hstuf.* Quintus de Veer, left from the railway station of Jöhwi towards Dorpat, where other units of the *Kampfgruppe* also arrived. Based on orders from the high command, the defensive line of *Kampfgruppe* Wagner was to run from Lake Wirz to south-east of Lake Peipus; the course of the River Embach (Ema), which connected the two lakes, was to constitute the natural combat line if the Soviets were able to advance close to the Tartu region.

THE BATTLE BEGINS

At Tartu *SS-Brigdf.* Wagner gathered as many men as possible to reinforce his *Kampfgruppe*; among the civilian population all men between the ages of sixteen and fifty were recruited and armed as best as possible with the little equipment that was available. The first units of the *Kampfgruppe* were deployed

Derk Elsko Bruins' *StuG* during a transfer march toward the Dorpat front; from the left, *SS-Uscha.* Rudolf Witte, *SS-Ustuf.* Römmelt, *SS-Rottenführer* Derk Elsko Bruins, and two other crewmembers.

Walter Seebach, here with the rank of *Hauptsturmführer* and with the Knight's Cross hanging from his neck.

Dorpat front, summer 1944: from the left, *SS-Brigdf.* Jürgen Wagner, *SS-Stubaf.* Léon Degrelle, and his adjutant, *SS-Ostuf.* Schäfer.

south of Tartu; *SS-Brigdf.* Wagner sent out many reconnaissance patrols throughout the area in order to intercept the enemy's leading elements in time. *II./SS-Art.Rgt. 54* emplaced its batteries on both sides of Dorpat, but was soon moved forward by some twenty kilometers to the southeast of the city on August 20 to provide supporting fire to the Estonian units of *11.Inf.Div.* The Soviets assailed the thin defensive line with enormous forces. The Estonians, who were poorly armed and equipped, were easily overrun. The 1st Company of *Fusilier-Bataillon 11* under Leutnant Bucholz on the left flank bore the brunt of the enemy attack. The battery commander of *4./SS-Art.Rgt. 54, SS-Ustuf.* Günther Horstmann, came to the aid of his army comrades, managing to throw back the Soviets. The enemy was quick to renew the attack with even greater forces. *SS-Ustuf.* Horstmann ordered his gunners to fire on the Soviets. In the space of forty minutes the Dutch battery fired 350 rounds, once again stemming the Soviet attack. The Soviets reacted with fire from their own anti-tank guns and mounted a new attack with fresh forces. The European volunteers pulled back in good order to a new defensive line, yielding little ground to the enemy. *II./SS-Art.Rgt. 54* then took up new firing positions at Meliste. On August 21, *SS-Brigdf.* Wagner had partial control of the situation on the Dorpat front. Along Lake Peipus and along the Werro-Dorpat road the presence of Soviet units indicated that the enemy was pushing to the north. Soon thereafter a report was received that the Soviets had reached Kambi on the Werro–Dorpat road. Wagner sent Degrelle's Walloons to block the Soviet penetration in the Kambi sector. Between August 21–22, there were no other enemy breakthroughs. On August 23, all hell broke loose again; the position at Noo fell into enemy hands. A small combat group led by the Wallonian *SS-Ustuf.* Léon Gillis was sent along the Dorpat road with three anti-tank guns. When the Soviets attacked, Gillis quickly lost his three *Pak* guns, but in a rapid counterattack the three guns were retaken by the Walloons, who lost no time in using them against the enemy tanks. With the Soviets continuing to push to the north, Wagner ordered Degrelle to hold the position at Kambi for as long as possible. From overhead, the Stukas under Major Rudel attacked the Soviet armored columns incessantly, but that was not enough. Despite that help, the Walloons were forced to withdraw to new positions west of Dorpat and south of the crest of Em.

On August 24, *Panzer-Brigade 101* and *SS-Panzer-Brigade Gross*, coming from Latvia, moved against Elwa and Noo. *SS-Panzer-Aufklärungs-Abteilung 11* under *SS-Stubaf.* Saalbach, as part of *Kampfgruppe Graf Strachwitz*, captured the city of Tamsa farther to the north. Also on the 24th, however, the Soviets reached the southern shore of Lake Wirz, separating the *Armee Abteilung Narwa* from *18.Armee.* The next Soviet objective now became the port of Parnu on the Gulf of Riga. In the meantime, Saalbach's *SS-Panzer-Aufklärungs-Abteilung* was attached to *Kampfgruppe Wagner* to be used as a quick reaction unit.

SS-Stubaf. Degrelle with his grenadiers on the Estonian front.

The Battle for Dorpat

On August 25, the battle for Dorpat began; the European volunteers were able to hold back the Soviet offensive for only one day, at the end of which the city fell into the hands of the Soviets. With the fall of Dorpat, the Soviets crossed the Em River, establishing a bridgehead on the northern bank. In an attempt to stop them both the Estonians and the Walloons were committed, engaging in battle near the village of Noela. To the east of Dorpat were Estonian units of little military value in which Wagner had no faith. *II./SS-Art.Rgt. 54* continued to provide fire support in an attempt to halt the enemy advance, but in the end the Dutch batteries had to displace to positions farther to the rear to avoid being surrounded. *SS-Stubaf.* Léon Degrelle was ordered to form a blocking position on the plain north of Dorpat, along the Parna-Lombi–Keerdu line. The Wallonian commander threw all available personnel into the front line, even those of non-combat units and wounded soldiers who were still able to hold a weapon. After having managed to gather together about sixty men, Degrelle led them to the outskirts of Dorpat where the leading Soviet elements had been reported, deploying them as best he could in defensive positions. When the first enemy units arrived they were met with a heavy volume of fire, following which they were forced to withdraw. Meanwhile, *Stubaf.* Degrelle had been able to recover two German artillery pieces that were quickly put into battery in the anti-tank role. Soon after he contacted Wagner on the telephone to update him on the situation at Dorpat and to ask for reinforcements. Wagner answered him, saying: "… Resist at all costs, as soon as I can I will send reinforcements!" Degrelle replied: "… As long as I am alive, the Soviets won't get past us."

After managing to pull together about forty more volunteers, *Stubaf.* Degrelle reorganized his men into two combat groups, positioning them on both sides of the road that led to Dorpat. At the same time he sent reconnaissance patrols to provide timely warning of enemy movements. Around 1300, Soviet tanks were spotted closing in; it was a good opportunity to use the two guns that had been recovered. *Stubaf.* Degrelle ordered the crew of the two German guns to open fire only when a hit was guaranteed, as there was not much ammunition on hand. As soon as the tanks were within range, the German gunners opened fire, destroying the first two tanks of the Soviet armored column.

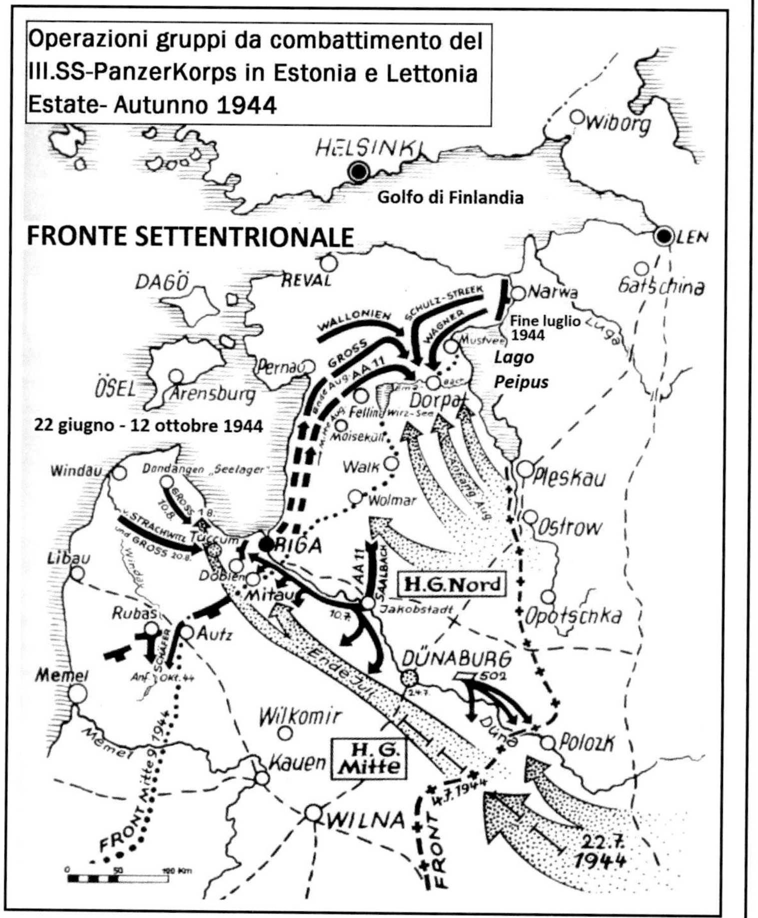

Combat Group Operations of III.SS-Panzerkorps in Estonia and Latvia, Summer–Autumn 1944

Fearing the presence of many anti-tank guns, the remaining Soviet tanks chose to withdraw, abandoning the field. With very little ammunition left with which to face a new enemy tank attack, Degrelle again called Wagner to ask for reinforcements. But the commander of *Nederland* offered him only words of encouragement and the order to continue to resist at all costs. The Soviets returned to attack in force, severely testing the ability of the defenders of Dorpat to hold on, but just at the moment that the Soviets were about to overrun the defenses, an entire squadron of *Stuka* dive bombers arrived to throw them back again. Many enemy tanks were destroyed on the ground while the Soviet infantry was forced to take cover in the nearby forest. Soon after some German *Tiger* tanks arrived to consolidate the defenses. For this exemplary conduct of defensive operations at Dorpat, on August 27, 1944, Degrelle was presented with the Oak Leaves to his Knight's Cross, followed in September of the same year with the gold pin for hand-to-hand combat. For three times, Degrelle's men were cited in the *III.(germ.) SS-Panzer-Korps* order of the day. The Soviet offensive, however, continued to be unstoppable; the three main objectives continued to be Reval in the north, Parnu in the center, and Riga in the south.

Reval

On September 10, 1944, *SS-Obergruppenführer* Felix Steiner had to report to Hitler's headquarters at Rastenburg: the *Führer* informed him of his intention to abandon Estonia, but at the same time ordered him to hold a bridgehead at Reval in order to enable all of the German forces to be evacuated by sea. This

Grenadiers in front of a *Josef Stalin* tank that was knocked out at close range, summer 1944.

Studying maps at Wagner's command post at Dorpat: from the left, Schäfer, Degrelle and Wagner.

A very nice aerial view of Dorpat dating back to the period of the war, with a clear view of the River Embach, which cuts the city in two.

mission was to be accomplished by the units of *III./SS-Panzer-Korps*: although Steiner was against the plan, he had to obey. When he returned to the Estonian front, he met with General Schörner, commander of Army Group North, to discuss the evacuation plans from Estonia, the operation which was codenamed *Aster*. The withdrawal of all German forces from Estonia began in September 14, 1944; units of *III.(germ.) SS-Panzer-Korps* began to withdraw to Latvia during the night between September 18–19, with cover being provided by the Wehrmacht II Army Corps. A grenadier company and an engineer platoon remained as a rear guard; the other units, one after another, left their positions seeking to hide their movements from the enemy as much as possible. At dawn the Danish and Norwegian grenadiers reached the bridge at Sillimäe, which was defended by Dutch volunteers; once they had crossed, the SS engineers blew the bridge. During the day of September 19,

SS-Ostuf. Max Schäfer

SS-Ustuf. Léon Gillis

Stefan Strapatin

An anti-tank gun in a firing position, camouflaged with branches.

units from *Nordland* and *Nederland* reached the Kothla–Järwe area. The area where III Corps was to gather was the region of Pernau, on the northern coast of the Gulf of Riga; the Germanic volunteers were to defend the capital of Latvia, Reval, and the port of Pernau (Parnu) for at least three days to ensure evacuation of the greatest number possible of the forces by ships of the Kriegsmarine. Along the entire western Estonian front the retreating German columns tried to escape the enemy's clutches, pushing towards the Baltic coast. At Reval the Geman military commander, General Gerok, was able to hold a bridgehead until September 22, thus enabling a large number of soldiers and civilians to make it to the port area. Thanks in part to the

Stubaf. Léon Degrelle personally presenting an Iron Cross to one of his valorous grenadiers who was wounded in combat on the Estonian front, summer 1944.

sacrifices made by the European Waffen-SS volunteers, in the space of a few days the German ships were able to evacuate more than 80,000 people from Reval before the city fell into Soviet hands. The next day the port of Parnu also fell after having been defended for three days by Dutch volunteers of the *Nederland* Brigade.

Parnu

Kampfgruppe Bunse, consisting of *I./de Ruyter* and other *Nordland* elements, continued to hold a small bridgehead at Parnu for more than three days, covering the embarkation of the German units in the small port. The new defensive line ran along the Parnu River south of the city. After the last bridge over the river had been destroyed, a small German reconnaissance detachment arrived on the opposite bank. The *Nederland* engineers quickly erected a crossing over the river using tree trunks, enabling the German recon personnel to cross to the friendly side. At the same time the *de Ruyter* motorcycle platoon stayed to defend the crossroads south of the city for a considerable period of time. The *Nederland* rear guard moved rapidly soon thereafter towards the southwest. Because of the traffic snarls along the few roads that were available, the *Nordland* reconnaissance battalion and *Kampfgruppe Bunse* from *Nederland* were detoured to the south. The *Nordland* reconnaissance battalion was assigned to block the road towards the Bay of Parnu east of Moiseküll, while *Kampfgruppe Bunse* was deployed to the area of Wolmar. On September 24, *Kampfgruppe Petersen (II./de Ruyter)* took up positions along the Lemmer River south of Parnu, blocking the coastal road to the south.

Kampfgruppe Report

"... During the day of September 24, 1944, *Kampfgruppe Petersen* held its positions along the Lemmer. Reconaissance conducted throughout the day reported no contact with the enemy. Around 1930, the outposts reported the approach of three enemy tanks and about twenty trucks with infantry aboard. Two enemy tanks were able to get through and reach the road south of the Lemmer, along the coast. The third tank was knocked out with hand grenades. The enemy infantry attempted to break through our positions, but was repulsed with heavy losses. The Soviets then made a massive tank attack along the coast and along the road with about twenty tanks. Our main line of resistance was penetrated, but more than five tanks were destroyed. The other tanks continued to advance towards an assembly area for our vehicles where there were only drivers and reserves. Even though these were not combat personnel they managed to knock out another four enemy tanks. *SS-Rottenführer* Strapatin particularly distinguished himself, and it is due only to his utter calm that our vehicles were spared from certain destruction. After having sustained heavy losses, the Soviets withdrew. Another two enemy tanks were knocked out as they were pulling back. Because of strong enemy pressure, the battalion itself also pulled back. *SS-Uscha.* Sporck was again engaged in covering the withdrawal of his countrymen, destroying yet another tank. The other two Soviet tanks that had been able to break through during the initial attack were knocked out by *4./SS-Art. Rgt. 54.* During the withdrawal the Soviets renewed their attack with several tanks in an attempt to wipe out or units. Two enemy tanks were destroyed with Panzerfaust rounds. To protect the battalion from further attacks by enemy tanks, the commander ordered the demolition of the bridge north of Haynach, even though his adjutant and several grenadiers were still on the northern bank acting as a rear guard."

The Following Dutch Volunteers Destroyed Enemy Tanks in Combat:

Name	Tanks	Unit
SS-Rottf. Strapatin	2	Stabs/II./de Ruyter
SS-Uscha. Seifholz	1	Stabs/II./de Ruyter
SS-Uscha. Schuur	3	5./de Ruyter
SS-Rottf. Kist	1	5./de Ruyter
SS-Ustuf. Teunissen	1	7./de Ruyter
SS-Sturmmann Rieger	1	8./de Ruyter
SS-Ustuf. Horstmann	1	4./SS-Art.Rgt. 54

SS-Rottenführer Stefan Strapatin, a volunteer originally from Romania, and a member of the *Nachrichtenzug* (signals platoon) *of II./de Ruyter*, was awarded the Knight's Cross on November 25, 1944.

On the morning of September 25, the Dutch volunteers of *Kampfgruppe Petersen* found themselves again along the coast road on the border between Estonia and Latvia. With the fall of Reval, the other German units also pulled back to the south along the coast, setting up defensive positions about thirty kilometers northeast of Riga, the capital of Latvia.

The following day, September 26, the units moved to southeast of the city, gathering in the large woods south of the Latvian

A Waffen-SS anti-tank gun ready to open fire.

A soldier preparing ammunition belts for machine guns.

village of Kelava. The men were granted a few hours rest. With the Soviets advancing towards the Baltic coast, it was necessary soon thereafter to plan offensive actions to stem the enemy pressure.

Tukums

With the road to Riga blocked, the Soviets shifted their attacks more to the west, in the direction of the small city of Doblen (Dobele), about sixty kilometers southwest of Riga. The units of III SS Corps had to reach the area of Tukums, the next pivot point in the defense of the Latvian front. *SS-Brigadeführer* Ziegler, commander of *Nordland*, was ordered to carry out a withdrawal to the south, to intercept the leading elements of the Soviet forces that had been pointed towards the sea. On September 28, 1944, both the *Norge* and *Danmark* regiments, along with units of the reconstituted *Nederland* Brigade (following the return of the *Kampfgruppe Wagner* elements), went to occupy defensive positions that had been prepared by Latvian and German labor companies north of Doblen. Beginning on September 30, the Soviets began to hit the positions held by the Gemanic volunteers with artillery fire; an infantry attack then followed, which was repulsed by the Germanic units. Between October 5–6, the units of III Germanic SS Corps received orders to transfer to the Autz sector. The *Nordland* command, however, was ordered to form a *Kampfgruppe* to be sent as soon as possible to the area north of Moscheiken; the combat group, known as *Sperrgruppe* (blocking group) *Schäfer*, named after its commander, *SS-Obersturmbannführer* Max Schäfer,[2] consisted of both of the engineer battalions of *Nordland* and *Nederland*, the *Nordland* reconnaissance battalion, the III SS Corps security company

Commander Wagner

and a group of three artillery batteries from *Nederland*. These forces took up positions in Moscheiken, between two *Wehrmacht* infantry divisions; the defensive line extended along the Vadakalis River, south of the hamlet of Roubas. On October 10, the Soviets attacked on the flanks, in the sectors defended by the *Wehrmacht*, overwhelming them. The leading Soviet armored elements quickly reached positions behind *Kampfgruppe Schäfer*; the grenadiers pulled back to escape the enemy's grip, covered by supporting fire from the Dutch artillery (*I./SS-Art.Rgt. 54*) and by the armored vehicles of the *Nordland* reconnaissance group. A new defensive line was established with all haste between the villages of Asvinsi and Bugisi; with the units still pulling back, the Soviets attacked the new positions, still trying to flank the positions held by the Germanic volunteers. Once again Schäfer was forced to order a withdrawal to the village of Micini; once the position had been reached and the danger of being surrounded had been prevented, thanks to the arrival of a few *Panzers* the grenadiers were able to counterattack, retaking the ground that they had just lost. The engineers from *Nordland* and *Nederland* were engaged in very tough fighting, first against infantry and then against tanks. *SS-Sturmbannführer* Voss, commanding the *Nordland* engineers, radioed a request for reinforcements and supporting fire. The artillerymen poured enfilade fire on the leading Soviet columns, inflicting very heavy losses and forcing them to retire. During the following two days the German artillery continued its powerful fire, keeping the Soviets far away from the area and allowing the units committed to the fighting, who were at the end of their tether, a bit of breathing space. *Kampfgruppe Schäfer* continued to hold its positons, giving them up only when relieved by a *Wehrmacht* unit.

The Dutch Fight on the Baltic

In Italy, the heroic behavior of the Dutch volunteers was carried on the pages of the Italian SS newspaper *Avanguardia*, in which there was a column entitled "The SS Fights for Europe," which regularly reported on the deeds of the various foreign volunteer formations. The piece dedicated to the *Nederland* Brigade was published in issue #27 dated September 27, 1944, and was titled "The Dutch Fight on the Baltic," signed by SS war correspondent Wim Sassen:

> Yesterday, having returned from the front for a few hours, we greeted another contingent of Dutch SS volunteers that had been sent into the combat zone. Sunshine spilled over the courtyard of an ancient Dutch castle. Today dense clouds hung over the Dutch countryside, but the armed forces communique cited the *Nederland* grenadier brigade, consisting of SS volunteers and our hearts are full of a dazzling sun. Oh, we are under no illusions about the situation; for weeks we have felt the ponderous attack by our enemies from the west, and we know that in these hours and days they are throwing the entire weight of their materiel against us, and that in the East the tidal wave of fire is approaching the borders of the Reich. Europe is shuddering under the power of her enemies, the skies rumble day and night with enemy aircraft, the soil of Europe is torn up by Russian and English shells, on the oceans of the world enemy warships pass by each other over the immense expanse of the sea, but nevertheless our hearts continue to be strong and full of faith. And this faith of the Dutch volunteers is at the same time fanatical and realistic. Many of us know the source of their strength, their potential, the enormous power of their industry, their colonies, the reserves of men that they have available; almost all of us have experienced the brutal force of the Soviet war machine in three years of warfare on the Eastern Front. However none of us doubt, for even an instant, the victory that will come to Germany and to our arms. In 1942 we found ourselves with other men from Flanders and from Denmark on the Mius in front of Kolodajevka. Our bunker was at the time the most advanced point on the European front against the Soviet Union. It had been a day of brutal fighting, and we were tired. Towards nightfall the door of the bunker opened. We leapt out; our division commander, then *SS-Gruppenführer* Steiner, appeared. That night we didn't talk very much with him but, even as we remained silent, many things were said. We can never forget even one of the words he told us: "You know, comrades, that our most formidable force is the resolve that we carry in our hearts; its reality is demonstrated by the fact that this bunker is the farthest position forward on the entire Eastern Front and that in it Dutch, Danish and German are spoken.

On June 17, 1944, an English prisoner asked me to speak with him a bit; I told him I could not do so without being a "traitor."

"Why a traitor?"

"Because I am Dutch and I wear the German uniform."

He was quiet for a while, and then said:

"If you are a traitor, it is not us who can decide, but only history."

This is one. Another asked me what rank I bore. When I told him I was an SS NCO and a tank commander, he asked me …

"Commander of a Dutch tank?"

"No, of a German tank."

"But with a Dutch crew?"

"No, my gunner is German, as is the radioman, the driver is Norwegian and the loader is a Fleming."

"Are all of them Dutch Germans or …?"

"No, they are Germans of the Reich"

"And how is it that in this Germanic Army you can command German soldiers?"

I answered: "We believe in a Germanic revolution; after this war Europe will be a precious truth. And thus I am equal to my German comrades."

He ended with the following words: "Incredible! Imagine a Dutch sergeant from the Legion, in England, commanding us!"

SS-Stubaf. Léon Degrelle

This the second reason why we have not and will not lose faith. If the Armed Forces communique cites the hard fighting on the Baltic, the men of the volunteer *SS "Nederland" Panzer-Grenadier Brigade* are well aware that their situation is more serious than ever. More than one Dutch mother will cast a fearful eye on the student atlas of one of her children and will look for names like Narva, Riga, Mitau and her night will be troubled, as even more will be the night of a German mother. But even this Dutch mother will have the peaceful certainty that victory will not escape her son's arms. Why? Because even though the Armed Forces Command had to announce the fighting in the Warsaw sector and we had to give up Kauen, in Holland hundreds of new volunteers were leaving for the front, at Anvers hundreds of future Flemish SS soldiers took leave of their families, and because everywhere in Europe a new spirit is taking hold. Three days ago using a telescope I saw the Dutch cruiser *Sumatra* on the Atlantic coast. It had been destroyed by European guns and had been forced to beach itself. The sight of one of our once superb Dutch cruisers saddened me under the circumstances, until I saw a symbol: we have to beach (give up) the old Holland and the old ideas. The new Holland is represented by the volunteers of the *"Nederland" Brigade* and by the SS grenadiers, cited in the Supreme Headquarters communiqué.

Chapter VIII
KURLAND

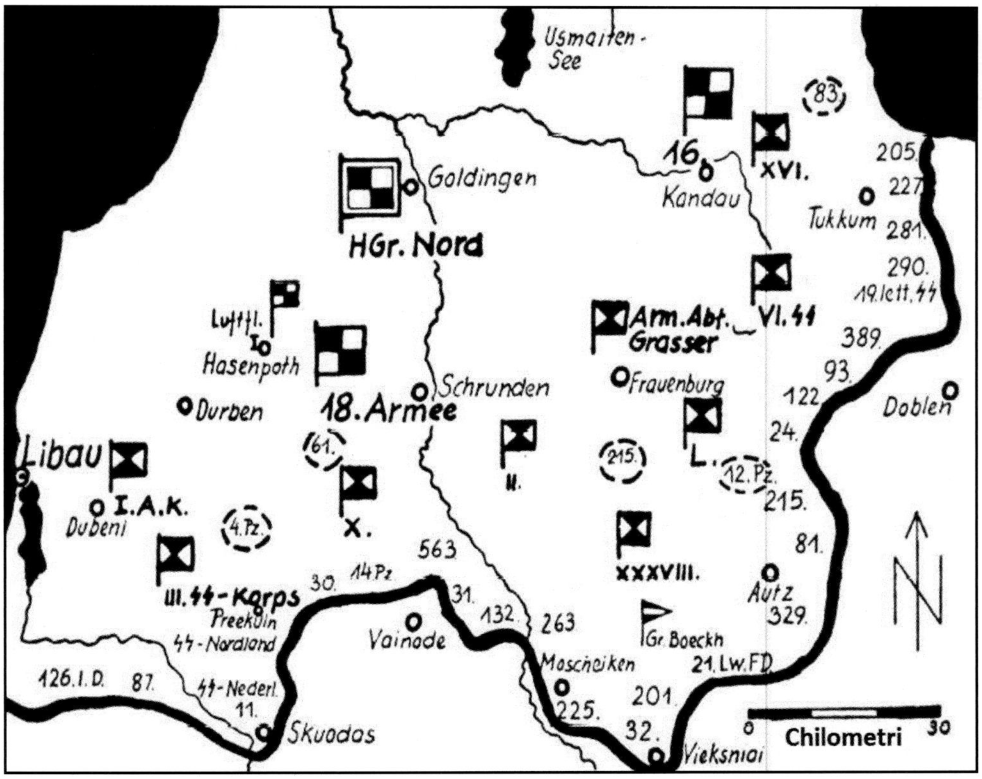

Dispositions of German forces in Kurland, October 1944.

Commander of Army Group North, Ferdinand Schörner.

In early October 1944, the German forces moved back from Estonia towards the Kurland Peninsula, which was the last German stronghold in the Baltic region; III SS German Corps followed the general withdrawal, leaving the region of Riga and taking up positions along a new defensive line between the villages of Skuodas to the south and Preekuln to the north. During the retreat to Kurland, the Germanic volunteers were assigned to act as the rear guard, continuing to fight against the enemy formations. From October 13, all of the bridges over the Duna River were blown up and the capital of Latvia was completely abandoned to the Soviets. Around the middle of October the German forces in Kurland found themselves again with their backs to the sea, restricted to the peninsula and surrounded by the Soviets; the only hope of survival was to escape by sea. To prevent that, the Soviets unleashed attacks against Libau, the last port in Kurland that could still be used by the *Kriegsmarine*. The commander of Army Group North, General Schörner, had proposed the evacuation of all of the troops from the pocket and a retreat to East Prussia.

Instead, Hitler ordered resistance to the last; Kurland was to be defended to the bitter end. Fortunately for the defenders the terrain in Kurland lent itself very well to defensive operations, as the western part was rich with forests and swamps while the eastern portion consisted mostly of mountains. The units of the *Nordland* Division and the *Nederland* Brigade took up positions in the southern part of the Kurland front. The first Dutch units reached the Batra area on October 14, 1944. The *Nederland* and *Nordland* units occupied positions in the *18.Armee* sector between the *11.Infanterie-Division* (*I. Armee-Korps*) and the *30.Infanterie-Division* (*X. Armee-Korps*). On October 15, 1944, the units of the III SS Germanic Corps were deployed as follows, from north to south: II and III Battalions of *Norge* were deployed on two hills along the Preekuln–Vainrode railway line, and II and III Battalions of *Danmark* to the east and west of the village of Trekni. The two remaining battalions of the *Nederland* Brigade were at the far end of this defensive line, that to the north ended with units of the German 30th Infantry Division and to the south with units of *11.Inf.Div. II./de Ruyter* was to the east of Annenhof along the Preekuln–Skuodas railway line and *I./de Ruyter* was also along the same Preekuln–Skuodas railway line as far as Ozoli. The Dutch brigade's command post was set up in a group of houses in Susten. *Kampfgruppe Aign*er (the remaining *Nederland* units plus a few German units) assumed positions between Ozoli and Flossen. The *Kampfgruppe* was commanded by *SS-Ustuf.* Anton Aigner, an expert artillery officer (born November 30, 1914, SS Number 353 043). The future commander of *Pz.Jg.Abt.54*, he had previously commanded *2./Art.Rgt.54*. Before arriving at the *Nederland* Brigade, he had been commander of *8./Art.Rgt.4* of the *Polizei* Division since November 1942.

Order of Battle of Heeresgruppe Nord – October 1944

III.(germ.) SS-Pz-Korps
SS-Pz.Gren.-Brig. "Nederland"
11.SS-Pz.Gren.-Div. "Nordland"

16.Armee – AOK 16
Reserven:
24. Inf.-Div.
31. Inf.-Div.
87. Inf.-Div.
132. Inf.-Div.
263. Inf.-Div.
300. Inf.-Div. Z.b.V.
II.Armee-Korps
227. Inf.-Div.
563. Inf.-Div.

XXXXIII.SS-Armee-Korps
23. Inf.-Div.
83. Inf.-Div.
18. Inf.-Div.
207. Sich.-Div.
90. Sich.-Div.
12. Lw.-Feld.-Div.

L.Armee-Korps
290. Inf.-Div.
281. Sich.-Div.

Korpsgruppe Kleffel
19. let. SS-Gren.-Div.

18. Armee – AOK 18
I.Armee-Korps
11. Inf.-Div.
126. Inf.-Div.
X.Armee-Korps
30. Inf.-Div.
14. Pz.-Div.
XXXIX.Pz.-Korps
61. Inf.-div.
225. Inf.-Div.
4. Pz.-Div.
12. Pz.-Div.

Armee-Abteilung Grasser
XXXVIII. Armee-Korps
32. Inf.-Div.
81. Inf.-Div.
121. Inf.-Div.
122. Inf.-Div.
329. Inf.-Div.
210. Sich.-Div.
21. Lw.-Feld.-Div.

Latvian SS grenadier armed with a *Panzerfaust*.

Dutch and Latvian volunteers in Kurland, 1944.

A Soviet tank knocked out in front of German positions.

A Dutch *Pak* in position at Vainode.

SS-Stubaf. Lohmann and *SS-Ustuf.* Ertel (in the center of the photo) with several *de Ruyter* award recipients, following the Second Battle of Kurland.

Early Encounters

The *Nederland* units reached their new positions just as the Soviets had managed to break through the positions of *11.Inf. Div.* north of the Tirs-Purvs swamps, gathering substantial forces for the next move towards Libau. The Dutch volunteers were soon called upon to reinforce the southern front. *I./de Ruyter* mached to the northeast of the Tirs–Purvs swamps, then turned to the east. *II./de Ruyter*, starting from the east, was able to establish contact with the other Dutch battalion. During the course of the action many enemy heavy weapons were captured. With help from elements of *11.* and *87.Inf.Div.*, the Soviet forces were pushed back after two days of intensive fighting. *SS-Ostuf.* Otto Petersen, commander of *II./de Ruyter*, distinguished himself particularly in leading the defensive fighting and was awarded the Knight's Cross on December 11, 1944. After the two Geman infantry divisions had sealed the gap in the defensive line, the *de Ruyter* Regiment returned to its earlier positions. Meanwhile, the Soviets had amassed forces in the area between Skuodas–Preekuln–Vainode, shifting their axis of attack farther to the south. At the end of October the *Nederland* units continued to defend the area around Kaleti. In view of the chronic shortage of men, the defensive line was based on several fortified positions that were on elevated ground. The *Nederland* units were to the north. The boundary between *III./Danmark* and *II./de Ruyter* was the small stream of Birkstal, about four kilometers south of Purmsati.

On October 27, the Second Battle of Kurland began. At 0600, more than 2,000 artillery pieces of all calibers opened fire simultaneously. Soon after, sixty Soviet divisions launched the assault. The sector between Skuodas and Vainode was attacked by the 5th Guards Tank Division under Marshal Rotmistrov, with about 400 armored vehicles. The sector that was most threatened was the sector defended by units of *Nordland*. Initially the Dutch positions were spared, but the respite lasted only a short while. In fact, before long the Soviet artillery began to shell the positions of Petersen's battalion in the area of Spuri, after which the infantry attack began. The Dutch grenadiers were able to push back the Soviet infantry after pitched battles all along the defensive line between the villages of Jostini, Puzi and Zarini. The enemy attack then shifted to Purmsati, where the Soviets were able to effect a breakthrough on the southern flank. *III./Danmark* under Ternedde managed at the last minute to stem the threat of a breakthrough. The following day the Soviets returned once again to attack the Dutch positions, as usual being preceded by a heavy bombardment by artillery and mortars. When the infantry charged against the positions of *II./de Ruyter*, several strongpoints were overrun, allowing the Soviets to penetrate the main defensive line. All of the available men were then rallied, including support unit personnel, to throw back the Soviets. When the situation seemed on the verge of deteriorating completely, an unexpected rainstorm stopped the enemy attack; the water and mud mired down the Soviet tanks, and without the support of the tanks the enemy infantry chose to withdraw. On October 29, the weather conditions improved, allowing the Soviets to resume their attacks with renewed vigor. With the skies free of clouds, the Soviet air force also joined in the fray, strafing and bombing the German positions. Losses were horrific. That day of October 29 also proved to be one of the worst days in the sector that was defended by the Dutch. The Soviet infantry broke through several places in the defensive line, forcing the *Nederland* and *Nordland* grenadiers to engage in continuous desperate counterattacks.

SS-Ustuf. Herbert Reith (born February 11, 1920, SS Number 490 026), commander of *5.Batterie* of *SS-Art.Rgt. 54*, had for days been engaged in directing the fire of his guns against the enemy. After having run out of ammunition for his entire battery, he led a counterattack with all of the men still available from his unit, forcing the Soviets to retire. For that exemplary conduct, he was cited for the Knight's Cross by *SS-Stubaf.* Schlùter, his regimental commander, and was officially awarded on December 11, 1944. However, Reith's success was only fleeting, as the enemy attack continued to be pressed. After the German bridgehead past the railway embankment was wiped out by the Soviets, *II./de Ruyter* itself was forced to pull back. At the same time the enemy attacked the positions of *I./de Ruyter* from the area of Rudbarzi.

The main offensive thrust developed against Hill 36.5 at Ozoli, on the battalion's southern flank. Defending the hill was 2nd Company of *de Ruyter*, whose positions were overrun by the enemy attack. Having lost their company commander and platoon leaders, who had been either killed or wounded, the few survivors abandoned the hill. At that point, *SS-Standarten-*

Herbert Reith

Stefan Strapatin

SS-Stubaf. Lohmann and *SS-Ustuf.* Schluifelder

SS troops in Kurland.

Oberjunker Georg Schluifelder, then in command of *1.Kompanie*, led a counterattack with all of the men he was able to rally, managing to retake the hill. The Soviets very quickly returned to attack the position, threatening to completely surround the Dutch grenadiers. At that point, Schluifelder decided to counterattack yet again to prevent the worst, and was able to hold the position and remain leading his men, despite the fact that he had been wounded.

For this action Schluifelder was promoted and decorated, first with the German Cross in Gold on November 4, 1944, for courage that he had shown during the fighting at Narva and on the *Tannenbergstellung*, and soon thereafter with the Knight's Cross on November 26, 1944, with the following citation.

Citation for the Award of the Knight's Cross to Georg Schluifelder Dated November 3, 1944, Signed by the Regimental Commander, and Approved by *SS-Brigdf.* Wagner

"*SS-St-Obj.* Schluifelder, with his *1./SS-Freiw.Pz.Gren.Rgt.49*, defended the northern sector of Hill 36.5, near Ozoli. On October 29, 1944, the Bolsheviks attacked south of the hill, managing to effect a breakthrough in the corps defensive line. During the attempt to stem the enemy advance, *2.Kompanie*, which was defending this hill, was overrun; following the loss of their commander and all of their other officers, the survivors withdrew. *SS-Std-Obj.* Schluifelder, having realized the seriousness of the situation, charged against the clearly superior enemy with his reserve company and with all of the other forces he had been able to gather. Always at the head of his men, Schluifelder engaged the enemy units in tough hand-to-hand fighting, moving from the starting point and managing to retake the hill with only eighteen men who were still able to fight. Owing to the small force, the enemy was able to penetrate our trenches several times. Schluifelder continued to counterattack, heavily engaging the enemy and inflicting heavy losses. Even though he was seriously wounded by a round to the shoulder, he continued to remain beside his men, spurring them on with his superb personal courage. Soon after, due to the wounds he had sustained, he lost his senses, and left his command post only when ordered to do so after a replacement had arrived. *SS-Std-Obj.* Schluifelder, thanks to his resolve and his superb personal courage, was able

A Germanic Waffen-SS volunteer of *Nordland*.

Rapid movement of German troops on the Kurland front, 1944.

to hold the sector around Hill 36.5, thus preventing a breakthrough of our lines."

The fighting around Ozoli lasted until early November 1944. During that same period, *SS-Stubaf.* Hanns Lohmann,[1] returning from a long convalescence after having been seriously wounded on the Oranienbaum front in February 1944 while commanding *III./Norge*, replaced Bunse as commander of the *de Ruyter* Regiment. The regimental command post was set up at Kaleti.

With the beginning of the rainy season, fighting in the *III.(germ.) SS-.Pz.Korps* lost much of its intensity for several weeks, but then on November 24, the Soviets resumed their attacks in the *I./de Ruyter* sector, without achieving any measurable success. For about another month the fighting was reduced to simple patrol activity and long-range encounters between the opposing artillery.

Graben Statt Graber

Once the front lines had been stabilized, the units were engaged mainly in strengthening their defensive position, according to the maxim of "*Graben statt graber*" ("better trenches than tombs"). The Dutch positions were baptized by the volunteers as "*Krimhilde-Stellung*," after the name of a noted female character in the saga of the Nibelungens. During this period the Dutch brigade received supporting fire from several army units, such as *Pz.-Jäger-Abt.563* and *Pz.-Jäger-Abt.667*. The Dutch *Flak* company emplaced its 20 mm guns in critical points of the defensive line. The *Nederland* engineers, in their continuing and back breaking work of strengthening the positions, were assisted by an emergency battalion and two Army engineer battalions, the 563rd and 591st. Most of the work was carried out at night, while during the day the engineers stayed under the cover of their positions. For a certain period infantry units

A *Panzerfaust* in action. A soviet tank is in the background.

of *563. Volksgrenadier-Division* (commanded by *Generalmajor* Ferdinand Brühl) were committed along the *Nederland* defensive front, before Schörner transferred it to another sector.

Testimony of a Dutch Waffen-SS Volunteer[2]

"... At the end of November 1944, the temperature fell drastically. Winter has arrived, the harsh winter in a continental climate. New elements are added to our already numerous privations. The blinding reflection of the snow, the biting cold, especially at night when the thermometer falls to thirty degrees below zero and maybe even lower. Finally, the layer of snow, ever deeper, more than a meter high. The mud in the trenches is transformed to ice [...] After weeks of the invariable grey sky, fog, rain and storms, the sun has finally appeared [...] It was as though we had seen it for the first time; completely filthy, with our eyes circled in black, most of us with long and shaggy beards, we were strange emaciated figures who moved slowly among the trenches."

In early December, with the arrival of the cold, the mud began to harden, allowing the Soviets to resume their attacks along the entire front. The enemy tanks were thus able to support the infantry attacks, severely testing the German anti-tank personnel, who were armed mainly with the *Panzerfaust* and a few *Panzerschreck*. Wherever action by the *Panzerjägers* was rendered impossible, artillery joined the action to repel the armor attacks. Despite their great superiority in men and equipment, the Soviets continued to achieve only limited success, remaining stalled along the main line of resistance.

New Awards

On December 11, 1944, the commander of the SS Brigade *Nederland*, Jürgen Wagner, added the Oak Leaves to his Knight's Cross for his exemplary leadership of his men during the fighting on the Leningrad front, at Narva, at Dorpat and in Kurland. In particular his continuous presence in the midst of his units engaged on the front line was commended and highlighted. On December 18, 1944, *SS-Ostuf.* Johannes Hellmers (born October 23, 1918, at Allerslev in Denmark), a veteran of *Frikorps Danmark* and commander of *6./de Ruyter*, was awarded the German Cross in Gold, with the following citation: "... During the withdrawal of *4./SS-Panzer-Grenadier-Brigade Nederland* from the Narva front to Latvia, *SS-Obersturmführer* Hellmers and several men from his company were cut off from their unit following a massive Soviet tank attack south of Pernau. The attempt to reach German lines failed after the enemy had seized all of the roads, villages and forests in the area. *SS-Obersturmführer* Hellmers, with great courage crossed through the enemy lines, moving at

A German defensive position in Kurland, 1944.

SS-Ustuf. Johannes Hellmers

SS-Ostuf. Klemens Behler

night. On several occasions the Soviets tracked the German group with dogs. It was only after ten days that *SS-Obersturmführer* Hellmers, along with *SS-Oberscharführer* Thyssen and *SS-Rottenführer* Kais reached the German lines, completely exhausted and weakened. *SS-Obersturmführer* Hellmers is a Germanic volunteer from Denmark. Since the time he was first assigned to *III.(germanisches) SS-Panzer-Korps*, he has repeatedly demonstrated exemplary conduct and a great ability to command. During the fighting southeast of Libau he continued to distinguish himself in a particular manner in combat. The two SS NCOs who returned with Hellmers have already been awarded the Iron Cross First Class for their courageous behavior during the action."

The Third Battle of Kurland

On December 21, 1944, the Third Battle of Kurland began, which was a new offensive carried out by fully four Soviet armies: the Third under Kasakov, the Fourth under Malyschev, the Tenth Guards under Korotkov, and the 42nd under Swiyidov. This time, the Soviets had a dual objective, as part of the force concentrated on Frauenberg and the rest against Libau. The pressure directed against the first objective was particularly strong, with a full twenty Soviet divisions thrown into the attack against the German positions in an attempt to reach the Frauenberg–Libau road; once again Soviet numerical superiority was unable to overcome the tenacity of the defenders. During the first two days of the offensive, the defensive front was penetrated in several points, but the quick reaction of the *12.Panzer-Division* and of the *227.Infanterie-Division* on the Frauenberg front dealt with the threat. During this third battle, the *III.(germ.) SS.Pz.Korps* remained relatively quiet; the Dutch volunteers were busy mainly staying under cover to avoid Soviet artillery fire as well as sniper fire. In response to the sniper threat several snipers from the brigade itself were assigned the difficult tak of "flushing out" their opposite numbers on the other side of the line. *SS-Unterscharführer* Steincke, one of the best snipers of the Dutch Brigade, in the first week of January alone managed to chalk up twenty personal kills. During the days that followed immediately he continued to add to his record.

The Fourth Battle of Kurland

The Fourth Battle of Kurland began on January 23, 1945, with a massive bombardment unleashed by Soviet artillery against the German positions; then eleven Red Army divisions attacked on both sides of Preekuln with the objective of reaching Libau. This time the greatest weight of the attack fell upon the positions defended by *30.Inf.Div.* and *III.(germ.) SS.Pz.Korps*. Naturally the positions of the *Nederland* Brigade were also subjected to heavy shelling. Along the Dutch defensive line there were two pivotal points that had to be defended at all costs: the Gross Gramsden–Kaleti road, with the Annenhof heights, and to the south, the hill of Ozoli. In order to reach the coast and the port of Libau, the Soviets would inevitably have to take these two key positions. *I./de Ruyter*, commanded by *SS-Ustuf.* Georg Schluifelder, was assigned to defend the hill of Ozoli. Despite numerous enemy attacks the hill remained firmly in the hands of the Dutch volunteers. *II./de Ruyte*r was positioned north of the Gross Gramsden-Kaleti road, while *I./de Ruyter* was to the south of the road. Fighting was concentrated primarily in the latter area. *SS-Art.Rgt. 54*, commanded by *SS-Stubaf.* Schlüter, provided very effective fire support to the Dutch grenadiers. Thanks to the proper and accurate fire direction provided by *SS-Ostuf.* Klemens Behler,[3] commanding the 3rd Battery of the *Nederland* artillery regiment, the Dutch were able to hold back

SS-Brigadeführer Jürgen Wagner, commander of the SS Brigade.

all Soviet attacks against the main line of resistance. During the first day of the Fourth Battle of Kurland the *Nederland* Brigade was able to hold all of its defensive positions in a dazzlingly effective fashion. On January 24, 1945, the Soviets opened up with another massive artillery barrage during which the Dutch positions were again heavily pounded. The *Nederland* Brigade had only four battalions on its defensive line, deployed as follows from north to south: *SS-Pionier-Bataillon 54* under *SS-Hstuf.* Wanhöfer; *II./de Ruyter* under *SS-Stubaf.* Petersen; *I./de Ruyter* under *SS-Stubaf.* Gerhard Unger (born December 12, 1912, SS Number 314 904); and *Kampfgruppe Aigner*, commanded by *SS-Hstuf.* Aigner. The *Kampfgruppe* consisted primarily of units of *SS-Pz.Jäg.Abt. 54*. The already heavy enemy pressure intensified noticeably during the course of the day and the first position to fall was that of the hill at Ozoli, following fierce fighting, which witnessed the death of most of the grenadiers of the Dutch 1st Company. *SS-Ustuf.* Schluifelder himself, after having been seriously wounded in the fighting, chose to commit suicide rather than to fall into Soviet hands as a prisoner.

The main line of resistance was then shifted more to the west, behind the railway line. Soon after, the enemy attacks focused on the Gross Gramsden-Kaleti road, where the Soviets were able to advance along both sides of the road after a series of furious close-quarter engagements with the Dutch volunteers. *SS-Ostuf.* Behler was able to withdraw with a few survivors only at the last minute. In that same area of the fighting, *6./de Ruyter* under *SS-Ostuf.* Hellmers clung doggedly to its positions. *SS-Pionier-Bataillon 54* was only lightly engaged in the fighting; deployed on the northern flank of the *Nederland* sector, it consisted of a reinforced engineer company, a reconnaissance company and two *Flak* platoons equipped with 20 mm guns. Wanhöfer's men also held their positions throughout the day. During the night, however, due to a new enemy breakthrough, they were forced to pull back to the west to a new defensive line. During that same night, other units arrived as reinforcements: *II./Inf.Rgt. 323 (218.Inf.Div.)* that took up positions east of Kaleti, and elements of *14.Panzer.Division*, which established themselves farther north in reserve. On 25 January the forces in Kurland were redesignated as *Heeresgruppe Kurland*; since January 15, 1945 *Generaloberst* Lothar Rendulic had taken over as commander of those forces. Also on January 25, the Soviets continued their attacks; the positions held by the Dutch *de Ruyter* Regiment were once again heavily pounded by Soviet artillery. When the Soviet infantry did attack, the hills around Annenhof, Meiri and Olzonieki were lost. Communications between the various units were completely disrupted because of the numerous enemy penetrations. The various platoons and more or less substantial mixed combat groups continued to fight as completely isolated units. The company under *SS-Ostuf.* Hellmers and *I./SS-Art. Rgt. 54* continued to fight doggedly. After fierce encounters, when the Soviets were on the verge of overrunning the positions of the Dutch SS volunteers, a simple gunner, *kanonier* Jenschke, led a handful of men in a counterattack, throwing back the Soviets. In the confusion of battle, in which the camouflage-pattern *Tarnjacke* he was wearing and which made his rank insignia difficult to see unwittingly had an interesting role, as the men who followed him only later realized that they had been led on a charge by an ordinary soldier. Meanwhile, the engineers under *SS-Hstuf.* Wanhöfer continued to hold their positions against continuous enemy attacks.

Diary Entry by *SS-Ustuf.* Horstmann 1, Dated January 25, 1945

"During two days of bitter fighting, the companies on the main line of resistance were completely overrun. Not a single man made it back to the rear. Right now only a few positions are still holding out, but they are completely surrounded by the enemy. The battalion command post has become a forward outpost and the road has become the new main line of resistance. Petersen and Unger, the two battalion commanders, and seven other men are all that is left to defend the village of Kaleti."

Also during the night of January 25, the Soviets worked their way around the southern flank of *Kampfgruppe Wanhöfer*, attacking the Dutch positions from the rear. Other Soviet units moved to the west along the Gramsden-Kaleti road. The *Nederland* Brigade engineers, however, were able to ward off all of the enemy's nighttime attacks, thanks in part to the providential arrival of two assault guns, which were also carrying additional grenadiers from *Nederland* aboard them. In the meantime, other enemy units had made their way close to the *de Ruyter* command post, two kilometers northwest of Kaleti. On the morning of January 26, the command post was displaced to Klein-Kaleti,

SS-Hstuf. Otto Petersen, *Kdr.* of *II./PzGr.Rgt. 49.*

A *Nebelwerfer* rocket launcher battery in action on the Eastern Front, 1945.

while the new defensive line was shifted to behind Kaleti. On the same day, while the *Nordland* sector remained relatively quiet, fighting continued in the sector defended by the Dutch volunteers, especially in the area around Kaleti, which continued to be attacked by enemy forces.

The last remaining *Nederland* assault guns managed to destroy a number of enemy tanks, but in the end had to pull back to avoid being knocked out themselves. North of Kaleti, a hasty counterattack with the support of several assault guns was repulsed by the Soviets. The fighting around Hill 42.4 was particularly vicious, during which the grenadiers of *7./de Ruyter* under *SS-Ostuf.* Emil Grabow (born September 11, 1913, SS Number 235 888) fought with particular distinction. *SS-Ostuf.* Grabow himself personally managed to knock out a T-34 with a *Panzerfaust* before being seriously wounded. His example was followed by his men, who were thus able to throw back the enemy attack against Hill 42.4. Having already distinguished himself in previous fighting, *SS-Ostuf.* Emil Grabow was awarded the German Cross in Gold on March 9, 1945. A new counterattack, this time by assault guns from *14.Panzer-Division,* temporarily threw back the Soviets.

Kampfgruppe Wanhöfer, which was still holding out northeast of Kaleti, was also attacked in the afternoon by enemy tanks. *SS-Hstuf.* Wanhöfer found himself forced to order a withdrawal in order to prevent the annihilation of his men; the Dutch engineers had to put up a stout fight to open a route to the area northwest of Kaleti, and during the fighting Wanhöfer himself was seriously wounded and was picked up by his men at the last moment before the arrival of enemy tanks. A new defensive position was established west of the Wartage River with several emergency units arriving from Libau. The *de Ruyter* command post was moved there. *SS-Stubaf.* Petersen, along with the *Nederland* survivors, took up positions at Klein–Kaleti. On January 27, a heavy Soviet artillery concentration hit Klein–Kaleti. *SS-Stubaf.* Petersen and his men clung tenaciously to their positions. A battalion of assault guns arrived as reinforcements to halt the Soviet tank attack. Petersen was able to defend the village for another night, until he was given the order to withdraw. The *Nederland* units continued to defend the line Krute–Klein–Kaleti–Kodeli until they were relieved by units from the *14.Panzer-Division* and *218.Infanterie-Division.* At the end of these last battles, the *de Ruyter* Regiment was left with about only eighty men still fit to fight, which amounted to the strength of less than a company!

DIARY ENTRY BY *SS-USTUF.* HORSTMANN 2

"... Everyone stayed in his position to the end. The enemy attacks broke up against the fire of our artillery! The guns became the main line of resistance. Not a one of us gave ground until we were relieved by other comrades."

On January 30, 1945, *SS-Obersturmführer* Johannes Hellmers was recommended for the Knight's Cross with the following citation: "... During the fighting in the area of Kaleti, the company occupied the line of the previous command post four hundred meters east of Kaleti as the main line of resistance. The company had been assembled from the survivors of a battalion *SS-Ostuf.* Johannes Hellmers commanded this company. During the day of January 25, the Soviets attacked with tanks and two thousand infantrymen from the forest facing the position. The enemy was able to break through the defensive positions, and when the situation appeared totally hopeless, *SS-Obersturmführer* Hellmers decided to launch an immediate counterattack with all of the remaining men. At the head of his soldiers, brandishing his machine pistol, he charged against the enemy, forcing them from the trenches and causing heavy losses. Despite the fact that he had been wounded twice during the action, he remained on the main defensive line and along with his men beat back all successive enemy attacks. It was thanks to his initiative and his personal courage that the main line of resistance in the Kaleti area was held on January 25,

German soldiers during a withdrawal movement.

SS-Stubaf. Hanns Erich Lohmann.

preventing the enemy from making any further breakthroughs. His resistance was decisive for the entire sector between Purmasti and Skuodas." *SS-Ostuf.* Hellmers was officially presented the Knight's Cross on March 5, 1945.

The Balance of Losses

Following the raging battles in Kurland, the *Nederland* Brigade had become a mere shadow of its former self because of the serious losses it had suffered.

A report dated January 26, 1945, compiled for Wagner by an officer of the brigade reflects the state to which the unit had been reduced:

Evaluation of units

1). *SS-Freiwilligen-Panzer-Grenadier 49 "de Ruyter"*: "The Regiment no longer has any combat capability following its retirement from the front line. The effective strength of each infantry battalion is around 10-20 men. The Regiment's heavy weapons for the most part have been lost and the crews that manned them cannot be employed completely as infantry after the loss of their weapons. The personnel of the service units are still essentially intact, as are the administrative personnel, so that they can be used for reorganization of the formation.

2). *SS-Artillerie-Regiment 54*: The personnel strength of the Regiment continues to fall drastically. Many men were lost during their use as infantrymen in several emergency units. With some reinforcements, however, the unit can be considered ready for action.

3). *SS-Pionier-Bataillon 54*: The Battalion has no remaining combat capability. Other than the adjutant and one company commander, there are no remaining officers or NCOs. The effective strength of the unit is around 10-15 men. The units that remained as rear guards for the Battalion are still essentially intact.

German soldiers in Kurland, 1945.

Retreat from Kurland

At the end of January, the remaining elements of *III.(germ.) SS-Panzer-Korps* were assembled in the area of Libau to be embarked aboard ships and transferred to Germany for their needed reorganization. In addition, the German high command had decided to use the corps on the front in Pomerania that was threatened by the Soviet forces. On January 26, Wagner had received the order that the brigade, along with *III.(germ.) SS-Panzer-Korps*, was to be transferred to the Vistula front. Beginning on January 30, units from *Nordland* and the *Nederland* Brigade were transported by the ships *Elbe*, *Ilmenau* and *Preussen*. Elements of the Brigade Staff and the Corps engineer battalion were loaded aboard the ship *R.O.I. II./de Ruyter*, *SS-Pionier-Bataillon 54* and *SS-Aufklärungs-Kompanie 54* were transported from Libau to Stettin aboard the *Michael Ferdinand*. Almost all of the ships, escorted by German submarines, were able to reach Germany; only one, the *Moira*, was torpedoed by a Soviet submarine. Aboard her were some *Nederland* Brigade personnel. Resistance by German and Latvian forces in Kurland continued until the surrender of March 8, 1945. The soldiers in Kurland thus ended the war without ever having been defeated, and as the Germans say, "*im felde unbesiegt*."

Chapter IX

THE POMERANIAN FRONT

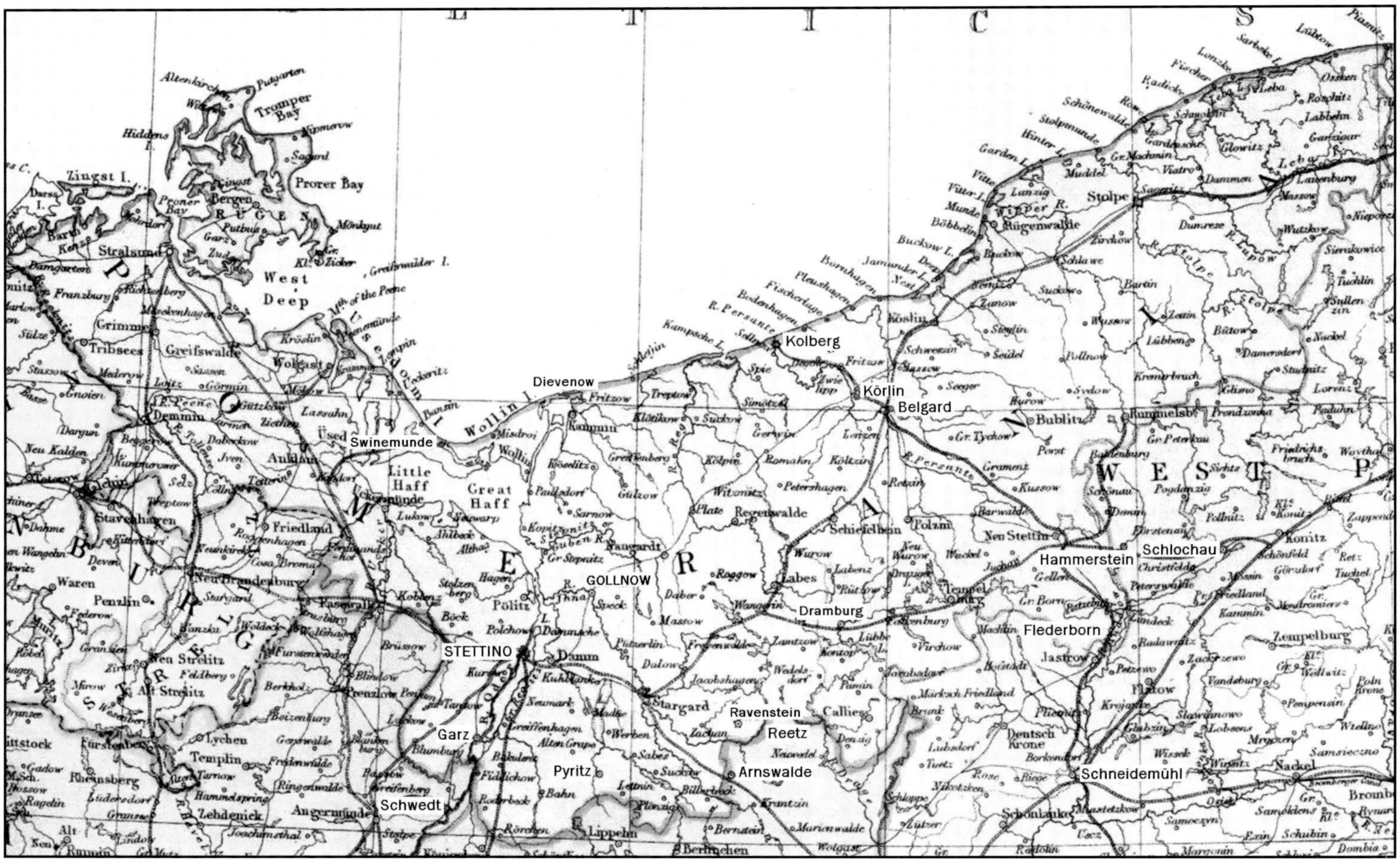

Period map of Pomerania, with the locations involved in the movements by *Nederland* units shown.

Around the middle of January 1945, Soviet forces overran the German positions along the Narev–Wichsel (Vistula) line, penetrating deeply into East Prussia. On January 26, the German 2nd Army was forced to withdraw behind the course of the Lower Vistula. Königsberg was surrounded. Farther to the south, in the Braunsberg–Heiligenbeil pocket, other German forces were engaged in a hopeless battle. Even Danzig found itself in the midst of a furious battle. To the north, along the Lower Vistula, while the forces of the Second Byelorussian Front under Rokossovski were taking a breather, those of the First Byelorussian Front under Zhukov went on the offensive in the direction of Posen and Frankfurt am Oder. Posen was surrounded but did not fall until February 23. Bromberg held out somewhat longer. The garrison of Schneidemühl, around which some units of *Nederland* also fought, was able to hold out until February 17. The Soviet First and Second Tank Armies reached as far as Küstrin on the Oder, bringing the front line up to the border of East Prussia and only a few hundred kilometers from Berlin. Only a counteroffensive in grand style would be able to push the Soviet armies out of the sacred territory of the *Reich*. To that end, on January 23, by order of Hitler, a new Group of Armies was formed, under the command of Heinrich Himmler; the *Reichsführer-SS* had been given the task of gathering all German formations between the Vistula and the Oder and to form a new defensive front along the Warta–Netze line. On January 24, Himmler established his headquarters at Deutsch-Krone. Gradually all of the German units available in Pomerania were attached to *Heeresgruppe Weichsel* (Army Group Vistula). For the most part it consisted of *Kampfgruppen* formed from second-line units and remnants of units that had been decimated in combat. At the same time, *General* Steiner assumed command of the new *11.Armee* while *General* Martin Unrein took over the command of *III.(germ.) SS-Panzer-Korps*.

The SS *Nederland* Division

While the leading units of *III.(germ.) SS-Panzer-Korps* were reaching Pomerania, the SS high command had decided to upgrade the Dutch Brigade into a new SS division, the *23.Freiwilligen-Panzergrenadier-Division "Nederland"* (*niederländische Nr.1*), which was to remain under the command of *SS-Brigadeführer* Jürgen Wagner. The unit identification number "23" had previously been assigned to the Bosnian SS *Kama* Division, which had been disbanded in October 1944. The first elements of *Nederland* were assembled in the area of Gollnow (now the Polish city of Goleniow), northeast of Stettin

An SS unit on the move in Pomerania.

A *StuG.III* and German grenadiers, 1945.

Visit by Felix Steiner at Hammerstein, February 1945.

and on the eastern bank of the Ihna River, where most of the unit's staff set itself up. The engineer battalion was formed with two *lehrkompanien* (training companies) from the *SS-Pionier-Schule* of Hradischko. At the end of the day, with new recruits, mainly *Volksdeutschen* and members of the Kriegsmarine, the strength of the new division was able to be brought up to a total of about 6,000 men. There was a shortage of at least 5,000 men to reach the theoretical strength of a simple Type 45 Wehrmacht infantry division. The division in question was an armored grenadier division, which should have consisted of (at least theoretically) of:

Two regiments of motorized infantry, each consisting of three infantry battalions, as well as of independent engineer, infantry support gun, *Flak* and motorcycle reconnaissance companies.

A regiment of motorized artillery, with two battalions of light howitzers and one of heavy howitzers.

A tank battalion equipped with assault guns, with four companies, each consisting of four platoons.

A battalion of anti-tank guns, with three batteries equipped with assault guns (about forty-five vehicles).

An armored reconnaissance battalion, with two motorized infantry companies, two companies mounted on half-tracks, and one heavy weapons company mounted on half-tracks.

A motorized anti-aircraft battalion with three 88 mm batteries and a 37 mm battery.

A motorized engineer battalion.

A motorized signal battalion with a telephone company and a radio company.

Around the middle of February 1945 the order of battle of the new *Nederland* Division was as follows (naturally many of the units were still in the process of being formed):

Divisionsstab

SS-Freiwilligen-Panzergrenadier-Regiment 49
I.-II. Bataillon

SS-Freiwilligen-Panzergrenadier-Regiment "Klotz"
I.-II. Bataillon

SS-Freiwilligen-Artillerie-Regiment 23
SS-Pionier-Bataillon 23
SS-Panzerjäger-Abteilung 23
SS-Nachrichten-Abteilung 23
SS-Wirtschafts-Bataillon 23
SS-Sanitäts-Kompanie 23
SS-Werkstatt-Kompanie 23
SS-Feldpostamt 23

Hetzer tank destroyers of the Waffen-SS in action in the area of Kallies.

A column of *Sturmhaubitze*, the new version of the *Sturmgeschütz III* assault gun.

SS grenadiers awaiting an enemy attack on the Pomeranian front.

The *SS-Panzerjäger-Abteilung* consisted only of 75 mm *Pak* guns and a few assault guns of the *Sturmhaubitze 42* type. The change in unit numerical designation from 54 to 23 became effective officially February 22, 1945, per order of the *SS-FHA* (SS operational command headquarters).

SS-Panzergrenadier Regiment Klotz

In early 1945, the formation of a new *Lehr-Regimentes* (training regiment) commanded by *SS-Ostubaf.* Rudolf Klotz[1] was begun at the *SS-Panzer-Grenadier Schule* at Kienschlag (in the Protectorate of Bohemia and Moravia). Most of the personnel were *Volksdeutschen* (foreigners of Germanic origin). The units were grouped together at Neudorf (now Networtschitz).

Order of Battle (Gliederung):

Regiments-Stab

Stabs-Kompanie

I.Bataillon

Stabs
Nachrichtenstaffel
Versorgungs-Kompanie
    1.-3. Gren.-Kp.
    4. schwere Kompanie

II. Bataillon

(same structure as I. Bataillon)
    13.Inf.Geschütz-Kp.
    14.Flak-Kp.
    15.-Aufkl.-Kp.

In early February, the *SS-Pz.Gren.-Lehr-Rgt*, by order of the *SS-FHA*, was transferred by train to Pomerania, to reinforce the *III.(germ.) SS-PzKorps*, which had withdrawn from Kurland. Between February 6–8, following orders from the headquarters of *III.(germ.) SS-PzKorps (Ia, TgbNr. 350/45 geh. V. 4.2.1945)*, the regiment was officially disbanded, to be used to reinforce

SS-Ostubaf. Max Schäfer on the Pomeranian front.

the SS *Nordland* and *Nederland* divisions, as follows:

a). |To *11.SS-Frw.PzGrenDiv "Nordland"* in the area of Freienwalde:

I.Btl. (minus its headquarters, signals and service companies)
13.(IG)-Kp. (personnel only, without their infantry support guns)

b). To *23-SS-FrwPzGrenDiv "Nederland"* in the area of Gollnow:

II.Btl. (minus its headquarters and service company)
15.(Aufkl)-Kp. (infantry personnel only, without vehicles)

On February 8, 1945, the roughly 800 men of the *SS-PzGren-Lehr-Rgt*, upon reaching the area of Gollnow, were mainly assigned to reinforce *SS-Freiw.Pz.Gren.Rgt. 49 "de Ruyter"* (BA-MA N 756)

The other units of the regiment, the headquarters, the headquarters company and the 14th *Flak* company, were left temporarily at the disposal of Headquarters, *III.(germ.) SS-PzKorps* in the area of Böck-Daber-Vörschendorf.

From February 12, 1945, beginning with these units and gathering up additional miscellaneous scattered units, the *SS-Panzer-Grenadier Regiment "Klotz"* was cobbled together, organized with two battalions and with the following *Feldpost* (field post office) numbers:

Degrelle with his Walloons on the front in Pomerania, 1945.

A *Panzerschreck*, a deadly weapon against enemy tanks.

SS-Panzer-Grenadier Regiment "Klotz"

Stab: 31 638
I.Btl. (1.-4.): 32 373
II.Btl. (5.-8.): 32 246

This new regiment was also transferred to *Nederland*, as the new *SS-Frw-Pz.Gr.Rgt. 48*, but officially designated *SS-Freiwilligen-Panzergrenadier-Regiment "Klotz"* (not to be confused with the other unit under formation at Schlochau), initially commanded by Klotz and then later, from February 25, by *SS-Stubaf.* Scheibe.

Kampfgruppe Lohmann

In view of the serious situation in the field, after having landed at Stettin the remnants of the *de Ruyter* Regiment who were veterans of Kurland were transferred to Ravenstein. There a *Kampfgruppe* was formed under the command of *SS-Ostubaf.* Lohmann and which consiosted of the *de Ruyter* regimental staff, *I./de Ruyter, II./Norge*, a cyclist company, an anti-tank company from the army, and a police detachment. At the same time a battery of the Dutch artillery was transferred to *the 4.SS-Pz.Gr.Division "Polizei,"* while the rest of the batteries were assigned between Fürstensee, Dramburg and Neu Weden. *Kampfgruppe Lohmann* was attached to the *Führer-Begleit-Division* commanded by *Generalmajor* Otto Ernst Remer. The engineers and some of the *Nederland* artillery were immediately committed to the front line. Between February 3–4, pitched battles flared up northeast of the city of Reetz (now Recz) following the arrival of strong enemy advance guard elements. The position of Gross Silber was recaptured by units of the *Führer-Begleit-Division*.

However, the Soviets counterattacked in force soon thereafter, retaking the position. During the day of February 7, the Soviets broke into Reetz. The small city represented an important road hub for all of the surrounding area. *Kampfgruppe Lohmann* was tasked with defending the position. In that same sector, because of operational necessities dictated by the deterioration of the military situation, a new combat group, *Kampfgruppe Schäfer*, was formed, under the command of the *III.(germ.) SS-Panzer-*

Lothar Hofer, commander of the *Nederland* artillery regiment.

Major Schacht, commander of *25.Fallschirmjäger-Regiment.*

Korps engineer commander, *SS-Ostubaf.* Max Schäfer, and consisted of the *Nordland* engineer battalion and some surviving units from *Nederland.* The next day the *de Ruyter* battalions were also sent to reinforce the defenses around Reetz. Meanwhile, the situation was also becoming critical in the area around Arnswalde; by now the city was completely surrounded by Soviet units and the besieged forces as well as the civilian population were waiting to be liberated. It was the same serious situation south of Stargard, where the defensive front was on the verge of collapsing from one moment to the next. There, to defend the slim defensive line were the remnants of the 28th *SS Wallonien* Division and some *Volkssturm* units.

Operation *Sonnenwende*

On February 14, 1945, the headquarters of all units of the *11.Panzer-Armee* were alerted to prepare for an imminent relief operation at Arnswalde; Operation Solstice was conceived to not only relieve the besieged garrison, but also to deal a severe blow to the northern flank of Zhukov's forces. The battalions of Germanic volunteers assembled under a driving rain that for days had been whipping the Pomeranian Plain. The *11.Panzer-Armee* attack forces took up positions south of the line Stargard-Reetz-Kallies. The German attack began on February 16. On the western flank, the *XXXIX.Panzer-Korps* with *10.SS-Panzer-Division Frundsberg* and the *4.SS-Polizei-Grenadier-Division* made rapid progress. In the center, the *Nordland* to the west and the *Nederland* to the east, aimed directly at Arnswalde. Behind them were the two remaining battalions of the *27.SS-Freiw.Gren.Div. Langemarck* and the *281.Inf.Div.* However, the units of *III.(germ.) SS-Panzer-Korps* soon ran into heavy enemy resistance. The *Langemarck* companies were hard pressed near Brallenthin and Petznick. Brallenthin was taken in the afternoon while at Petznick the Soviets continued to put up stiff resistance. The *Danmark* Regiment of *Nordland* was stalled on the heights south of Reichenbach, while *Norge* was engaged at Schlagenthin, managing to wrest only a portion of the position from the enemy. The attack on Stolzenfelde was also stymied by Soviet units.

The Dutch volunteers of the *de Ruyter* Regiment fought unsuccessfully around Reetz; the 1st Company attacked along both sides of the Ravenstein-Reetz road, supported by *SS-Panzerjäger-Abt. 54* under *SS-Ustuf.* Aigner. The attack was halted by a massive Soviet artillery barrage in the cemetery north of the city. During the attack a lone Dutch assault gun that was attempting to force its way into the city from the west was right at the cemetery gate. *II./de Ruyter* was called back from its positions north of Reetz, to be shifted to the south to support the attempt by *I./de Ruyter* to capture the city from the south from the area of Altenwedell and to thus open a gap in the Soviet defenses. While the Dutch units were crossing the Ihna, the Soviets attacked with tanks, stopping the attack by *II./de Ruyter* even before it began. During the day of February 17, *I./de Ruyter* made a series of repeated attacks from the cemetery of Reetz towards the center of the city, but without any results. The Soviets had dug themselves in well in the town and also had many heavy weapons, and above all artillery, which from the hills to the southeast dominated the city in the valley. Any frontal attack was doomed to failure. *SS-Ostubaf.* Lohmann thereofore decided to avoid any further frontal attacks, ordering his men to first eliminate the enemy gun positions on the hills by making a flank attack. Meanwhile *II./de Ruyter* was once again displaced to the north of Reetz to occupy new positions along the Walkmühle-Konraden railway line. Between February 18–28, all of the attacks that were carried out by the Dutch grenadiers continued to meet with negative results. Beginning on February 28, it was the Soviets who went on the counterattack. In the Ihna sector the Dutch volunteers were able to hold their positions in the Reetz cemetery and on *Reichstrasse 104.* It was during this period that a new artillery group was being formed for *Nederland* (*III./SS-Art.Rgt.54*) under *SS-Stubaf.* Lothar Höfer. However, the guns and their transport vehicles had not yet been

A Waffen-SS *Panzerzerstörerkompanie* anti-tank company, offloading at Pyritz in Pomerania, February 1945.

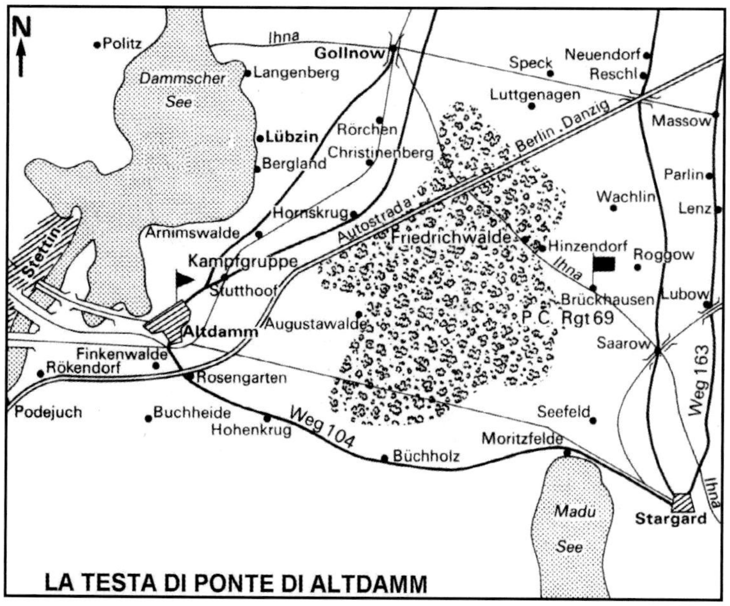

The Altdamm bridgehead

issued. One of the batteries, the 9th, was supposed to be equipped with 88 mm Flak guns. The new Soviet offensive severely impacted the plans to form this new unit, however.

The Soviet Counteroffensive

On March 1, 1945, the positions of *III.(germ.) SS-Panzer-Korps* were literally turned upside-down by Soviet artillery fire and soon thereafter they were subjected to attack by enemy tank formations. Two positions were particularly hard hit, the first, in the area of Petznick, Brallenthin and Repplin was defended by the Flemish volunteers, and the second in the area of Reetz, which was held by the Dutch volunteers. The defenses at Reetz collapsed under the weight of the Soviet shelling and tank attacks. Most of the units of the *de Ruyter* Regiment were forced to pull back to the north, after the Soviets reached *Reichstrasse 104*. The Dutch volunteers dug in to defend Falkenwalde, where the regimental command post and that of the *II./SS-Art.Rgt. 54* were also established. Some grenadiers of *II./de Ruyter* who were defending Konraden, northeast of Reetz, in the confusion of the fighting lost contact with the rest of the battalion while they were withdrawing to the north. The personnel *of III./SS-Art.Rgt. 54* also reached Falkenwalde, without any of their guns and still in a training status, joined also by elements of *SS-Panzer-Jäger-Abt. 11* who took an active part in the defense of the position. On March 2, 1945, a new assembly area for the units of *Nederland* was established in the village of Kasshagen, two kilometers north of Jakobshagen. At dawn of that same day, *de Ruyter* units began to pull out of Falkenwalde. *SS-Ostubaf.* Lohmann established new defensive positions at Jakobshagen. About twenty Soviet tanks struck the new Dutch positions out of nowhere, before the units had been able to be properly deployed; ten of the tanks were knocked out at close range by *Panzerfaust* rounds. *SS-Ostubaf.* Lohmann was himself wounded during the fighting. Meanwhile, isolated elements of *II./de Ruyter* that had pulled back from Konraden managed to link up with the battalion. The bulk of the *Nederland* units made their way towards Freienwalde, passing through Ball and Langenhagen. Other Dutch units reached Rehwinkel in the early afternoon.

A Dutch *Unterscharführer* at the Altdamm bridgehead, March 1945.

General Hans von Tettau

SS-Staf. Karl Burk

A formation of *Stalin* tanks attacked the position at Charlottenfelde where several batteries of *SS-Art.Rgt.54* had withdrawn and where they had remained stalled because of the clogged roads. The Soviet tanks were able to destroy numerous vehicles of the Dutch unit as well as all of the guns of *SS-Art.Rgt.54*.

In the hours that followed, the position at Freienwalde, which was also threatened by the imminent arrival of the Soviets, was also abandoned by the *Nederland* units. Kannenberg was defended by *II./Danmark*, by the *Nederland* engineers, and by paratroopers of *Fallschirmjäger-Regiment Schacht* (25th Parachute Regiment commanded by Major Schacht of the *9. Fallschirmjäger-Division*). The remaining *Nederland* units assumed positions along a new defensive line east of Massow on March 5. *SS-Pionier-Bataillon 54* secured the northern flank towards Freiheide. *Fallschirmjäger-Regiment Schacht* covered the road to Falkenberg. Southeast of Daarz the defense was taken up by other Dutch volunteers. Also on March 5, the Soviets attacked from the southeast, but were held back by Schacht's paratroopers. The *Nederland* units that were farther to the south also found themselves under enemy attack, but they were able to hold their positions. Soviet artillery began to hammer the area between Massow and Daarz before launching a new assault against the two cities, but the attack was thrown back by the European volunteers. Their advance halted to the south, the Soviets moved their axis of attack farther to the north, engaging units of *Frundsberg* at Neuendorf, northwest of Massow. After bloody fighting the Soviets captured the small city of Speck on the road to Gollnow. The *Nederland* engineers were called upon to attempt to eliminate the dangerous enemy penetration. On March 6, *Frundsberg* units were still engaged in the area of Neuendorf, while those from *Nederland* continued to hold back the Soviet attacks in the area of Daarz.

Enemy forces were able to infiltrate between Neuendorf and Massow, threatening the *Nederland* artillery batteries. The Dutch gunners had to fight as simple grenadiers to defend their guns and their very lives. Massow was once again unexpectedly under enemy attack and almost surrounded. The commanders of the German units engaged in the sector, among them *SS-Stubaf.* Sörensen and *Major* Schacht, reported to *SS-Brigadeführer* Wagner at his command post at Lüttenhagen to plan a new withdrawal. But when Wagner, via radio, requested authorization from the Corps headquarters, the reply was quite eloquent: "... The current line of resistance must be held at all costs!" Shortly after that radio message, bitter fighting erupted again around the position at Daarz. In the face of the enormous enemy superiority in men and machines, the Dutch volunteers were not able to do much, and accordingly they began to pull back despite orders from higher headquarters to continue to hold their positions.

The Altdamm Bridgehead

Between March 7–8, what remained of *III.(germ.) SS-Panzer-Korps* took up positions at the Altdamm bridgehead, southeast of Stettin. Defending the northern area of the bridgehead, from Lübzin to Hornskrug, were a naval infantry company, the remnants of *Frundsberg*, *II./Danmark*, Schacht's paratroopers, and the remnants of *Nederland*. *SS-Art.Rgt.54* set up in the area of Birkhorst. Command of the sector was assumed by the *Nederland* commander, *SS-Brigadeführer* Wagner. In the central sector, between Hornskrug and the highway, were the *Nordland* reconnaissance detachment and the survivors of the *Norge* Regiment. Farther to the south were *III./Danmark*, elements of *SS-Pionier 11* and *SS-Flak.Abt.11*. The remaining units of *Langemarck* and *Wallonien* took up positions between Höckendorf and Finkenwalde. On March 10, the surviving men of the *de Ruyter* Regiment were forced to give up the position at Chirstinenberg. During the following night the batteries of *SS-Art.Rgt.54* abandoned their positions at Birkhorst, displacing to the area south of Arnimswalde. A new line of resistance was established along the Bergland–Friedrichshof axis. *SS-Brigadeführer* Wagner remained in command of the sector. Elements of *de Ruyter* were still at Hornskrug, led by *SS-Ostubaf.* Klotz, the

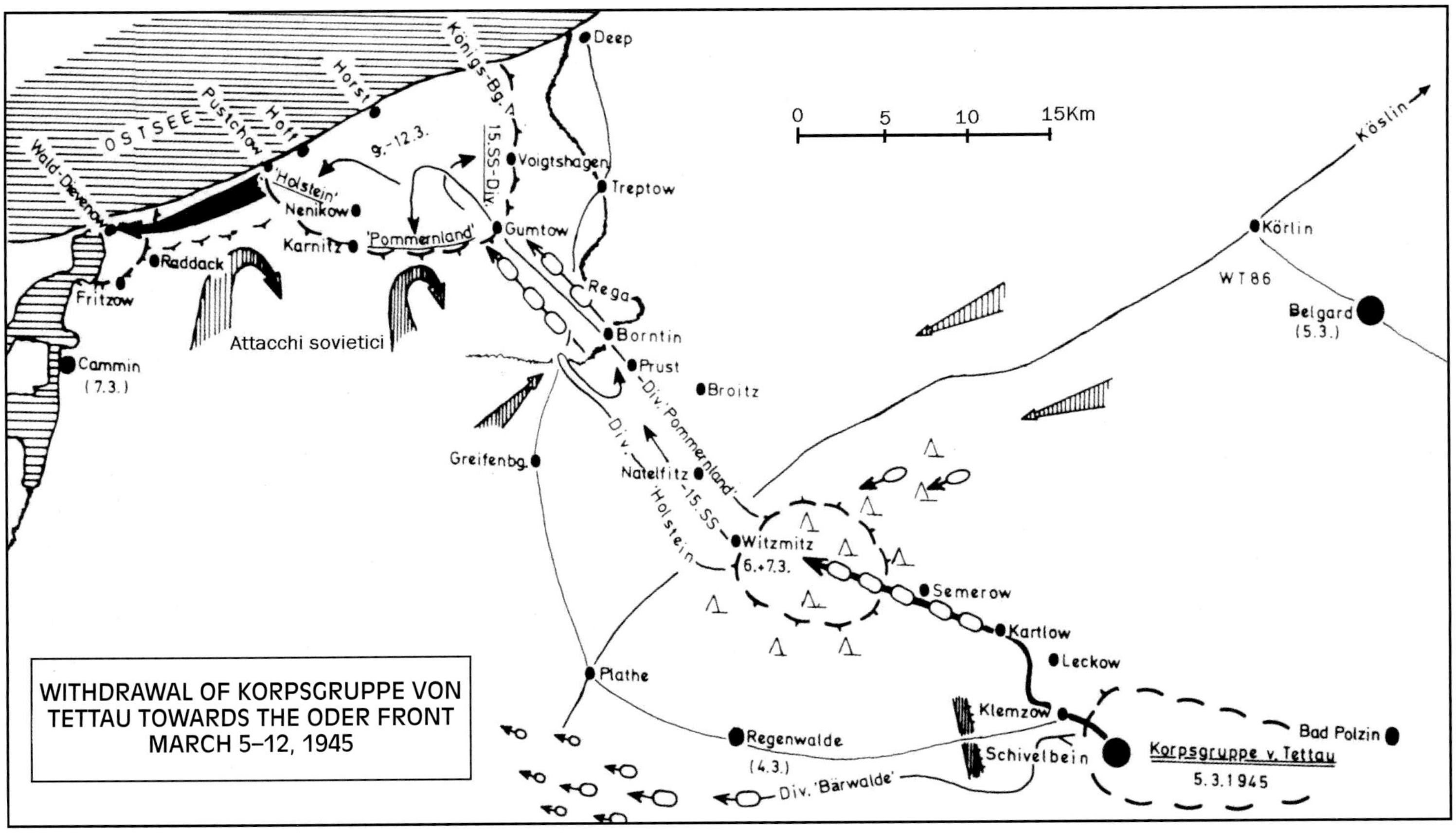

WITHDRAWAL OF KORPSGRUPPE VON TETTAU TOWARDS THE ODER FRONT MARCH 5–12, 1945

Oberst Joachim Hesse, commander of *Panzer Division Holstein*, here pictured in the Carpathians as commander of *Panzer Regiment 64* (first on the left).

new commander of the regiment, who had recently arrived from Kienschlag with other replacements. Early in the morning of March 11, the Soviets sallied forth from positions they had occupied during the night and broke through on both sides of Friedrichsdorf. This forced the German units to withdraw once again. On March 15, the batteries of *I.* and *II./SS-Art.Rgt.54* were redeployed to Altdamm, while *III.Abteilung* of the same regiment was reorganized west of the Oder.

The *General Seyffardt* and *Korpsgruppe von Tettau*

Since October 1944, at the Hammerstein training area, formation had been under way of a new *General Seyffardt* Regiment, consisting of two battalions: I Battalion was formed based on the few survivors of the terrible retreat from the bridgehead at Narva, with new volunteers coming from Holland and with other personnel from the division who had completed their convalescence. II Battalion was formed with reserve troops from the *SS-Panzergrenadier-Lehr-Regiment* from Neweklau and personnel from the Kriegsmarine. Even before formation of the new *SS Nederland* Division began, the Dutch regiment, along with other reserve units of *III.(germ.) SS-Panzer-Korps* at the Hammerstein training area, the *Offiziergruppe Scheibe*[2] (officer training group) and the *Unterführer-Ausbildungs-Bataillon Hämel*[3] (NCO training battalion) were immediately committed from the end of January to the front line against advanced Soviet forces that were within only a few kilometers from the training camp itself. A combat group under *SS-Ostubaf.* Paul Massell,[4] the new commander of the *General Seyffardt* Regiment, consisting mainly of personnel from I Battalion, was initially employed in the area east of the Oder River, later to displace to the area of Schneidemühl (now Pila, in Poland). The Dutch *Kampfgruppe* was engaged in pitched battles for "*Festung Schneidemühl*." Commanding the garrison, which consisted of *Volkssturm* elements, two machine gun battalions, troops coming from the NCO schools at Kolberg, Euberg and Teptow, a naval infantry battalion and also an assault gun battalion (*StuGAbt. Graf Dohna*), was *Oberst* Heinrich Remlinger. In early February, the remaining elements of *Kampfgruppe Massell* withdrew towards Flederborn, where they continued to fight against Soviet forces. It was at Flederborn, on February 2, 1945, that *Ostubaf.* Massell died in combat. On February 4, the remnants of the *Kampfgruppe* were attached to what was left of the *General Seyffardt* Regiment under the command of *SS-Stubaf.* Tröger, forming a new combat group, initially commanded by *SS-Hstuf.* Vieweger and attached to the 15th Latvian SS Division.

Later, around the middle of February, elements of *General Seyffardt* along with other reserve units of *III.(germ.) SS-Panzer-Korps* at the Hammerstein training area (Scheibe and Hämel)

From the left, Siegfried Scheibe and Rudolf Klotz wearing their *SS-Ustuf.* rank.

Ss-Ostuf. Henri Fenet

Waffen-SS grenadiers retreating on the Pomeranian front, March 1945.

were pulled together to form *Kampfgruppe Scheibe*, commanded by *SS-Ostubaf.* Siegfried Scheibe, who had also officially been appointed as the new commander of the 48th Dutch SS Regiment. This combat group was detached from *Gruppe Ax* due to the deteriorating situation on the Pomerania front, following the failure of Operation Solstice and the approach of Soviet troops close to the Hammerstein training area. *Gruppe Ax* consisted of the remains of the 15th Latvian SS Division that was also undergoing reorganization in Pomerania, and since February 15, 1945, under the command of *SS-Oberführer* Karl Burk. The name Ax that had been assigned to the *Kampfgruppe* referred to the name of the former commander of the Latvian division, *SS-Oberführer* Adolf Ax.

Gruppe Ax Order of Battle[5]

Stab/15.Waffen-Grenadier-Division der SS

Kampfgruppe "Scheibe"

Reste Grenadier-Regiment 59
Reste SS-Freiw.-Panzergrenadier-Regiment 48
2 Alarm-Bataillon[6]

Kampfgruppe "Janums"

Reste 15.Waffen-Grenadier-Division der SS
2 Alarm-Bataillon

On February 24, the 19th Soviet Army of the Second Byelorussian Front punched a wide gap through the German defensive front in Pomerania, separating the German 2nd Army and the *3.Panzer-Armee*. The initial attack hit the German positions along the railway line between Könitz and Hammerstein, in the area defended by *Gruppe Ax*. Poorly armed and for the most part consisting of troops who were experiencing their initial exposure on the front line, the German units were forced to pull back quickly in the face of the Soviet attack. The Dutch regiment and all of the other reserve and training units at Hammerstein sustained heavy losses. On February 26, following the fall of Baldenburg, a new combat group made its appearance, the *Korpsgruppe von Tettau*, commanded by *General der Infanterie* Hans von Tettau. The corps, that initially consisted only of the *Division z.b.V. 604* (604th Special Task Division), had been transferred to Pomerania to prepare defensive positions just as the Soviets arrived. From February 1, 1945, it was subordinated to *11.SS-Armee of Heeresgruppe Weichsel*, whose units consisted of the *Division "Köslin"* and *Division "Bärwalde."* On March 1, it was subordinated to *3.Panzer-Armee*, receiving as reinforcements the *15.Waffen-Grenadier-Division der SS* (to which *Kampfgruppe Scheibe* had always been attached) and elements of *33. Waffen-Grenadier-Division der SS "Charlemagne" (franz. Nr.1)*. The *"Köslin"* Division had in the meantime been renamed the *Division "Pommernland."*

After having attempted unsuccessfully to counterattack

A *Panther* tank assigned to *Nordland* in Pomerania, February 1945.

north-west of Baldenburg, *Korpsgruppe von Tettau* again found itself surrounded in the area between Bad Polzin and Schivelbein, along with units from the *Panzer Division "Holstein"* led by *Oberst* Joachim Hesse. On March 5, the general ordered a breakthrough maneuver to try to establish contact with the German forces to the west in the direction of Regenswalde. The *Panzer Division "Holstein"* advanced on the right, the *Division "Pommernland"* in the center, and the*"Bärwalde"* on the left. Units of the *15.SS* and *Kampfgruppe Scheibe* formed the rear guard. After having gotten past the first of the Soviet blocking positions, the road to Regenswalde was found to be blocked by strong enemy units. In keeping with orders issued by von Tettau to attempt to avoid encounters with enemy forces as much as possible, the units made their way to the northwest, passing through the villages of Leckow, Kartlow and Semerow, in the wooded area southeast of Witzmitz. It was only the units belonging to *"Bärwalde"* that were forced to withdraw to the south, splitting up into small groups that independently continued to make their way back to the west. While elements of *Panzer Division "Holstein"* were establishing a new bridgehead along the Körlin-Plathe road, on March 6, the bulk of the *Korpsgruppe* made it to the forest southeast of Witzmitz. Once radio contact was finally established with *3.Panzer-Armee*, it was learned that the bridgehead at Wollin had already been reached by the Soviets, which meant that the new objective became Dievenow, farther to the west along the coast. *General* von Tettow decided to push to the north and to gather his forces together at Horst on the Baltic coast, and from there, to move along the coast in the direction of Dievenow. During the course of the march to Horst, *Panzer Division "Holstein"* established a new bridgehead on the Rega River, north of Greifenberg. However, due to heavy enemy pressure, this bridgehead could not be held for long. Units of the *Division "Pommernland"* then joined the action at Borntin, which was successfully held and which allowed all of the units of the *Korpsgruppe* to pass through, while the advance guard of *Pommernland* reached the area of Gumtow, and from there made it to Horst on the coast. In the meantime, the Latvian units and *Kampfgruppe Scheibe* remained as a rear guard south of Witzmitz. There the remaining units of *X.SS-Armee-Korps* (*SS-Standartenführer* Herbert Golz) and of *Charlemagne* also arrived, coming from the Belgard area.

During the nights of March 7–8, 1945, sixteen Luftwaffe Ju 52 transport aircraft dropped containers with ammunition and fuel in the areas through which the *Korpsgruppe* was passing. During the night between March 7–8, the *Korpsgruppe* finally was able to occupy the bridgehead at Horst, barely in the nick of time, to defend it against an unexpected Soviet attack. Von Tettau deployed his forces to protect the defensive perimeter; to the east were the Latvian units and *Kampfgruppe Scheibe*, to the south was *Pommernland*, and to the west was *Panzer Division "Holstein."* The Soviets attacked the bridgehead incessantly, causing heavy losses to the *Korpsgruppe*. During the night of March 10, the German units began to march towards the bridgehead at Dievenow, which was stubbornly defended by two Kriegsmarine infantry battalions. *Panzer Division "Holstein"* led the attack, with an infantry battalion and the *Artillerie-Fahnejunker-Regiment* coming from Gross Born. Command of the combat group was assumed by *Major* Friedrich Buchenau, former commander of the 4th Regiment of the *Division "Bärwalde."* The French SS battalion commanded by *SS-Ostuf.* Henri Fenet was ordered to cover the withdrawal of the German troops, but also to protect the numerous columns of civilians.

For this mission *SS-Ostuf.* Fenet divided his battalion into two groups; the first, under Fenet himself, was to march along the upper part of the coast. The second smaller group, led by *SS-Hstuf.* Roy and *SS-Ustuf.* Leune, was to closely follow the civilian columns along the beach. The Soviet units tenaciously opposed the withdrawal to the west by the *Korpsgruppe* units, initiating a series of fierce and bloody encounters that resulted in elevated casualty counts on both sides. During the day of March 11, the leading elements reached Wald-Dievenow. Following orders, *Panzer Division "Holstein,"* which by now had lost all of its tanks, established a defensive line along the southern flank of the coastal "corridor," defending it from continuous enemy attacks. The retreating columns, which had been joined by thousands of civilians, continued to march to the west, along the coast, under the constant fire of enemy heavy weapons. From the sea, the cruiser *Admiral Scheer* and the destroyer *T-33*, along with naval artillery batteries on the island of Wollin, provided supporting fire. The rearguard of the *Division "Pommernland"* and of the 15th Latvian SS Division were to continue to defend the area of Hoff, halfway between Horst and Divenow, until the morning of March 12, but strong enemy pressure forced the units to pull back at dawn's first light. For the entire day of March 12, units of *Korpsgruppe von Tettau* continued to arrive at Wald-Dievenow. There were only a few hundred survivors from the *General Seyffardt* Regiment. *SS-Hstuf.* Vieweger, commander of *I./48*, along with twenty five other men, was captured by the Soviets. Thirteen of them were shot on the spot.[7] In practice, the new regiment was decimated even before it was assigned to the newly formed *Nederland* Division. From the area of Dievenow the remaining personnel of the 48th SS Regiment were transferred to Swinemünde and from there, by train on March 19, to the area of Heinersdorf, about five kilometers northwest of Schwedt, where they rejoined what was left of the *Nederland* Division units.

CHAPTER X
THE ODER FRONT

Dutch personnel in the area north of Berlin.

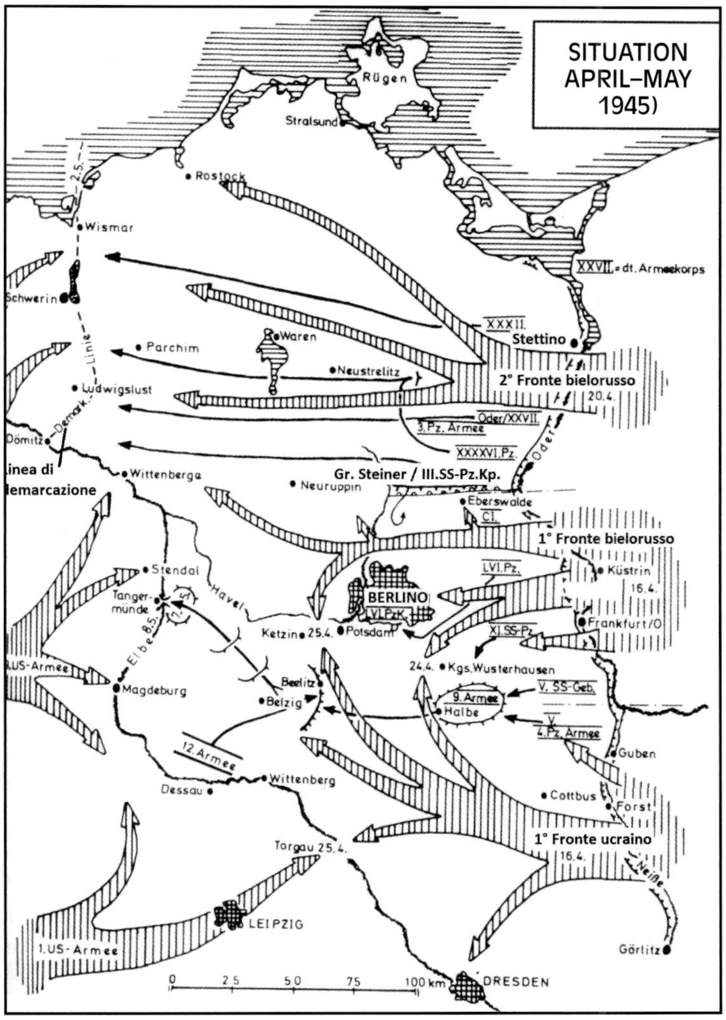

Soviet offensives between April and May 1945. The moves of the two separated groups from *Nederland* can be seen clearly, one to the north and one to the south of Berlin.

Following the failure of the offensive at Arnswalde, the *Nederland* units were transferred to the western bank of the Oder. In particular, towards the end of March 1945, the units of *III. (germ.) SS-Panzer-Korps* were assembled in the area between Wussow, Sommersdorf and Wattin, southwest of Stettin. On March 27, the units moved to the area of Altüstrienchen, Schwedt and Garz, as the Soviets had concentrated their 61st Army on the eastern bank of the Oder, directly opposite the positions at Schwedt and Garz. At that time, *III.(germ.) SS Panzer-Korps* became subordinate to *3.Panzer-Armee* commanded by von Manteuffel, who had issued the following proclamation to his troops: "*The Oder is the front line, not just a stop along the line of retreat.*" Following the evacuation of the bridgehead at Altdamm, the Dutch artillery batteries and those of *Nordland* were dug in on the western bank of the Oder, with *SS-Art.Rgt. 11* in the area southwest of Schwedt, and *SS-Art.Rgt. 54* northwest of that. The other units of *Nederland* also took up positions northwest of Schwedt, where training was resumed for the new recruits who had just been assigned to the division. *SS-Frw. Pz.Gren.Rgt. 48 General Seyffardt*, under *SS-Ostubaf.* Scheibe, which had returned to the division (with only a few survivors), after having been employed in the area between Polzin and Dievenow, was reorganized with three battalions, mainly with personnel from *SS-Freiwilligen-Panzergrenadier-Regiment "Klotz"* and other personnel from the Waffen-SS, Luftwaffe and Kriegsmarine. The *de Ruyter* Regiment was also reorganized in the area of Garz under the supervision of *SS-Ostubaf.* Lohmann who had returned from his hospital stay. The regimental command post was established at Gasekow.

SS-EINSATZ-BATAILLON REHDER

In light of the seriousness of the military situation, it was decided, in agreement with the hierarchy of the Waffen-SS, chief among whom was the chief of the *SS-Hauptamt, SS-Obergruppenführer und General der Waffen-SS* Berger and the head of the *SS-Führungshauptamt*, Jüttner, to collect all of the personnel possible, including non-combat personnel from the offices of the Waffen-SS as well as all soldiers assigned to homeland duties in order to form emergency units to send to the front line. The same order was also given to the offices of the Kriegsmarine and the Luftwaffe. Adopting this method, not only in the city of Berlin itself, about 10,600 men were recovered from various military administrative offices. One of these emergency units, with the strength more or less of a battalion and consisting mainly of Waffen-SS administrative personnel which included many older personnel, was placed under command of *SS-Sturmbannführer* Werner Rehder,[1] a veteran of the fighting on the westen front. This is how Rehder himself described the formation, composition and armament of this battalion:

> The soldiers and NCOs come from every part of Germany and were thrown together at Oranienburg. From there, they were transported to Angermünde, where I took over the battalion. It is a ragtag bunch of all shades, a final offering, convalescents and half cripples, office personnel, all of whom are unfit, who had been put out to pasture. Most of them have had sedentary jobs for a long time. Their morale is not the best. To that must be added the

A soldier armed with an assault rifle and a *Panzerfaust*.

SS-Stubaf, Hand Kempin, for a time commander of *547. Volksgrenadier-Divison*.

inadequate equipment and armament: rifles from almost every part of Europe and only a few automatic weapons. When I spoke with the chief of Waffen-SS supplies, Berger, on March 23, 1945, he assured me that later on other weapons would arrive as well as an artillery unit, but none of this was ever to happen.[2]

The unit was designated *Kampfgruppe Rehder*. The discussion between Rehder and the *Chef des SS-Hauptamtes*, *SS-Obergruppenführer* Gottlob Berger, leads one to believe that the *Kampfgruppe* consisted mainly of personnel of the *SS-Hauptamt*. The headquarters of *9.Armee* reflected in its *Tagsmeldung* (Order of the Day) dated 3/23/45, on page four: "Encountered *SS-Einsatz-Bataillon* (SS Task Battalion) as part of the *Oder-Korps*." This likely was reference to *Kampfgruppe Rehder*.

Again, in the words of *SS-Sturmbannführer* Rehder: "At the end of March, the Battalion relieved several *Volkssturm* units on the Oder, in and around Friedrichstahl, south of Gartz. The men were soon busy building and reinforcing the defensive positions."[3]

In late March *II./de Ruyter* took up positions just to the south of Rehder's battalion. Soon thereafter, the battalon was integrated into the Dutch regiment, becoming the 1st Battalion, but still commanded by Rehder. Along with II Battalion under *SS-Stubaf.* Petersen, the regiment once again became the strongest unit within the division. From March 11 to April 7, 1945, *SS-Stubaf.* Klotz commanded the regiment during the period when Lohmann was recovering from his wounds.

547. Volks-Grenadier Division

The Dutch 49th SS Regiment was shortly thereafter attached to the *547 Volks-Grenadier Division.*[4] Commanding that unit until the end of March was *SS-Standartenführer* Hans Kempin, replaced on April 1, by *Generalmajor* Erich Fronhöfer. Kempin was replaced because of disputes he had with the local *Gauleiter* (the NSDAP party official), Emil Stürtz. The *547 Volks-Grenadier Division* had been deployed along the Oder front alongside the *1.Marine-Division* with the following units:

Grenadier-Regiment 1091
Grenadier-Regiment 1093
Artillerie-Regiment 1547
Füsilier-Kompanie 547
Divisionseinheiten 1547

3. Panzer Armee deployed the *XXXII.Armee-Korps* in the area of Stettin and *SS-Korps Oder* farther south, while *XXXXVI. Armee-Korps* was in the Schwedt area. *Nederland*, *Nordland* and *18.Panzergrenadier-Division* formed the operational reserve of *Heeresgruppe Weichsel* (Army Group Vistula).

German defensive position on the Oder front, April 1945.

An SS unit ready for combat.

A group of German grenadiers crossing a river, April 1945.

New Separation of Units

Following the umpteenth Soviet offensive, on April 16, 1945 the two Dutch regiments were again separated to be employed in different operational areas because of the confused military situation at the time. While the *General Seyffardt* moved to the south, the *de Ruyte*r remained in its positions. Some units of *Nederland*, including the *General Seyffardt* Regiment that had barely been reorganized, and *II.* and *III./SS-Art.Rgt. 54* and other lesser units were transferred to the area southwest of Seelow, following the units of the *Nordland* Division. The *de Ruyter* Regiment continued to be subordinated to the *547. Volks-Grenadier Division*, holding positions at Gatow and Garz, as did also *I./SS-Art.Rgt. 54*. On April 20, the Soviets attacked along the Oder front, in the area south of Stettin, forcing *3. Panzer Armee* to retreat. A new defensive line was established on both sides of Schmölln between April 25–26. Positions were established there by the remainder of *Langemarck*, by *Wallonien* and by the Dutch *de Ruyter* Regiment. The next day the *Jugend-Bataillon* of *Langemarck*, manned with young recruits led by *SS-Hstuf.* Hans Stange, fought valiantly at Prenzlau. Beginning on April 25, the *de Ruyter* units were relieved by Wehrmacht units, and began to withdraw towards Pinnow south of Schwedt. The roads were completely clogged by columns of fleeing civilians,

SS-Hauptsturmführer Otto Petersen

Surrendering to the Americans, May 1945.

A young SS grenadier.

leaving the Dutch volunteers no alternative but to act as a rear guard for that deluge of old people, women and children, to protect them from indiscriminate attacks by Soviet soldiers. After having engaged in other defensive fighting, the units continued to withdraw to the west, north of Berlin. The remnants of the two battalions under Rehder and Petersen marched along the Fürstenberg–Güstow road, with the Soviets always at their heels. On April 28, with the imminent fall of Berlin and the end of the war itself, the retreat of the units to the west continued, towards Schwerin. On May 2, 1945, the leading units of *3.Panzer-Armee* crossed the demarcation line (established between the Anglo-Americans and the Soviets), surrendering to the Allied forces.

Parchim

On May 3, 1945, the remnants of the Dutch *de Ruyter* Regiment reached the Parchim area. The Soviets were very close. Lohmann ordered his men to hold the positions they had reached until the German units had crossed the demarcation line. The commander of *II./de Ruyter, SS-Stubaf.* Petersen, noted in his diary: "… Once again, my battalion and what was left of de Ruyter had to cover the retreat of other German forces and wait for them to cross the demarcation line. For the last time, our men dug holes and trenches west of Parchim. Two assault guns were in support, which took up positions right on the line with the grenadiers. Further back were the regiment's three remaining guns, ready to open fire. We all prepared ourselves to give the Soviets a warm welcome. When they attacked, they seemed sure of their victory. Eight, nine, ten enemy tanks descended into the valley. Our grenadiers were ready with their weapons in their hands. Everyone maintained strict discipline, waiting for the order to open fire. The lead Soviet tank stopped in front of a destroyed bridge over the stream in front of our positions. Not suspecting anything, the other eleven tanks moved forward one behind the other. Only at that point was the order to fire given and in a matter of a few seconds all hell broke loose. The assault gun on the left hit the lead tank, and the assault gun on the right hit the tank at the tail end of the column. Our *StuG* guns knocked out all of the enemy tanks, one by one, with speed and precision. The steep terrain prevented the Soviets from pulling back quickly. There was complete chaos. At that same moment two armored vehicles with a white star came from Parchim. Our men hoped that the Americans were also about to attack the Soviets. Instead, the two vehicles stopped on the road and two officers from the 7th Armored Division stopped to obseve the battle with their binoculars." That same day of May 3, *General* Hörnlein thanked *SS-Ostubaf.* Lohmann for the efforts made by *de Ruyter* acting as the rear guard of *XXVII. Armee-Korps*. The next day, May 4, 1945, the Dutch volunteers surrendered to the Americans.

Chapter XI

THE HALBE POCKET

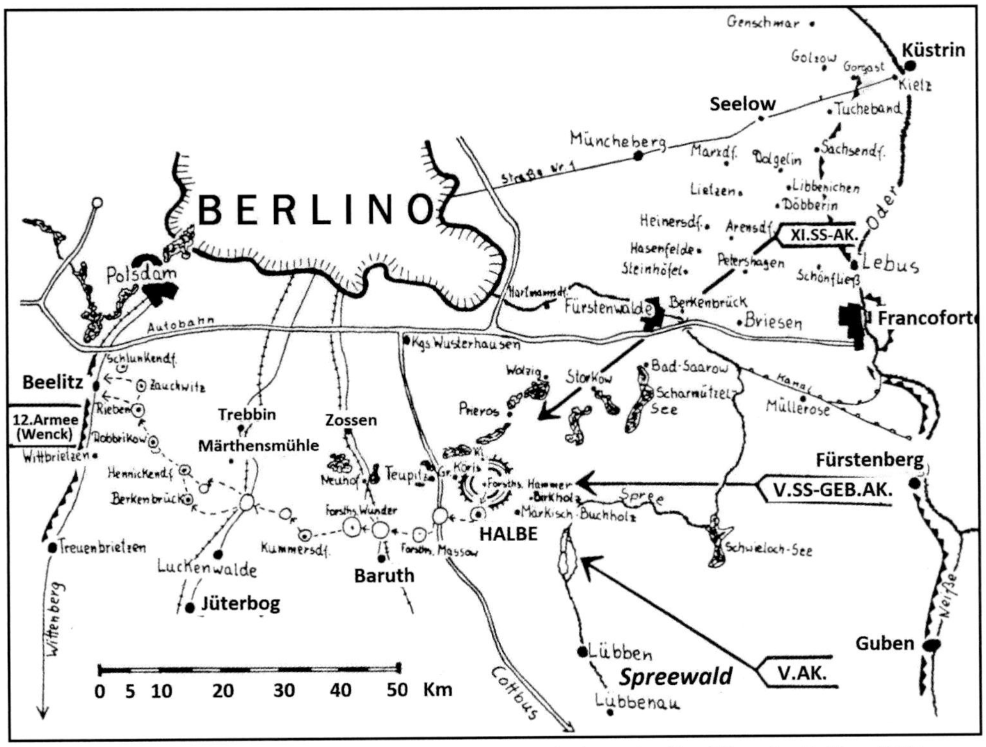

Map of German troop movements in the Halbe Pocket, up to the Elbe, April–May 1945.

General Theodor Busse

Soviet heavy artillery in action, April 1945.

The remnants of *Nederland*, around 4,000 men, including the *General Seyffardt* Regiment, after having been sent to the south of Berlin to challenge the Soviet offensive, found themselves surrounded in the Halbe Pocket along with all of the other units of *9.Armee* under General Busse. The Dutch regiment was commanded by Wagner. The German Army, after having been engaged in defending the Seelow heights and after having sustained heavy casualties, had pulled back southeast of Berlin,

General Walter Wenck

SS-Ostubaf. Rüdiger Pipkorn

on April 20, finding itself completely surrounded by Soviet forces that were headed towards Berlin from the south and the east. Busse's forces were deployed in the *Spreewald*, a region full of lakes and forests southeast of Fürstenwalde, in the clutches of the First Byelorussian Front under Zhukov and the First Ukraininan front under Konev. When the encirclement began the German Army had about 80,000 men, many of whom belonged to the remnants of numerous Waffen-SS formations. Alongside the military units were thousands of civilians seeking to flee from the Soviets.

9.Armee Order of Battle, Until the End of April 1945

V. SS-Gebirgs-Korps (*SS-Obergruppenführer* Friedrich Jeckeln)

Kampfgruppe 21.Panzer-Division
Panzer-Grenadier-Division "Kurmark"
23. SS-Freiwilligen-Panzergrenadier-Division "Nederland"
32. SS-Freiwilligen-Grenadier-Division "30.Januar"
35. SS-und Polizei-Grenadier-Division
36. Waffen-Grenadier-Division der SS

XI. SS-Armeekorps (*SS-Obergruppenführer* Kleinheisterkamp)

337. Volks-Grenadier Division
169. Infanterie-Division
214. Infanterie-Division
275. Infanterie-Division
286. Infanterie-Division
342. Infanterie-Division

V. Armeekorps (*Generallleutnant* Eduard Wagner)

712. Infanterie-Division
303. Infanterie-Division (Infanterie-Division "Döberitz")
Feldausbildungs-Division 463
Feldausbildungs-Division 541
Feldausbildungs-Division 619

Among the SS units not officially listed in the *9.Armee* organization chart were the remnants of *SS-Panzer Aufklärungs 10* and other units of the *SS Frundsberg* Division commanded by *SS-Stubaf.* Heinz Brinkmann. There were more than a thousand heavy weapons including guns and mortars, 79 tanks, and 150-200 other armored vehicles. Among the 36 tanks available to *XI.SS-Armeekorps*, there were fourteen *Royal Tigers* of *Schwere SS-Panzer Abteilung 502* (*SS-Sturmbannführer* Kurt Hartrampf). Between 25 and 26 April a first attempt was made by the *Luftwaffe* to drop supplies in the pocket, but as it had not been possible to establish contact with the besieged forces, suitable drop areas had not been found.

Early Relief Attempts

On April 24, *General* Wenck, commander of *12.Armee*, had ordered his *XX.Armee-Korps* to try to establish contact with the *9.Armee* forces. During the night, units of the *"Theodor Körner"* Division (formed with youngsters belonging to the RAD, (the *Reich* Labor Service) attacked near Treuenbrietzen, clashing with the Soviets of the Fifth Guards Mechanized Corps. The following morning it was the turn of the *"Scharnhorst"* Division to attack in the direction of Beelitz, setting off a pitched battle with Soviet units that lasted for two days. During the night between April 25–26, Hitler issued a personal order for Busse's 9th Army and Wenck's 12th Army establishing that:

1). The 12th Army was to eliminate the Soviet Fourth Guards Tank Army, reaching the line from Beelitz to Ferch, then to attack to the east to establish contact with the 9th Army.
2). The 9th Army was to continue to defend its eastern front between Spreewalde and Fürstenwalde, then to attack to the west to establish contact with the 12th Army.
3). Once the two armies had made contact, they were to attack north towards Berlin to liberate the city that was besieged by Soviet forces.

General Busse, after having consulted with Wenck, was in agreement to attack to the west, but after linking up with 12th Army it was his intention to withdraw with it towards the Elbe in order to surrender to Allied forces. Accordingly, on April 26, Busse organized two *Kampfgruppen* that were to attack simultaneously in two directions, to the south from Halbe towards Baruth and to the north, from Teupitz. These two combat groups were *Kampfgruppe von Luck* and *Kampfgruppe Pipkorn.* The first group, commanded by *Oberst* von Luck, consisted mainly of *Panzergrenadier Regiment 125* and the tanks of *Panzer Regiment 22* of *21.Panzer-Division.* The second group, under *SS-Standartenführer* Rüdiger Pipkorn, consisted of the remnants of *35. SS-Polizei-Grenadier-Division* and some tanks from *10.SS-Panzer-Division Frundsberg.* There are no reliable reports concerning the participation of *Nederland* units in this action. Initially the units of *Kampfgruppe von Luck* advanced without any problem along the Berlin-Dresden highway until they ran into strong resistance from the 50th Guards Rifle Division, reinforced with numerous *Josef Stalin* tanks, at Baruth. *Kampfgruppe Pipkorn* was quickly embroiled in bitter fighting against forces of the Soviet 329th Rifle Division, during which

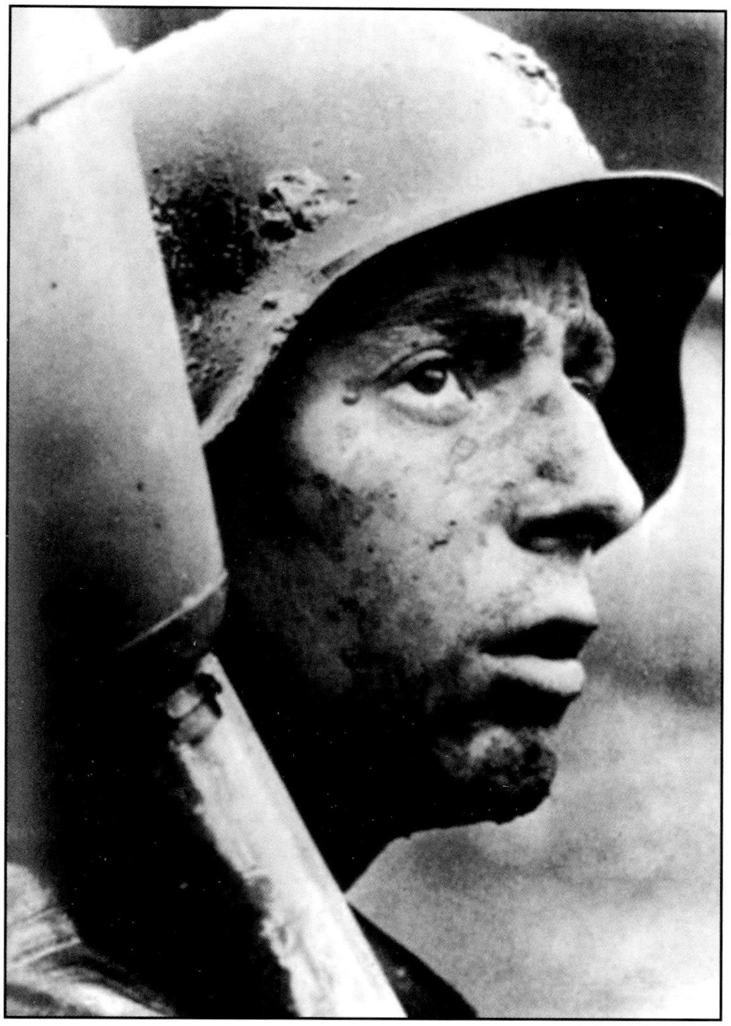

A German tank hunter with a *Panzerfaust*.

A German tank killer team in action.

SS-Standartenführer Pipkorn himself was killed; the units broke up into small groups and the soldiers attempted to pass individually through the Soviet lines, while others went to join *Kampfgruppe von Luck*. Most of the men ended up being taken prisoner by the Soviets.

The following is a testimony by *SS-Stubaf.* Helmut Diehl, commander of *SS-Pol.Gren.Rgt.90* of the *35.SS*, provided following his capture:

> Although the first attempts at breaking out of the encirclement were successful, the units that passed through the enemy lines were soon wiped out by fire from Soviet aircraft and artillery. Losses were enormous. It literally was not possible to raise your head and I was never able to direct the fighting. All that I could do was to stay huddled under a tank with my adjutant and study the map.[1]

The bombardment by artillery and aircraft sowed panic amongst the German columns that were moving under the shelter of trees. The Soviet tank gunners and artillerymen aimed at the top of the trees so that they could shower a myriad of wood splinters over the surrounding area, splinters that were the principal cause of death and wounds. Men who were hit in the chest or stomach died from loss of blood without being able to receive any aid. The sandy terrain that characterized the area prevented the digging of foxholes to shelter in, the only shelter available being the very craters that had been made by enemy shellfire. In the meantime at Baruth the fighting intensified noticeably; a few *Panther* tanks reached the area to lend a hand to the German units. Busse ordered von Luck to continue to stay in the Baruth area, but strong enemy pressure forced von Luck to allow his men to attempt to flee individually to the west. However, in order to do that, they still had to fight against Soviet infantry and tanks that continued to flow into the combat area in ever-greater numbers. The German tank killer teams, armed with *Panzerfaust* and other anti-tank weapons and camouflaging themselves effectively in the forest, managed to knock out numerous Soviet tanks. Supplies were dropped from the air, mainly ammunition, but they amounted to very little, and by now the greater part of the two combat groups had been destroyed. The Soviets claimed to have captured more than five thousand prisoners, among them *Oberst* von Luck, and to have destroyed forty enemy armored vehicles. Only a few lucky survivors of the various German formations managed to cross the Elbe River.

On April 27, the Germans were able to discover a gap along *Reichstrasse 96*, south of Zossen and north of Baruth, through which many men made their way before the Soviets began to use air attacks to close the gap. A Luftwaffe aircraft spotted the escapees from the air. Once the news reached Hitler, the *Führer* became furious when he realized that Busse's troops were pulling back to the west rather than pushing towards Berlin. His headquarters sent numerous messages to *9.Armee* but did not receive any reply. Throughout the night and during the following

German soldiers captured by the Soviets.

A forest road in the Halbe Pocket. Note the fleeing civilians and abandoned vehicles and artillery pieces, April 1945.

day the Germans renewed their attacks along the same axes, south of the village of Halbe towards Baruth and to the north, from Teupitz.

A New Breakthrough Attempt

During the night of April 28, the Germans again attempted to make a breakthrough around the village of Halbe, managing to overrun the positions of the 50th Guards Rifle Division, creating a corridor from Halbe to the west, after furious engagements with exceedingly high losses for both sides: "It was like a carpet of corpses around the crossroads, a grey-green carpet."[2] Between April 28–29, the fighting continued to increase in intensity around the village of Halbe and the surrounding forests, which were bombarded mercilessly by Soviet artillery and aircraft. While the rear guard of *9.Armee* was still at Storkow, the advance elements had finally been able to make contact with *12.Armee* at Beelitz. The situation at Halbe continued to worsen, with German units continuing to flow to the west through the open corridor, all the while clashing with the Soviets. In the confusion of the flight, there were many incidents reported between *Wehrmacht* units and Waffen-SS units, with each accusing each other of helping and giving medical assistance only to their own respective wounded. In the end, about 25,000 German soldiers out of the initial 80,000[3] were able to escape from the Halbe Pocket and join with *12.Armee* units on the eastern side of *Reichstrasse 2*. From there they continued to fight alongside each other and march to the west towards the Elbe to surrender to American forces. For their part the Soviets suffered about 20,000 soldiers killed during the battle. Also not to be forgotten are the thousands of German civilians that were killed during their desperate flight to the west. The men of the *Nederland* also continued to fight valorously along with the advance point units of *9.Armee*. On April 29, 1945, *SS-Stubaf.* Scheibe, commander of the *General Seyffardt*, fell in combat along the road between Zossen and Baruth.[4] On May 9, 1945, he was posthumously awarded the Knight's Cross. In the area around Mäertensmühle the last survivors gathered around their commander, Wagner;

The bridge over the Elbe at Tangermünde, May 1945.

A *Schwimmwagen* trying to cross the Elbe.

Troops crossing the Elbe River, May 1945.

there were only about a hundred men still able to march and fight.

During the night of April 30, after having giving them what final medical care possible, between forty and fifty seriously wounded men who could not be moved because of a lack of transport were left behind in the local school at Mäertensmühle. The rest of the men resumed their march, along with *Brigadeführer* Wagner, rallying again three miles farther to the northeast, near Forsthaus Mäertensmühle, where units of the 32nd SS Division had established a rally point. From there they continued towards the bridgehead at Beelitz.

Towards the Elbe

The units of Wenck's *12.Armee* continued to doggedly defend the area of Beelitz, where the linkup had been made with the *9.Armee* forces and where the remnants of the so-called Army Group Spree of *General* Reymann, from the Potsdam sector, were also arriving. The Soviets continued to violently shell and bomb the entire area, while other Soviet units had reached Elsholz, only six kilometers south of Beelitz, which was a vital point for the passage of German troops who were withdrawing from the southeast. The appearance of the last of the *Panther* tanks of the *Kurmark* Division kept the enemy threat at bay, allowing the civilian and military columns to rest and eat for a moment before resuming their march. *General* Wenck had managed to scrape together around a hundred vehicles of all types to transport the exhausted German troops. *General* Busse himself had lost so much weight that he was unrecognizable. Only a few Waffen-SS units, among them the *Nederland*, chose to cross through the village without pausing to rest. Wagner established a rally point for his units at Redeken, near Genthin. On May 3, with the news of the death of the *Führer* coming from Berlin and the signing of the surrender, Wenck ordered his troops to pull back to the Elbe as soon as possible, to establish a bridgehead against Soviet attacks. At the same time he sent one of his corps commanders, *General* von Edelsheim, to negotiate with the American 9th Army on the other side of the river. That same day, von Edelsheim crossed the Elbe on board an amphibious vehicle near Tangermünde, meeting with General William Simpson. The commander of the US 9th Army allowed the German officer passage only for his wounded and disarmed soldiers, refusing to accept civilians or to assist the Germans to build bridges to allow crossing the river. During the morning of May 5, the German troops began to cross the Elbe River in three places: on the damaged railway bridge between Stendal and Schönhausen, over the remains of the road bridge near Tangermünde, and on the ferry at Ferchland about a dozen kilometers farther south.

The first troops to cross were the soldiers of Busse's *9.Armee*, tired and battle-scarred, while units of *12.Armee* continued to defend the defensive perimeter against Soviet attacks. Soviet

May 1945: *SS-Brigdf.* Wagner discussing the surrender of his men.

German soldiers crossing the Elbe, May 1945.

A German officer, followed by SS soldiers, May 1945.

German soldiers surrendering to American forces.

artillery fire caused heavy losses among the masses of civilians and military personnel waiting to cross the river.

The American soldiers received orders to seek foreign SS combatants, and especially Russian anti-communist volunteers. In accordance with the recent Yalta agreement these "traitors" in German uniform had to be handed over to the Soviets. The American soldiers were concerned mostly with stripping the German soldiers of everything they could in the way of decorations, medals, insignia, watches and anything else that they could bring home as war trophies. Until May 7, 1945, the last remaining units of *12.Armee* continued to cover the crossings over the Elbe, and then they also began to ferry across to the opposite bank. The men who had been stopped by the Americans and sent back tried to cross the river with makeshift means in other places; they used canoes, tree trunks, wooden planks, or whatever could keep them afloat. *SS-Ostuf.* Joost van Ketel, a dentist with *Nederland*, made it through a US checkpoint at Dessau, passing himself off as a foreign worker in Germany and showing a Dutch passport.

A Sad Epilogue

The rest of the Dutch units attached to *9.Armee* who escaped the terrible battle of annihilation by the Soviets crossed the Elbe between Lenzen and Tangermünde between May 5–6. Their commander, Wagner, had to have many discussions with the Americans so that his soldiers would be accepted as normal prisoners of war. After having been imprisoned, in June 1947, Wagner was turned over to the new Yugoslav government, which condemned him to death by firing squad for atrocities committed by units under his command. The charges against him probably were connected to the period spent by the Dutch SS Brigade in Croatia in 1943, when it was employed against partisan groups, but information concerning the charges is not clear. Some sources state that the commander of the *Nederland* Division, Wagner, was condemned to death by hanging.

APPENDICES

APPENDIX A: UNIT INFORMATION

Designations

SS-Freiwilligen-Panzergrenadier Brigade "Nederland"	July 1943
4.SS-Freiwilligen-Panzergrenadier Brigade "Nederland"	November 1943
23.SS-Freiwilligen-Panzergrenadier Division "Nederland" (neiderländische Nr.1)	February 1945

Commanders

SS-Brigadeführer Jürgen Wagner	May 1943 – May 1945

Knight's Crosses Awarded to the Division: 19

Divisional Insignia
The runic symbol of Odal, with arrowheads

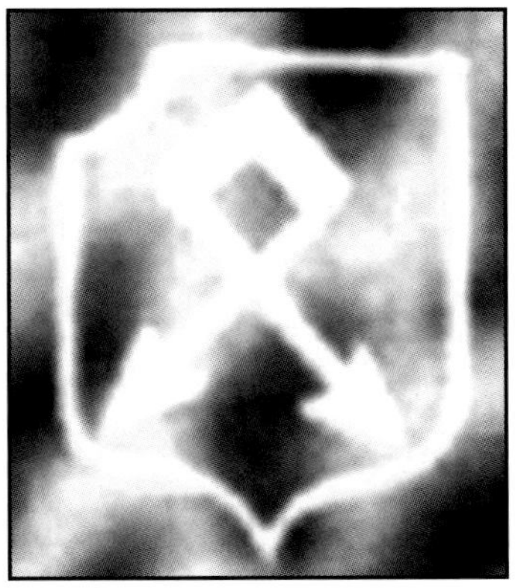

Vehicle Insignia
The division's crest enclosed within a shield could be encountered in various shapes, such as sharply pointed, squared, or other variations.

APPENDIX B: WAR DIARY

1943

Period	Army Corps	Army	Heeresgruppe	Area
August	*being formed*	Germany		
September	*being formed*	*2.Panzerarmee*	*F*	Croatia
December	*transferring*		*Nord*	Leningrad

1944

Period	Army Corps	Army	Heeresgruppe	Area
January	*III.SS*	*18.Armee*	*Nord*	Leningrad
March	LIV	*Armee Abt. Narwa*	*Nord*	Narva
April	*III.SS*	*Armee Abt. Narwa*	*Nord*	Narva
October	*In reserve*	–	*Nord*	Kurland
November–December	*III.SS*	*18.Armee*	*Nord*	Kurland

1945

Period	Army Corps	Army	Heeresgruppe	Area
February	*III.SS*	*11.Armee*	*Vistula*	Pomerania
March	*III.SS*	*3.Panzerarmee*	*Vistula*	Pomerania
April		*3.Panzerarmee*	*Vistula*	Pomerania

APPENDIX C: ORDER OF BATTLE

Naturally the final organization chart shown below is very theoretical, as many of the units were never actually formed.

SS-Freiwilligen-Panzergrenadier-Brigade 4 "Nederland" (December 1943)

Brigadestab

SS-Freiw.Panzergren.Rgt.48 "General Seyffardt"
- *Stab und Stabskompanie*
- *I.Bataillon (1.-4. Kompanie)*
- *II.Bataillon (5.-8. Kompanie)*

SS-Freiw.Panzergren.Rgt.49 "de Ruyter"
- *Stab und Stabskompanie*
- *I.Bataillon (1.-4. Kompanie)*
- *II.Bataillon (5.-8. Kompanie)*

SS-Freiw.Artillerie Rgt.54
- *Stab*
- *I.Abteilung*
- *II.Abteilung*

SS-Panzer-Aufklärungs-Kompanie 54
SS-Panzerjäger-Abteilung 54
SS-Pionier-Bataillon 54
SS-Nachrichetn-Kompanie 54
SS-Feldersatz-Btl. 54 (Stab, 1-5 Kp.)
SS-Sanitäts-Kompanie 54
SS-Wirtschafts-Kompanie 54
SS-Nachschub-Truppen 54

Kampfgruppe Wagner (September 1944)

SS-Freiw.Panzergren.Rgt.49 "de Ruyter"
SS-Freiw.Artillerie Rgt.54
SS-Panzer-Aufklärungs-Kompanie 54
SS-Panzerjäger-Abteilung 54
SS-Pionier-Battailon 54
SS-Nachrichetn-Kompanie 54
SS-Feldersatz-Btl. 54 (Stab, 1-5 Kp.)
SS-Sanitäts-Kompanie 54
SS-Wirtschafts-Kompanie 54
SS-Nachschub-Truppen 54

Kampfgruppe SS-Freiw. Sturmbrigade Wallonien

I./Waffen-Grenadier-Regiment der SS (estn. Nr.3)
23.SS-Freiwilligen-Panzergrenadier-Division "Nederland" (February 1945)

Divisionsstab

SS-Freiwilligen-Panzergrenadier-Regiment 49
I.-II. Bataillon
SS-Freiwilligen-Panzergrenadier-Regiment "Klotz"
I-II Bataillon
SS-Freiwilligen-.Artillerie-Regiment 23
SS-Pionier-Battailon 23
SS-Panzerjäger-Abteilung 23
SS-Nachrichetn-Abetilung 23
SS-Wirtschafts-Bataillon 23
SS-Sanitäts-Kompanie 23
SS-Werkstatt-Kompanie 23
SS-Feldpostamt 23

23.SS-Freiwilligen-Panzergrenadier-Division "Nederland" (March 1945)

Divisionsstab

SS-Freiwilligen-Panzergrenadier-Regiment 48
I.-II. Bataillon
SS-Freiwilligen-Panzergrenadier-Regiment 49
I-II Bataillon
SS-Freiwilligen-.Artillerie-Regiment 23
SS-Pionier-Battailon 23
SS-Panzerjäger-Abteilung 23
SS-Nachrichetn-Abteilung 23
SS-Wirtschafts-Bataillon 23
SS-Sanitäts-Kompanie 23
SS-Werkstatt-Kompanie 23
SS-Feldpostamt 23

APPENDIX D: III. (GERMAN) SS-PANZER-KORPS

Formed on April 15, 1943, at the *Truppenübungsplatz* at Grafenwöhr.

War Diary

1943

Period	Army	Heeresgruppe	Area
July	*BdE*	Bavaria	
September	*2.Panzerarmee*	*F*	Balkans
December	-	*Nord*	Oranienbaum

1944

Period	Army	Heeresgruppe	Area
January	*18.Armee*	*Nord*	Oranienbaum
March	*Armee-Abteilung Narwa*	*Nord*	Narva
October	*z. Vfg*	*Nord*	Kurland
November	*18.Armee*	*Nord*	Kurland

1945

Period	Army	Heeresgruppe	Area
January	*18.Armee*	*Nord*	Libau
February	*11.Armee*	*Weichsel*	Pomerania
March	*3.Panzeramee*	*Weichsel*	Oder

Commanders:

15 April 1943: *SS-Obergruppenführer* Felix Steiner
9 November 1944: *SS-Obergruppenführer* Georg Keppler
4 February 1945: *SS-Obergruppenführer* Matthias Kleinheisterkamp
11 February 1945: *SS-Gruppenführer* Martin Unrein
5 March 1945: *SS-Brigadeführer* Joachim Ziegler

Order of Battle

a). Korpstruppen (units directly subordinate to the Corps)

Artillerie-Kommandeur 138
SS-Nachrichetn-Abteilung 103
schwere SS-Panzer-Abteilung 103
SS-Werfer-Abteilung 103
SS-Sanitäts-Abeilung 103
SS-Nachschubtruppen 103

b). Unterstellte Divisionen (units subordinate directly to the Corps)

December 26, 1943

9.Luftwaffen-Feld-Division
10.Luftwaffen-Feld-Division
SS-Panzer-Grenadier-Division "Nordland"
Kampfgruppe SS-Polizei-Division

September 16, 1944

Division z.b.V. 300
20.Waffen-Grenadier-Division
11.SS-Freiwilligen-Panzergrenadier-Division "Nordland"
4.SS-Freiwilligen-Panzergrenadier-Brigade "Nederland"

March 1, 1945

11.SS-Freiwilligen-Panzergrenadier-Division
23.SS-Panzergrenadier-Division
27.SS-Freiwilligen-Grenadier-Division
28.SS-Freiwilligen-Grenadier-Division

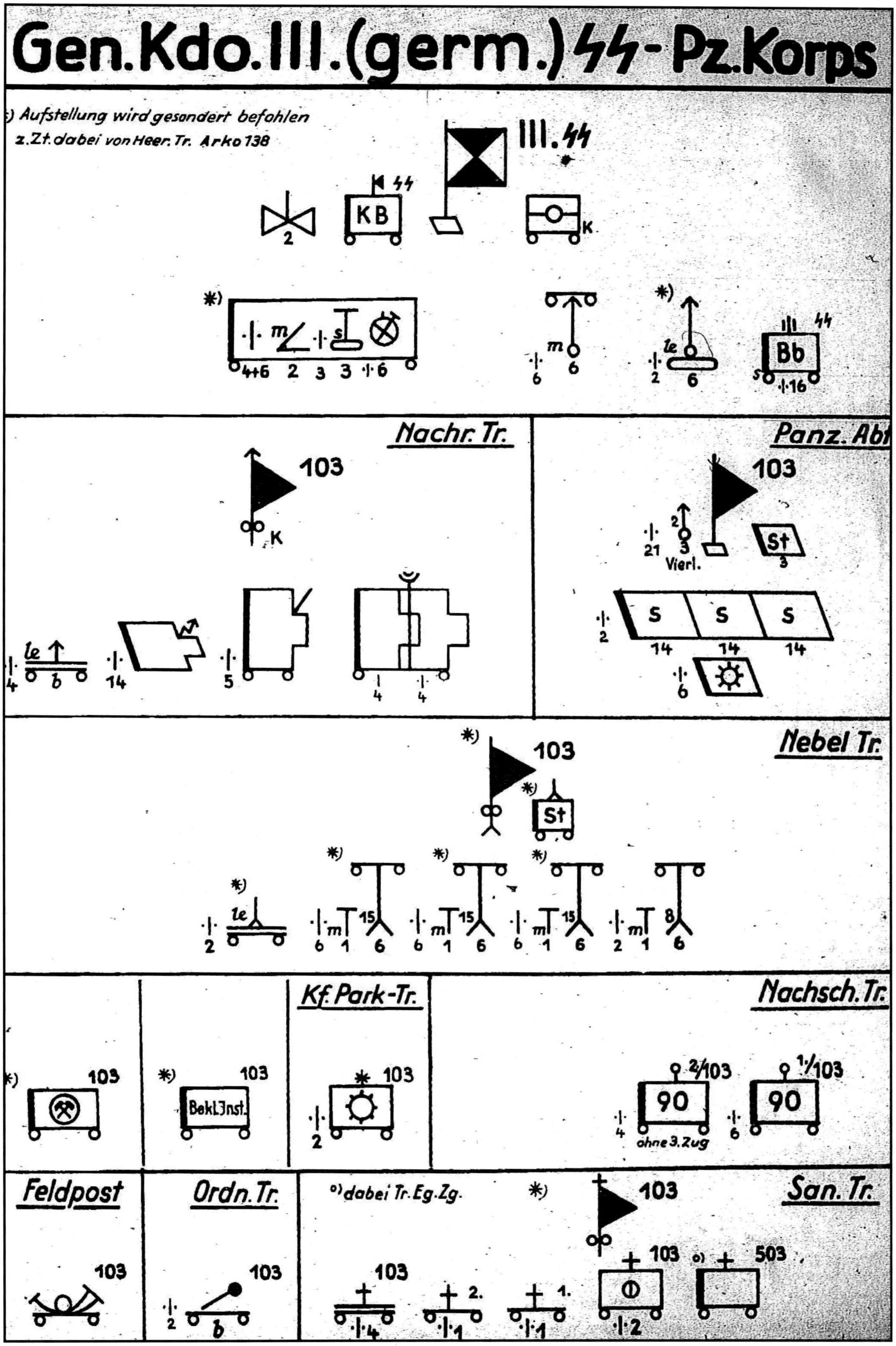

Taktische gliederung of the *Generalkommando* of the Corps

APPENDIX E: FELDPOST NUMBERS

The *Feldpost* (field post office) number served to identify a unit within the German military postal system. This system served above all to hide a soldier's affiliation with a specific unit, but even more so to identify the exact location of the unit itself. This is why, even for families to be able to correspond to loved ones, they had to use a *Feldpost* number.

SS-Freiwilligen-Legion "Nederland"

Unit	Feldpostnummern
Legions Stab	40112
I.Bataillon (1.-4. Kompanie)	40899
II.Bataillon (5.-8. Kompanie)	41450
III.Bataillon (9.-12. Kompanie)	42278
13. Kompanie, Infanterie Geschütze	43156
14.Kompanie, Pak	43990

SS-Freiw.Panzergren.Brigade 4 "Nederland"

Unit	Feldpostnummern
Brigadestab	57720

SS-Freiw.Panzergren.Rgt. 48 "General Seyffardt"

Unit	Feldpostnummern
Stab und Stabskompanie	40112
I.Bataillon (1.-4. Kompanie)	40899
II.Bataillon (5.-8. Kompanie)	41450
III.Bataillon (9.-12. Kompanie)	42278
13. Kompanie	43156
14.Kompanie	43990
15.Kompanie	44277
16.Kompanie	58770

SS-Freiw.Panzergren.Rgt. 49 "de Ruyter"

Unit	Feldpostnummern
Stab und Stabskompanie	59176
I.Bataillon (1.-4. Kompanie)	56387
II.Bataillon (5.-8. Kompanie)	58547
III.Bataillon (9.-12. Kompanie)	57711
13. Kompanie	56045
14.Kompanie	58298
15.Kompanie	57651
16.Kompanie	59222

SS-Artillerie Rgt. 54

Unit	Feldpostnummern
Stab	56420
I.Abteilung	59048
II.Abteilung	57362
SS-Aufklärungskp. 54	56084
SS-Panzerjägerabteilung 54	57173
SS-Pionierbataillon 54	58308
SS-Flakbatterie 54	46140
SS-Nachrichtenkp. 54	58949
SS-Feldgendarmerie	47428

SS-Feldersatz Btl. 54 (Stab 1-5 Kp)*	40004
SS-Sanitätskp. 54	59719
SS-Wirtschafts-Kp. 54	59884
SS-Instandsetzungs-Kp. 54	58651
SS-Nachschub-Abt. 54	57881
SS-Feldpostamt 54	56655

SS-Artillerie Rgt. 54

Unit	Feldpostnummern
Stab	56420
I.Abteilung	59048
II.Abteilung	57362
SS-Aufklärungskp. 54	56084
SS-Panzerjägerabteilung 54	57173
SS-Pionierbataillon 54	58308
SS-Flakbatterie 54	46140
SS-Nachrichtenkp. 54	58949
SS-Feldgendarmerie	47428
SS-Feldersatz Btl. 54 (Stab 1-5 Kp)*	40004
SS-Sanitätskp. 54	59719
SS-Wirtschafts-Kp. 54	59884
SS-Instandsetzungs-Kp. 54	58651
SS-Nachschub-Abt. 54	57881
SS-Feldpostamt 54	56655

23.SS-Freiwilligen-Panzergrenadier-Division "Nederland" SS-Freiw.Panzergren.Rgt. 48 "General Seyffardt"

Unit	Feldpostnummern
Stab und Stabskompanie	57720
I.Bataillon	40899
II.Bataillon	41450
III.Bataillon	42278

SS-Freiw.Panzergren.Rgt. 49 "de Ruyter"

Unit	Feldpostnummern
Stab und Stabskompanie	59176
I.Bataillon	56387
II.Bataillon	58547
III.Bataillon	57711

SS-Artillerie Rgt. 23

Unit	Feldpostnummern
Stab	56420
I.Bataillon	04528
II.Bataillon	57362
III.Bataillon	59048
SS-Aufsklärungskp. 23	56084
SS-Pionier-Bataillon 23	58308
SS-Nachrichtenkp. 23	58949
SS-Sanitätskp. 23	59719
SS-Wirtschafts-Kp. 23	59884
SS-Nachschub-Abt. 23	57881

* Disbanded in October 1944.

APPENDIX F: RANK EQUIVALENTS, WAFFEN-SS/HEER

SS Rank	Collar tab	Corresponding Collar tab used	Heer rank until 1941
Oberstgruppenführer		Generaloberst	
Obergruppenführer		General der Infanterie	
Gruppenführer		Generalleutnant	
Brigadeführer		Generalmajor	
Oberführer		-	
Standartenführer		Oberst	
Obersturmbannführer		Oberstleutnant	
Sturmbannführer		Major	
Hauptsturmführer		Hauptmann	
Obersturmführer		Oberleutnant	
Untersturmführer		Leutnant	

Sturmscharführer		Stabfeldwebel	
Hauptscharführer		Oberfeldwebel	
Oberscharführer		Feldwebel	
Scharführer		Unterfeldwebel	
Unterscharführer		Unteroffizier	
Rottenführer		Obergefreiter	
Sturmmann		Gefreiter	
Oberschütze		Oberschütze	
Schütze	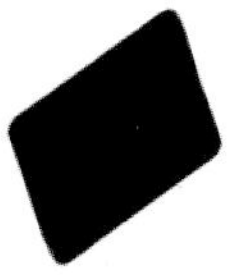	Schütze	

APPENDIX G: KNIGHT'S CROSS RECIPIENTS

The institution of the Iron Cross (*Eisernes Kreuz*) hearkens back to the period of the Napoleonic wars, during Prussia's fight for independence, and in the following years remained as the highest decoration of the German and Prussian armies. The decoration was awarded to soldiers of every branch and rank. There were two classes, 1st class (*EK I Klasse*) and 2nd class (*EK II Klasse*). For higher ranks there was the Grand Cross (*GrossKreuz*). With the beginning of the Second World War, Adolf Hitler modified the rules for decoration as well as its appearance. The Iron Cross of 1939 differed from earlier versions because of the presence of the swastika in its center (in place of the Prussian crown) and because of the year of its adoption (1939) displayed in the lower portion. The degrees of the decoration rose to four: in addition to the 1st class, 2nd class and Grand Cross, the Knight's Cross was added (*Ritterkreuz des Eisernen Kreuzes*), which like the Grand Cross was worn on the neck with a ribbon (which was 45 mm wide) in the colors of the *Reich*: black, white and red. For veterans of the First World War who had already been awarded the Iron Cross, a special badge was instituted (*Spange 1939*) to be attached o the award's ribbon, representing a National Socialist eagle, with the year 1939 indicated at the bottom of the badge. The dimensions of the Iron Cross were 44 mm x 4 mm, while those of the Grand Cross were 63 mm x 63 mm. The Grand Cross was awarded only once, to Air Marshal Hermann Göring. Awarding the various decorations was strictly sequential, in the sense that a given degree of the Iron Cross could only be awarded if the preceding degree had already been awarded. This meant that, for example, to receive the Knight's Cross it was not enough to distinguish oneself in combat, but that the recipient already had to have been awarded the Iron Cross 1st and 2nd classes. In particular the *Ritterkreuz* was awarded for, "... acts of particularly decisive heroism in combat along with great personal determination." Hitler personally ordered that the population was to show gratitude toward those who were awarded the *Ritterkreuz*. The Iron Cross and the Knight's Cross were very similar in appearance, but were easily distinguished by how they were worn on the uniform. The Iron Cross was "pinned" to the left side of the uniform. When the Iron Cross First Class was awarded, the Second Class was represented by a small ribbon attached to the second uniform button from the top. Because of the lengthening of the war, in 1940 degrees higher than the Knight's Cross were instituted. On July 3, 1940, the "Oak Leaves" (*Eichenlaub*) was instituted, consisting of three oak leaves in silver to be affixed to the eyelet that held the Knight's Cross. On June 21, 1941, the "Oak Leaves with Swords" (*Eichenlaub und Schwerten*) was added, which consisted of two crossed swords below the oak leaves. On July 15, 1941, diamonds were added to the oak leaves (*Ritterkreuz des Eisernes Kreuzes Mit Eichenlaub, Schwerten und Brillanten*).

Nederland Recipients

Eichenlaub zum Ritterkreuz des Eisernen Kreuzes: Knight's Cross with Oak Leaves

Name	Rank and position	Unit	Date
Scholz, Helmut	SS-Ostuf and Kdr.	II./de Ruyter	09/21/44
Wagner, Jürgen	SS-Brigf. And Kdr.	4.SS-Frw.Pz.Gr.Brg.Ned.	12/11/44

Ritterkreuz des Eisernen Kreuzes: Knight's Cross

Name	Rank and position	Unit	Date
Behler, Klemens	SS.Ostuf and Kdr Batterie	3./SS-Artillerie –Rgt.54	03/17/45
Bruins, Derk Elsko	SS.Rittf. and geschützfhr.	1./SS-Pz.Jäg.Abt.54	08/23/44
Collani, Hans	SS-Ostubaf. and Kdr.	SS.Frw.Pz.Gr.Rgt.49	08/19/44
Ertel, Karl Heinz	SS-Hstuf. and Adj.Rgt.	SS.Frw.Pz.Gr.Rgt.49	08/23/44
Frühauf, Karl-Heinz	SS-Hstuf. and Kdr.	II./de Ruyter	06/04/44
Hellmers, Johannes	SS-Ostuf. and Kdr.Kmp.	6./SS-Frw.Pz.Gr.Rgt.49	03/05/45
Hofer, Lothar	SS-Stubaf. and Kdr.	II./SS-Artillerie-Rgt.54	04/05/45
Jenschke, Walter	SS-Kanonier	Flak-Zug II./SS.Art.Rgt 54	12/18/44
Jörchel, Wolfgang	SS-Otubaf. and Kdr.	SS-Frw.Pz.Gr.Rgt.48	04/21/44
Meyer, Hans	SS-Hstuf. and Kdr.	I./de Ruyter	09/02/44
Mooyman, Gerardus	SS-Sturm. and geschützfhr.	SS-Pz.Jäg.Kmp.Leg.Ned.	02/20/43
Petersen, Otto	SS-Stubaf. and Kdr.	II./de Ruyter	12/11/44
Rieth, Herbert-Albert	SS-Ustuf. and Kdr. Batterie	2./SS-Artillerie-Rgt.54	12/11/44
Rühle von Linlienster, Hans Joachim	SS-Hstuf. and Kdr.	I./General Seyffardt	02/12/44
Scheibe, Siegrfried	SS-Stubaf. and Kdr.	SS-Frw.Pz.Gr.Rgt.49	05/09/45
Schluifelder, Georg	SS-Hascha. and Kdr.	I./de Ruyter	11/26/44
Schlüter, Wilhelm	SS-Stubaf. and Kdr.	SS-Artillreie-Rgt.54	08/23/44
Scholz, Helmut	SS-Ustuf. and Kdr.	I./de Ruyter	06/06/44
Strapatin, Stefan	SS-Rottf.	SS-Frw.Pz.Gr.Rgt.49	11/16/44
Wanhöfer, Günther	SS-Hstuf. and Kdr.	SS-Pionier-Bataillon 54	08/27/44

APPENDIX H: DOCUMENT RECOMMENDING THE OAK LEAVES FOR JÜRGEN WAGNER

The recommendation (*Vorschlag*) for the award of the Oak Leaves to Wagner, signed by *SS-Obergruppenführer und General der* Waffen-SS Felix Steiner on October 20, 1944:

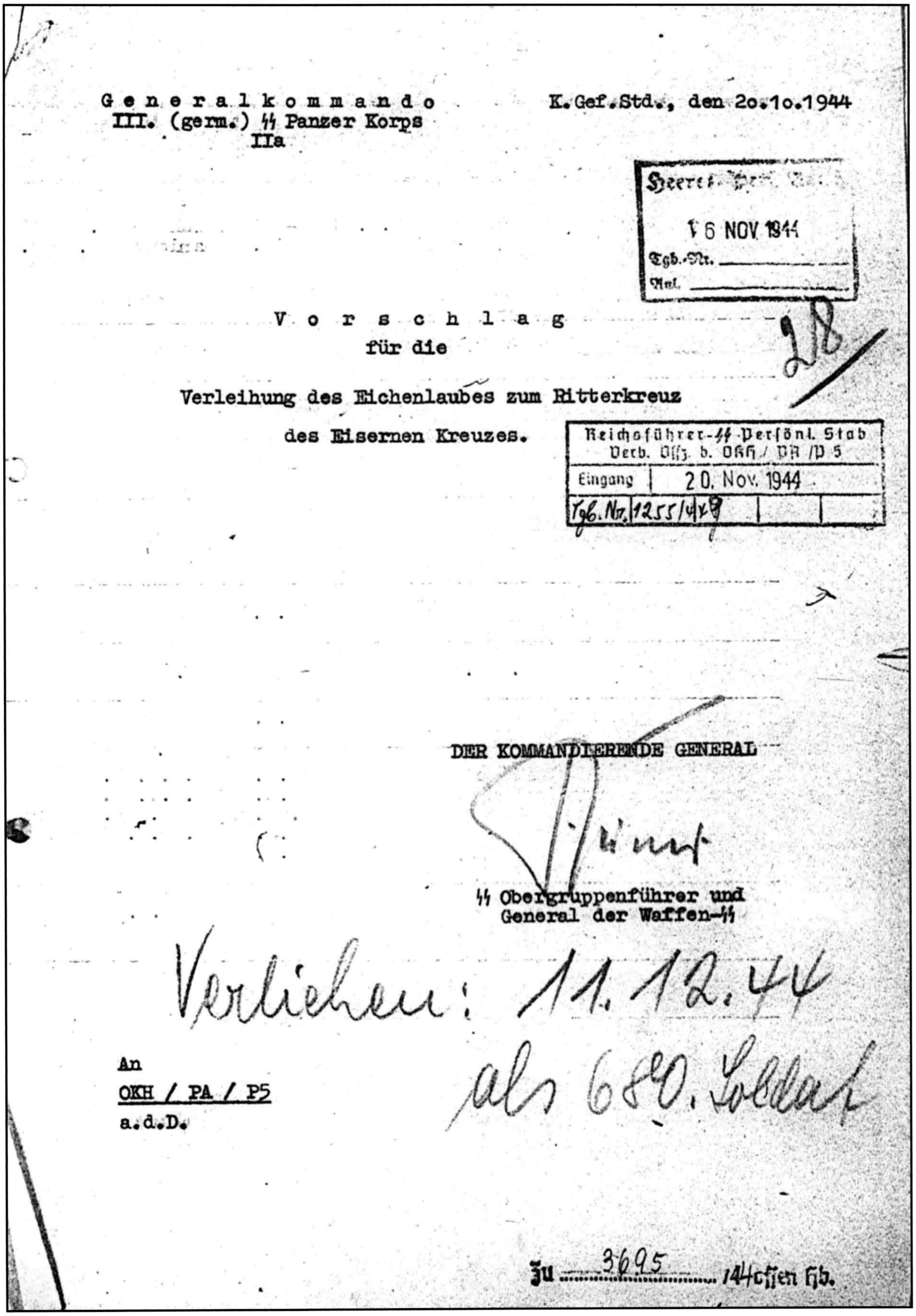

Generalkommando
III. (germ.) SS Panzer Korps
IIa

K.Gef.Std., den 20.10.1944

Heeres-Pers.-Amt
16 NOV 1944
Tgb.-Nr.
Anl.

218

Vorschlag
für die
Verleihung des Eichenlaubes zum Ritterkreuz
des Eisernen Kreuzes.

Reichsführer-SS-Persönl. Stab
Verb. Offz. b. OKH / PA / P 5
Eingang 20. Nov. 1944
Tgb.Nr. 1255/44

DER KOMMANDIERENDE GENERAL

Steiner

SS Obergruppenführer und
General der Waffen-SS

Verliehen: 11.12.44
als 680. Soldat

An
OKH / PA / P5
a.d.D.

zu 3695 144cfsen Hb.

Frontispiece of original document from the official Waffen-SS archives.

Translation of the Recommendation from the Original

SS-*Brigadeführer* Wagner, since the award of the Knight's Cross on July 20, 1943, in continuous action as commander of *4.SS-Freiw.Pz.Gren.Brig. Nederland*, has repeatedly demonstrated exceptional behavior. Following the difficult withdrawal from the Oranienburg front, the young Brigade was charged with the defense of the Narva bridgehead. Well aware of the fact that the critical point of the defensive line would be in the area of Lilienbach, working tirelessly and animated by unbounded energy, Wagner personally supervised all of the arrangements necessary for effective defensive measures. Despite the serious effects of enemy fire, he was able always to personally determine the critical point of the direction of the enemy assault. The main attack, which began on March 8, 1944, preceded by a double nighttime bombardment lasting ten to eleven hours, made by a formation of enemy bombers and followed by an attack by a much larger tank and infantry force, was thus able to be repelled. The enemy continued to attack until the end of March, paying no heed to his heavy losses of men and equipment, with the objective of overrunning the bridgehead at Narva. *Brigadeführer* Wagner was the heart of the defense. From his command post, which was only eight hundred meters behind the main combat line, he would travel on foot to the critical points of the fighting and was by his personal example able to incite officers, NCOs and troops to stubborn resistance, so that the enemy was not able to force the bridgehead and thus to break through the Narva front.

When on August 12–13 strong enemy forces were able to break through the *18.Armee* front west of Lake Pleskau, thus threatening Dorpat and the southern flank of *Armee-Abteilung-Narwa*, between August 14–15, a mixed group was organized under the command of *SS-Brigadef.* Wagner, consisting of various units that assembled at Dorpat. On August 16, at 0415, the enemy launched a surprise attack with significant forces near Meihkoorma on the Seenege River, between Lake Peipus and Lake Pleskau, continuing to push in the direction of Dorpat. Wagner went on the counterattack with all of the forces available to him, pushed the enemy to the east, and made possible the withdrawal of the *207.Sicherungs-Division* which was threatened with being surrounded by the enemy. During the following days the enemy repeated his strong attacks in the direction of Dorpat from the east, southeast and south with all of the forces at his disposal. By his personal example and by his ability to lead, Wagner was able to inflict upon the enemy such losses that the attacking forces lessened day after day. He did this to enable an attack to be prepared by the newly formed *87,J.D.*, with whose help the enemy attack along the Embach was able to be repulsed.

During the advance by *III.(germ.) SS-Panzer-Korps* from the Estonian region, the enemy managed to break through northeast of Wolmar, in the *L.Korps* sector, and to occupy the city of Wolmar with strong tank forces. On September 23, 1944, the *4.SS-Freiw.Panz.Gren.Brig. Nederland* was detached from *III. (germ.) SS-Panzer-Korps* and was attached to *L.Korps*. On September 23, towards nightfall, in the area northwest of Wolmar, the Brigade was involved in closing the enemy breach. In three days of fighting the Brigade, under the leadership of *Brigadef.* Wagner, was able to push back the overwhelming enemy forces and to inflict high losses of men and equipment on the adversary. All of the critical situations in that sector of the front were overcome and *L.Korps*, as well as *II.Korps* coming from the north were able to disengage from the enemy according to plan.

Following its action near Doblen, *4.SS-Freiw.Panz.Gren. Brigade Nederland* was ordered to assemble in the area south of Grobin, during the night of October 14, 1944, and from there to reach the area of Barta and to report to the *11.J.D.* to close the gap in the front north of the Tirs–Purvs swamps and to wipe out the enemy forces that were advancing from the northern forests. The enemy, with a strength of about two regiments with heavy weapons, had established itself across a gap in front *of Gren.Reg. 23* in the impenetrable wooded areas. Some weak units kept watch over the eastern edge of the forest, to the north of which some artillery and emergency units had been placed. There was a risk that the enemy, who had reinforced his infantry with tanks and assault guns, would bypass these weak lines and thus succeed in his intent of breaking through in the direction of Libau. During this critical situation, *SS-Brigadef.* Wagner decided to attack the enemy forces in the forest with four assault groups from the *Nederland* Brigade while at the same time sealing the gap in the front with these same forces. The Brigade conducted the attack and became involved in difficult nighttime fighting in the forest, and after three days was able to clear out the forested area. The enemy force there and all of its vehicles were completely wiped out. This success is clearly attributable, in addition to the courage of the troops, to the exceptional leadership ability of SS-*Brigadef.* Wagner, who in the crucial moments always showed himself to be fearlessly in command of the situation. These actions prevented the enemy from realizing his intention of achieving a breakthrough in the direction of Libau.

APPENDIX I: GERMAN CROSS IN GOLD RECIPIENTS

The German Cross (*Kriegsorden*) was instituted on September 28, 1941, by Adolf Hitler (*Führer und Oberster Befehlshaber der Wehrmacht*) to honor acts of heroism by German units on the eastern front. The award existed in two classes, Gold and Silver, independent of each other, with no hierarchy. The Gold class was awarded for repeated acts of heroism in the face of the enemy, which however did not justify the award of the Knight's Cross. The Silver class was not an award for valor, but was instead for meritorious service, and was in fact considered to be a lesser award than was the *Ritterkreuz Des Kriegsverdienstkreuzes* (Knight's Cross for meritorious service).

List of *Nederland* Personnel Awarded the German Cross in Gold

Aigner, Anton	SS-Hstuf., Chef	2./SS-Art.Rgt. (mot) 54	02/07/44
Bosch, Johann	SS-Ustuf.	2./SS-Pionier-Bataillon (mot) 54	18/12/44
Collani, Hans	SS-Ostubaf, Kdr.	SS-Pz.Gren.Rgt.49	24/04/44
Deck, Eugen	SS-Ostuf	6./SS-Pz.Gr.Rgt.49	12/03/44
Diener, Walter	SS-Hstuf., Chef	14./SS-Pz.Gr.Rgt.49	24/04/44
Faasz, Dr. Albert	SS-Hstuf.d.Res.	Stab/SS-Pz.Gr.Rgt.48	23/05/44
Fitzthum, Josef	SS-Staf., Kdr.	SS-Frw.Leg. "Niederlande"	24/08/44
Grabow, Emil	SS-Ostuf.	7./SS-Pz.Gr.Rgt.49	09/03/45
Hellmers, Johannes	SS-Ostuf.	6./SS-Pz.Gr.Rgt.49	18/12/44
Hensgen, Theodor	SS-Hscha.	Stab I./SS-Pz.Gr.Rgt.49	18/12/44
Hofer, Lothar	SS-Hstuf., Kdr.	I./SS-Art.Rgt.(mot) 54	24/04/44
Ilgner, Gerhard	SS-Ostuf.	i./SS-Pionier-Bataillon (mot) 54	17/09/44
Jauss, Hans-Robert	SS-Ostuf.	4./SS-Pz.Gr.Rgt.48	24/04/44
Jepp, Siegfried	SS-Hstuf., Chef	1./SS-Art.Rgt. (mot) 54	15/04/45
Laszakovits, Franz	SS-Uscha.	2./SS-Art.Rgt.(mot) 54	26/09/44
Meyer, Hans	SS-Stubaf.	1./SS-Pz.Gr.Rgt.49	23/05/44
Meinke, Artur	SS-Oscha.	3./SS-Art.Rgt.(mot) 54	15/04/45
Pölzbauer, Karl	SS-Oscha.	2./SS-Pz.Gr.Rgt. 48	08/05/44
Pulles, Gerrit-Jan	SS-Ustuf.	3./SS-Pz.Gr.Rgt. 49	18/12/44
Rüschoff, Josef	SS-Hstuf.	SS-Art.Rgt.(Mot) 54	23/09/44
Schluifelder, Georg	SS-Oscha.	II./SS-Pz.Gr.Rgt. 49	14/11/44
Steifeld, Gustav	SS-Ustuf.	Brigadestab	08/11/44
Sülberg, Ludwig	SS-Hscha.	II./SS-Pz.Gr.Rgt. 49	09/03/45
Thissen, Wilhelm	SS-Hstuf., Chef	SS-Nachrichten-Kp.(mot) 54	19/10/44
Venemen, Frans	SS-Hscha.	3./SS-Pz.Gr.Rgt. 48	24/04/44
Vieweger, Wolfgang	SS-Hstuf.d.Res.	I/SS-Freiw.Pz.Gr.Rgt. 48	27/04/45
Vossenberg, Wilhelm	SS-Uscha	1./SS-Art.Rgt.(mot) 54	22/03/45
Ziemssen, Dietrich	SS-Stubaf.	1.Generalstabsoffizier	16/06/44

APPENDIX J: CITATION FOR THE GERMAN CROSS IN GOLD FOR GEORG SCHLUIFELDER

Citation for the award of the German Cross in Gold for Georg Schluifelder, presented on October 6, 1944, by *SS-Hstuf.* Fritz Tröger. The document is important from a historical point of view for the *Nederland* Brigade, because it attests to the presence of *Kampfgruppe Tröger*, consisting of veterans of the *General Seyffardt* Regiment as part of the brigade itself on the *Tannenbergstellung* front and in Kurland.

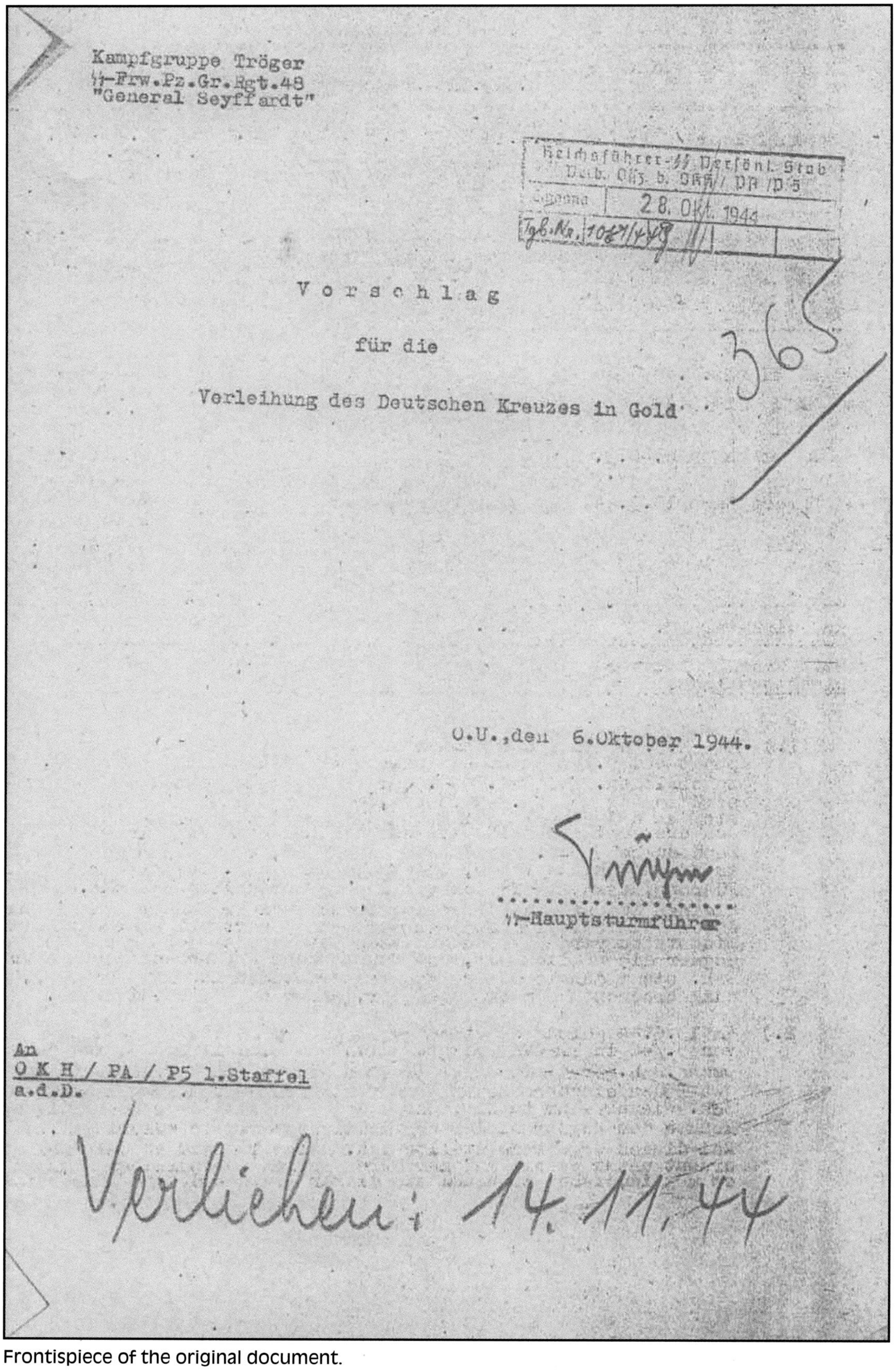

Kampfgruppe Tröger
SS-Frw.Pz.Gr.Rgt.48
"General Seyffardt"

Reichsführer-SS Persönl. Stab
Eingang 28. Okt. 1944

365

V o r s c h l a g

für die

Verleihung des Deutschen Kreuzes in Gold

O.U., den 6. Oktober 1944.

SS-Hauptsturmführer

An
O K H / PA / P5 1. Staffel
a.d.D.

Verliehen: 14.11.44

Frontispiece of the original document.

Translation of the Citation

1). On 3/21/44, the enemy attacked in the *II./48* sector, directing its greatest effort against the positions of the *7./48*, and managing to break through. *SS-Oberscharfùhrer* Schluifelder, in reserve at the headquarters of the motorcycle rifle platoon of *II./48*, went on the attack with his men, managing to repel the enemy, inflict heavy losses, and reestablish the main line of resistance. During that counterattack, which was decisive for the entire bridgehead, Schluifelder demonstrated great command ability, extraordinary valor and spirit of sacrifice. With his small platoon he charged against the enemy at the head of his men, leading them by his personal example; it was due to his personal and fearless action that this attack succeeded and that by it the enemy was denied the opportunity to overwhelm the bridgehead. Schluifelder found himself with his men facing an enemy force of 150 men, wiping out two thirds of them.

2). On 6/15/44, an enemy attack force was able to break through the left flank of *5./48*, near Popovka and to entrench itself. *SS-Oscha.* Schluifelder went on the counterattack with a small combat group and evicting the enemy from the trenches. Once again he demonstrated valor, ably leading the counterattack and managing to inflict heavy losses on the enemy. In this counterattack, Schluifelder once again put his valor and ability to the test and thanks only to his personal action was it possible to oppose this breakthrough with his small combat group.

3). During the nighttime hours of 6/17/44, the enemy, following a heavy preparatory artillery fire, broke into the point of contact between *5./48* and *6./48*, with orders (according to statements by prisoners) to take and hold Popovka. Schluifelder quickly became aware of the danger, and once again went on the counterattack, and once again managing to oust the enemy from the position, inflicting heavy losses. Later, Schluifelder and his men had to defend themselves against enemy assault troops, once again testing his capacity for action, his courage and his command ability.

4). On 7/22/44, the "*Sommerfest*" assault group was given the mission of breaking into enemy lines and taking prisoners. Schluifelder led an assault group and was able to break into the enemy trenches. As the enemy recognized the intentions of the assault group, it withdrew from the positions that had been breached and then directed heavy mortar fire on them. Favored by a heavy fog, the enemy then attacked with the intention of cutting off and overwhelming Schluifelder's assault group.

Schluifelder immediately grasped the situation and decided to attack the clearly numerically superior enemy force, which in the meantime was encircling him, but he broke out of the encirclement and brought his group back with negligible casualties. In this action, despite the fact that the unexpected fog had rendered visibility difficult and that all conditions favored the enemy, Schluifelder showed himself to be resolute and the master of the situation. Yet again, through his ability to command, he demonstrated his personal action and his superb valor.

5). When after 7/26/44, a new defensive line (the Tannenberg positions) had been established on the Narva front, Schluifelder was designated as adjutant of Tröger's combat group. The *Kampfgruppe* was on the Narva-Reval road and defended itself against four enemy attacks, during which eight tanks were hit. Schluifedler was the liaison officer between the sector of the *HKL* (*HauptKampfLinie*, main combat line) and the command post, as both radio and telephone communications had broken down. During the enemy attack, that continued almost without any letup from 1400 to 2230, and consisting of battalion or regimental size units that were supported by tanks and artillery covering fire, Schluifelder showed cold-blooded determination and valor. He was always in the areas of hottest fighting and managed to drag along a navy unit that was part of the combat group and which was experiencing combat for the first time; thanks to his personal and decisive action, to his high example and to his resourcefulness, the units of the combat group, some of which were facing enemy tanks for the first time, overcame their fear of the tanks and repelled all of the strong attacks.

Schluifelder is a capable front-line soldier and in consideration of his repeatedly proven valor and his unconditioned capacity to act, he has shown himself to be worthy of being awarded the German Cross in Gold.

APPENDIX K: TAKTISCHE GLIEDERUNG, NEDERLAND BRIGADE, MARCH 1944

A "graphic" order of battle of the *SS Nederland* Brigade on March 10, 1944. The document is read left to right, from top to bottom, displaying the organization of the components of a specific unit at a given point in time. The weapons and equipment assigned to each unit are shown within the rectangles.

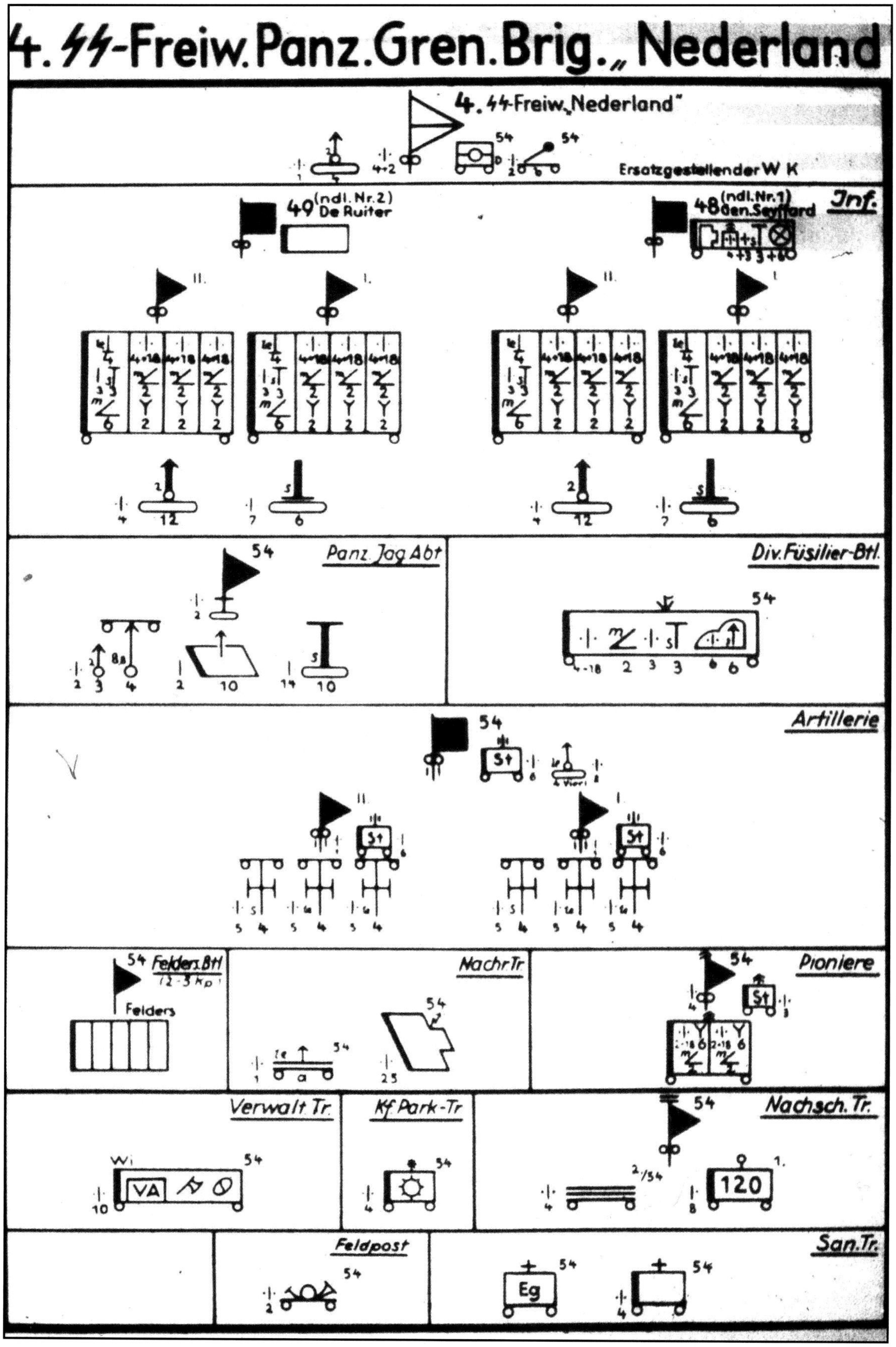

APPENDIX L: "NEDERLAND" BRIGADE AND DIVISION UNIT COMMANDERS

The names of the unit commanders are listed in chronological order.

Brigade/Division Commander: *Brigf.* Jürgen Wagner (October 1945 – May 1945)

Adjutant	Stubaf. Christian Steenhold-Schütt
Ia	Stubaf. Dietrich Ziemssen
	Hstuf. Helmut Kordts
	Stubaf. Jürgen von Bock
	Stubaf. Erich Hartmann
	Stubaf. Reinhardt Wörner
Ib	Stubaf. Gerhard Noatzke
	Ustuf. Konrad Bläss
	Ostuf. Henri van t' Hof
	Ostuf. Alfons Graf
	Hstuf. Fritz Beist
	Ostuf. Walter Heggblum
Ic	Ostuf. Paul Koopman
	Hauptmann Schorr
	Ostuf. Horst Kühn
	Ustuf. Gerhard Närger

SS-Pz.Gren.Rgt. 48 "General Seyffardt"

Commanders	Ostubaf. Josef Fitzthum (May 20, 1943 – November 3, 1943)
	Ostubaf. Wolfgang Joerchel (January 8, 1944 – May 1944)
	Stubaf. Herbert Garthe (May 1944 – July 1944)
	Ostubaf. Richard Benner (July 1944 – July 27, 1944†)
	Ostubaf. Siegrfried Scheibe (July 29, 1944 – ?)
	Ostubaf Paul Massell (? – 2 February 1944†)
	Ostubaf Siegfried Scheibe (1945 – March 17, 1945†)
I./48	Hans Joachim Rühle von Lilienstern (November 1943 – January 1944)
	Stubaf. Fritz Geiger (? – June 1944)
	Stubaf. Karl Betzwieser (? – July 1944) taken prisoner
	Hstuf. Fritz Tröger (remnants of I./48 following withdrawal from Narva)
	Hstuf. Wolfgang Vieweger (to Hammerstein)
II./48	Stubaf. Helmut Breymann (November 1943 – July 27, 1944†)
	Hstuf. Karl Wald
III./48	Formed in 1945
	Stubaf. Fritz Geiger
	Hstuf. Karl-Heinz Frühauf
	Hstuf. Johannes Riegl

SS-Pz.Gren.Rgt. 49 "de Ruyter"

Commanders	Ostubaf. Hans Collani (August 1, 1943 – July 29, 1944†)
	Hstuf. Karl Heinz Ertel (July 29, 1944 – August 5, 1944)
	Stubaf. Fritz Bunse (August 5, 1944 – November 8, 1944)
	Ostubaf. Hans Heinrich Lohmann (November 8, 1944 – March 10, 1945)
	Ostubaf. Rudolf Klotz (March 11, 1945 – April 7, 1945)

	Ostubaf. Hans Heinrich Lohmann (April 7, 1945 – May 8, 1945)
I./49	Hstuf. Eduard Voorwinden (November 1943 – December 1943)
	Hstuf. Werner Mosenthin (December 1943 – August 1944)
	Stubaf. Franz Lang
	Hstuf. Hans Meyer
	Stubaf. Rudolf Walther
	Stubaf. Gerhard Unger
	Stubaf Werner Rehder
II./49	Stubaf Karl Göttsche (November 1943 – January 1944)
	Hstuf. Hans Bürmeister (January 1944 – March 1944†)
	Hstuf. Walter Diener (March 12, 1944†)
	Hstuf. Karl-Heinz Frühauf
	Ostuf. Helmut Scholz
	Hstuf. Karl Heinz Ertel
	Stubaf. Otto Petersen (August 1944 –?)

SS-Artillerie Regiment 54

Commanders	Staf. Karl Diebitsch (? – November 1944)
	SS-Obf. Kurt Brasack (November 1944 –May 20, 1944)
	Stubaf Schlüter (May 1944 – August 1944)
	Stubaf Lothar Hofer
I./ArtRgt 54 10/5cm	Stubaf. Joseph Rüschoff
II./ArtRgt 54 I.FH 18	Hstuf. Fritz Topeters † Hstuf. Quintus de Veer
III./ArtRgt 54 sFH/Flak	Stubaf. Lothar Hofer

SS-Aufklärungs Kompanie 54

Ostuf. Erich Kuhne (– July 1944)
Hstuf. Erich Hildebrandt (July 1944 – August 14, 1944†)

SS-Pionier Btl. 54

Hstuf. Karl-Heinz Frühauf (January 1944)
Hstuf. Adolf Wolff (March 1944)
Stubaf. Ernst Wendtland (?)
Stubaf. Adolf Wolff (March 1945)
Stubaf. Günther Wanhöfer
Hstuf. Gerhard Ilgner (April 1945)
Hstuf. Karl-Joachim Schütte (April 1945)

SS-Panzerjäger Abt. 54-StuG

Stubaf. Knud Schock
Hstuf. Paul Krauss
Hstuf. Anton Aigner (February 1945 –)
Hstuf. Philipp Rösser (February 1945 – May 21, 1945†)

SS-Sanitäts Abteilung 54

Stubaf. Dr. van Heutsz
Hstuf. Johannes Dr. Krey
Stubaf. August Dr. Loderhose

SS-Nachrichten Kompanie 54

Hstuf. Wilhelm Thissen
Hstuf. Anton Schuler
Ustuf. Botho Kattoll

SS-Flak Kompanie 54

Ustuf. Cornelius Nieuwendijk-Hoek
Ustuf. Edmont Le Roux

SS-Feldgendarmerie Trupp 54

Ustuf. Fritz Neukamm

SS-Ausbildungs-und Ersatz Btl. 54

Stubaf. Kurt Pachur

APPENDIX M: SERVICE RECORD OF PAUL MASSELL

This exceptional document attests to service by Paul Massell, commander of the *General Seyffardt* Regiment, who was killed in battle on February 2, 1945, near Flederborn in Pomerania, and bears his photograph in civilian attire.

The information in the page above reports the following data in sequence: Date (Datum), rank (*dienstgrad*), unit of assignment (*Einheit*), and the function within the unit (*Art…*). It should be noted that Massell's last official duty goes back to August 9, 1944, and reflects that he is at the disposition of the General Headquarters of *III.SS-Pz.Korps*.

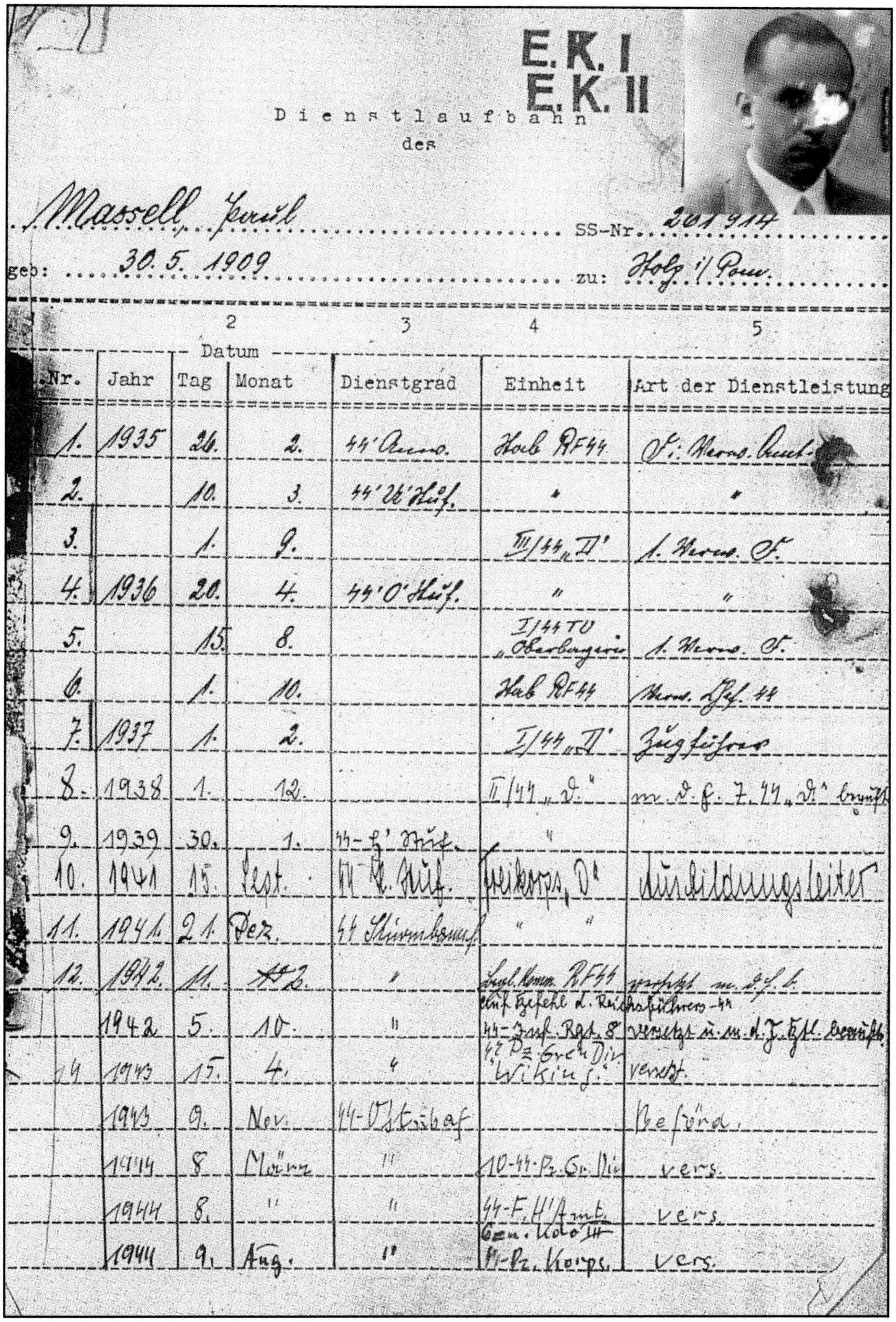

E.K. I
E.K. II

Dienstlaufbahn
des

Massell Paul SS-Nr. 201 914

geb: 30. 5. 1909 zu: Holz i/Pom.

Nr.	Jahr	Tag	Monat	Dienstgrad	Einheit	Art der Dienstleistung
1.	1935	26.	2.	SS-Anw.	Stab RFSS	[illegible]
2.		10.	3.	SS-Ue'Stuf.	"	"
3.		1.	9.		III/SS „D"	1. Verw. F.
4.	1936	20.	4.	SS-O'Stuf.	"	"
5.		15.	8.		I/SS TV „Oberbayern"	1. Verw. F.
6.		1.	10.		Stab RFSS	Verw. Ref. SS
7.	1937	1.	2.		I/SS „D"	Zugführer
8.	1938	1.	12.		II/SS „D"	m. d. F. [illegible] beauftr.
9.	1939	30.	1.	SS-H'Stuf.	"	
10.	1941	15.	Sept.	SS-H. Stuf.	Freikorps „D"	Ausbildungsleiter
11.	1941	21.	Dez.	SS Sturmbannf.	" "	
12.	1942	11.	[illegible]	"	[illegible] Komm. RFSS auf Befehl d. Reichsführers-SS	[illegible] m. d. F. b.
	1942	5.	10.	"	SS-Inf.-Rgt. 8	versetzt u. m. d. F. [illegible] beauftr.
14	1943	15.	4.	"	SS Pz. Gren. Div. „Wiking"	versetzt
	1943	9.	Nov.	SS-O'Stubaf		Beförd.
	1944	8.	März	"	10-SS-Pz.Gr.Div	vers.
	1944	8.	"	"	SS-F.H'Amt.	vers.
	1944	9.	Aug.	"	Gen. Kdo III SS-Pz. Korps	vers.

APPENDIX N: SPECIAL FLASHES

From the outset the Dutch legionnaires wore the Waffen-SS uniform with a special collar flash, the runic sign of the wolf hook (*wolfsangel*), that they wore on the uniform lapel in lieu of the SS double runes. There were two types of this flash: horizontal or vertical. The latter type could be made with white cotton thread and sometimes with silver thread, and only occasionally with silver wire thread. The horizontal type, of white cotton, was the regulation style introduced by the Germans in November 1941 to replace all of the previous types, but many legionnaires continued to wear the older type of vertical flash.

When the Dutch volunteers were transferred to the new *SS Nederland* Brigade they adopted the regulation Waffen-SS flash, which had in reality been used by most of the legionnaires since 1942.

Official flash, German production.

Dutch flash with *wolfangels* rune in metal.

Dutch flash with embroidered *wolfangels* rune.

Dutch volunteer with official German collar flash (horizontal).

Dutch style collar flash (vertical).

APPENDIX O: CUFFTITLES

Cuff- or sleevetitles, reflecting the name of the unit of affiliation, were worn not only by members of the Waffen-SS, but also by other elite army and Luftwaffe units. These bands of black cloth with letters embroidered either by hand or by machine, measured 28 mm wide by 490 mm long and were worn on the left sleeve of the uniform almost at wrist level. For some Waffen-SS divisions, more than one title was produced, various versions for the division itself or specific versions for the various regiments within the division. The cuff titles represented a unique element of the SS uniform. They served to identify the unit affiliation and were thus issued to all members of SS formations as an integral part of the uniform. Throughout the war the cufftitles became increasingly important and were issued during solemn ceremonies to glorify belonging to various military formations.

Cufftitle Types

Based on their manner of production, cufftitles were divided into four categories:

1st Type: Hand embroidered with aluminum wire thread. This type was produced from 1933 until June 1942. It was used by all NCOs until 1936, but thereafter only by officers.

2nd Type: Machine embroidered with white cotton thread or silver grey thread. This type, designated *RZM* (*ReichZeugMeister*, produced by machine) was produced between 1936 and 1943 specifically for NCOs and enlisted troops.

3rd Type: Machine woven with aluminum wire thread, produced between 1939 and 1943, for use only by officers.

4th Type: Machine woven with thin grey cotton or silk thread. This type, called the *Bevo* (*Beteiligung Vorsteher*) type, was produced between 1943 and 1945 for all ranks.

Cufftitles for the Dutch Legion

In November 1941, a cufftitle for the Dutch legion was authorized with the inscription "Frw. Legion Niederlande" (Dutch Volunteer Legion). Prior to that date the Dutch had produced their own cufftitle. There is another German version with the inscription "Nederland" (using the Dutch spelling) rather than the German Niederlande.

Cufftitle for the Legion.

Nederland Cufftitle

Produced by BeVo and introduced in 1943.

Nederland cufftitle.

General Seyffardt Cufftitle

Produced by BeVo, it was developed as the result of a request by veterans of the First Company of the Frw. Legion Nederland in memory of the general who was assassinated by the Dutch resistance movement. It was almost certainly introduced in October 1943, and the existence of a Dutch-produced version is certain. The *General Seyffardt* cuff title can be described as very rare.

General Seyffardt cufftitle.

de Ruyter Cufftitle

The *de Ruiter* Regiment cufftitle was also introduced in 1943, and is possibly even more rare than the *General Seyffardt* title. Unfortunately, there are no known photographs that show this cufftitle in use, but based on accounts by veterans it is certain that they were indeed worn.

de Ruyter cufftitle.

APPENDIX P: SLEEVE PATCHES FOR THE DUTCH LEGION, BRIGADE, AND DIVISION

The volunteers of the European volunteer Legions wore German uniforms, and as a sign of national identity wore a patch with their national colors on the left sleeve. In the case of the Dutch Legion there were several types of patches of Dutch and German production. The patch was normally worn above the cuff title, although early on it was placed higher up, at mid-sleeve. There are at least four Dutch produced versions (A, B, C and D), and one German version (E).

Type A: Horizontal rectangle with the red, white and blue colors, surrounded by a yellow border.

Type B: A small shield in orange, white and blue. The diagonal begins at the upper left.

Type C: A larger shield whose diagonal runs in the opposite direction than that of the previous shield, with a rounded base.

Type D: As for type C, but with the diagonal running in the opposite direction, as in Type B.

Type E: The German type, introduced in November 1941; laid out as the Type C but with red instead of orange, and with a blue border.

Type A

Type B

Type C

Type D

Type E

Patch for the *Nederland* Brigade

APPENDIX Q: PROPAGANDA POSTERS

Propaganda recruiting posters for the *Westland* Regiment aimed at attracting young Dutch men.

Posters to encourage recruitment in the Dutch Legion.

Another recruiting poster for the Dutch Legion.

The Dutch version of the most famous Waffen-SS poster. Note that model used for this poster was *SS-Ostuf*. Klemens Behler, awarded the Knight's Cross while serving with *Nederland*.

"Join the Waffen-SS if you want to fight against Bolshevism!"

"Your place is in the Waffen-SS."

"Join the Waffen-SS yourself."

Another propaganda poster appealing to Dutch volunteers, with the picture of Paul Krüger, a hero of the Anglo-Boer War, in the background.

In this poster, the background figure is Admiral de Ruyter, who was victorious over the British fleet.

Poster for the Dutch Legion.

APPENDIX R: VEHICLES USED BY NEDERLAND

SdKfz 251 Mittlerer Schützenpanzerwagen

Technical Characteristics

Crew	12
Weight	7,810 kg
Motor	Maybach HL 42 six cylinder gasoline, 100 HP
Dimensions	Length 5.8 meters; Width 2.1 meters; Height 1.75 meters
Performance	• Maximum road speed: 52.5 km/h • Range on road 300 km • Fording 0.6 meters; Slope 24°

The *SdKfz 251* was classified as a medium (*mittlerer*) vehicle weighing three tons. It was produced by *Hanomag* of Hannover, but the chassis and superstructure were built by *Büssing-NAG*. The *SdKfz 11 leichter Zugkraftwagen 3t* was used as the basis for the *SdKfz 251* and the first examples to come off the production line were assigned to the *1.Panzer Division* in early 1939. The *SdKfz 251* was mainly an armored troop transport vehicle, capable of carrying up to twelve men (a complete infantry squad). In Waffen-SS units it was assigned primarily to armored grenadier units. The most widely produced version was the *SdKfz 251/1*. Armed with at least two machine guns, plus the squad's weapons, the *SdKfz 251/1* was an excellent support vehicle for fast-moving armored formations. At least four different versions of the body were produced, mostly as a result of having to produce vehicles that were better able to cope with the increasingly demanding requests from front-line troops, not to mention the overall number of variants that were produced. Armor thickness varied from 6 to 14.5 mm. At least twenty-two different variants were produced, including weapons carrier, ambulance, artillery observation vehicles, command vehicles and signals vehicles (more radio than telephone); there were also versions fitted with infrared searchlights, anti-aircraft guns, and even a self-propelled anti-tank version mounting a long-barrelled 75 mm anti-tank gun.

Sturmgeschütz III SdKfz 182

Technical Characteristics

Crew	4
Weight	24 tons
Armor	80/20 mm
Armament	75 mm KwK 34 L48 main gun; 2 x MG-34 machine guns
Motor	Maybach HL 120 TRM twelve cylinder V, 300 HP
Dimensions	Length 6.7 meters; Width 2.96 meters; Height 2.17 meters
Performance	• Maximum road speed: 45 km/h • Range on road 200 km

Development of the *Sturmgeschütz III (SdKfz 142)* assault gun began in 1935 in order to produce an infantry support vehicle that could provide close artillery support, in accordance with the *Sturmartillerie* (assault artillery) concept. Production of the first series version (version 0) did not, however, begin until five years later until February 1940 with an initial order for thirty examples. The new assault gun was based directly on the *Panzer III* tank, whose chassis it maintained basically unaltered. Armament consisted of a 75 mm L/24 gun installed in a low casemate affixed to the chassis. The casemate, being fixed, allowed only limited traverse of the main gun. There was no secondary armament other than an MP 38 machine pistol issued to the crew. The armor, which was considerably thicker than that on the *Panzer III*, reached a thickness of 50 mm frontally and 30 mm on the sides. The 75 mm gun was installed in a simple mounting that was bolted to the floor of the fighting compartment, which itself was covered by a simple canvas cover which left the crew exposed to injury from shrapnel. The crew consisted of a vehicle commander seated in the right rear of the compartment, a driver seated in front on the left, a gunner and a radioman-loader positioned alongside the driver. Following production of the A version, the *Ausf B* was put into production, equipped with a new and better transmission and a new type of running gear with 40 cm wide tracks that was followed in 1941 by the C, D and E versions. From the very outset of the campaign on the Eastern Front these guns were used almost exclusively in an anti-tank role against the fearsome Soviet tanks; having realized that the 75 mm gun was inadequate, in September 1941 Hitler personally requested a new self-propelled gun armed with a more powerful gun and with improved armor. The new version, the *Ausf F*, which was unveiled in March 1942 by the Alkett company, had a new larger superstructure, improved armor protection, and a 75 mm L/43 gun with improved performance. In February 1944, during the reorganization of the Dutch brigade to a division, its *PzJägAbt* was issued several *Sturmhaubitze 42* assault howitzers, designed and produced by Alkett, based on the chassis of the *StuG III Ausf* F and *F/8* and armed with a 105 mm *StuH 42 L/28* (*L/30*) gun. Production began in October 1942, but in 1943 they were built using the *Ausf G* chassis. The early vehicles were fitted with a muzzle brake, but this was deemed to be superfluous as of September 1944. From October 1942 to February 1945, 1,212 were produced and their principal roles were to support the infantry and the *StuG III* batteries.

PanzerKampfwagen Panther V Heavy Tank

Technical characteristics

Crew	4
Weight	45,500 kg
Armor	80/20 mm
Armament	75 mm KwK 42 L/70 main gun; 2 x MG-34 machine guns
Motor	Maybach HL 230 P30, twelve cylinder Diesel, 700 HP
Dimensions	• Length 8.86 meters (with gun forward), 6.88 meters (hull only) • Width 3,43 meters• Height 3.1 meters
Performance	• Maximum road speed: 46 km/h • Range on road 177 km • Fording depth 1.7 meters • Slope 60% • Vertical obstacle 0.91 meters • Trench 1.91 meters

The sudden setbacks to German fortunes on the eastern front were undoubtedly due in large measure to the surprise appearance on the battlefield of the revolutionary Soviet T-34 tank. Its performance profoundly shocked the High Command of the German Army, rudely awakening them from their dreams of easy victories and the excessive faith they had placed in German tanks, above all in the *Panzer IV*. Steps had to be taken immediately. Work on development for a "successor" to the *Panzer IV* had begun as early as 1937, when Henschel and other firms were asked to prepare several designs for a tank weighing 30–35 tons. In 1941 the Henschel (VK.3001H) and Porsche (VK.3001P) prototypes had already been completed, but when the Soviet T-34 tanks were encountered, it was decided to make significant modifications. In fact, the choice was made to arm the new tank with a heavy 88 mm gun and to adopt an armor layout similar to that of the T-34, with sloped plates; another tank was thus designated, the VK.4501. In April 1942, the two companies presented their designs to *Waffenprüfamt 6*, the section of the army's armament department that was responsible for design and acquisition. The differences between the two designs were stark: the Daimler-Benz, VK.3002 (DB) was an alter ego of the Soviet tank with the addition of some features typical of German production. The shape of the hull was almost identical to that of the T-34; the driver sat inside the turret, with hydraulic transmission controls. The engine was an MB507 Diesel with rear drive sprocket wheels (as on the Russian tank). The bogies were doubled, with no rubber tire rims, with leaf spring suspension. The hull had side doors (for escape) and fuel tanks were located on the hull near the exhaust, again copied from the T-34. This design was undoubtedly functional; the leaf springs, for example, were easier to produce than were torsion bars, the use of road wheels entirely of steel avoided the problem of the shortage of rubber at that time, and even the diesel engine was advantageous. If we compare it to the MAN version (VK.3002 M) we can see that it is definitely not as simple a type but one that was designed in the spirit of the German tradition in that armaments category. Its hull was higher and wider than that of the Daimler-Benz model as well as of the Soviet model; a larger turret was mounted slightly towards the center of the hull (rather than more forward) to preclude an excessive overhang of the heavy 75 mm main gun. The torsion bar suspension used interleaved road wheels; a Maybach HL 210 V-12 gasoline engine was proposed, with power transmitted through front sprocket wheels. When the models were presented, Hitler was more impressed with the Daimler-Benz version, ordering however that a 75 mmL/70 gun be mounted rather than a 75 mm L/48. Accordingly, 200 vehicles based on this model were ordered, but the *Waffenprüfamt* commission preferred the MAN entry (which was more in line with the classic Teutonic type), and MAN was requested to produce a prototype in mild steel as quickly as possible for May 1942; the Daimler order was later cancelled. In September 1942, the first model of the MAN (VK.3002 M) was completed and was examined at Nuremberg. The second model was examined and tested at Kummersdorf by the *Heereswaffenamt* for army trials. The first vehicle was produced in November 1942, with a goal of producing 250 per month, but at the end of 1942 that figure was raised to 600 vehicles monthly. It was thus necessary to put together a large group of men and machines dedicated to its production and thus Daimler was also ordered to produce the tank according to the MAN design; the first tanks left the Daimler plant in early 1943. In January of that year, *Maschinenfabrik Niedersachsen* of Hannover, and Henschel also began to work on production of the *Panther*; in February, numerous other subcontractors became involved, making production of this tank one of the largest and most focused armaments programs of the *Reich*. The 600 monthly production figure was never reached; in May 1943, a production of 324 vehicles was achieved, but the monthly average for 1943 was 154. In 1944, an average of 330 tanks was reached and by February 1945, a total of 4,814 *Panthers* had been built.

The first series models were the *PzKpfw V Ausf A*, even though they were still pre-production vehicles. *The PzKpfw V Ausf B* and *C* were never put into production. The successive version, the *PzKpfw V Ausf D*, followed by another *PzKpfw Ausf A*, were employed on the Normandy front. The final definitive version was the *PzKpfw V Ausf G*. Adding to all of the already excellent characteristics of the original design, the final version of the *Panther* incorporated changes suggested by units that had used the earlier versions in front-line service. The most significant modifications made to the *Panther* had to do with the front glacis, which was characterized by a hemispherical machine gun mount and elimination of the driver's visor, who used a periscope instead. The side plates were redesigned and consisted of a single steel plate that was thicker but which was better angled to allow the interior space of the fighting compartment to be increased and the fuel tanks in the rear of the hull to be enlarged. The exhaust system was improved so that a valve prevented ignition of returning gases. The crew access hatches on the turret roof were fitted with a simplified mechanism that consisted of a simple hinge with auxiliary springs. The left side-cooling fan was redesigned to carry a heating system for the crew, and from the end of 1944, the gun mantlet was modified in order to eliminate the problem of deflecting rounds to the top of the hull. A total of 3,126 *Panther Ausf G* were produced.

GLOSSARY

Abteilung: detachment, military unit
Abwehr: defense
Allgemeine: general, overall, generic
Armee: Army
Armeekorps: Army Corps
Aufklärung: reconnaissance
Ausbildung: training (unit)
Bäckerei-Kompanie: bakery company
Bataillon: battalion
Bau: construction (unit)
Befehlshaber: commander of
Beobachter: artillery observer
Beobachtung: divisional observation unit
Betriebstoff: fuel
Brigade: brigade
Brücke: bridge
Datum: data
Einheit: unit (referred to a unit, military unit)
Einschiess: marksmanship training
Ersatz: replacement (unit)
Fallschirmjäger: paratrooper
Feld-ersatz-Bataillon: divisional replacement battalion
Feldhaubitze: field howitzer
Feldlazarett: field hospital
Fernsprech: telephone system
Flak (Fliegerabwehrkanone): anti-aircraft gun
Freiwillige: volunteer
Funk: radio
Gefechtsgruppe: combat group
Genesung: convalescense
Geschütz: cannon
Gewehr: rifle
Gliederung: organization
Granatwerfer: mortar
Haus: house
Heer: army
Heeresgruppe: group of armies
Hilfwillige (hiwi): auxiliary volunteer
Hitlerjugend: Hitler Youth
Instandsetzungs: divisional repair unit
Kampfgruppe: combat group
Karten: maps
Kolonne: column (of vehicles or troops)
Kompanie: company
Krad or Kraftrad: motorcycle
Kradschützen or Kraftradschützen: motorcycle rifleman divisional
Kraftfahrer: driver
Kraftradmelde: motorcycle courier
Krankenwagen: ambulance
Kriegsberichter: war correspondent
Kriegstagbuch: war diary
Landser: soldier
Lehrgang: course, training
Leicht: light (type of unit or weapon)
Maschinengewehr (MG): machine gun
Mitarbeiter: assistant
Nachrichten: signals, communications
Nachschub: supply
OKH (Oberkommando des Heeres): Army High Command
OKW (Oberkommando des Wehrmacht): Armed Forces High Command
Ort: place, area
Pak (Panzer Abwehr Kanone): anti-tank gun
Panzerfaust: anti-tank weapon (literally, "armored fist")
Panzergrenadier: armored grenadier
PzKpfw (Panzer Kampfwagen): tank
Schlächterei-Kompanie: animal slaughter company
SdKfz (Sonderkraftfahrzeug): special vehicle; armored car
Selbstfahrlafette (sf): motorized self-propelled guns
Sperrgruppe: barrier group (a type of kampfgruppe)
SS (Schutz Staffeln): protection squad; bodyguard
SS-Hauptamt: SS central office
SS-Führung-Hauptamt: SS-HA office responsible for organization and training of new Waffen-SS units
Spiess: company sergeant major
SPW (Schützenpanzerwagen): armored personnel carrier
Standarte: regiment
Sturmgeschütz: assault gun (self-propelled)
Sturmgewehr: assault rifle
Tierartzt: veterinarian
Turmnummer: turret number (on tanks)
Tross: pack animal train
Trupp: squad
Vermessungs: topographical survey
Vermittlung: liaison
Verpflegungsamt: commissary office
Versorgungs: services, supplies
Verwaltung: administrative office
Volkssturm: citizen militia
Werkstatt: repair unit
Wetter: weather station
Wirtschafts: economic section (divisional level)
Zug: platoon

BIBLIOGRAPHY & ENDNOTES

Primary Sources

Public Archives

Bundesarchiv-Militärarchiv Freiburg, Germany
Rijksinstituut voor Oorlogsdocumentatie, Amsterdam, Holland
US National Archives and Records Administration (NARA), Washington, DC

Period Magazines and Publications

Signal magazine, various editions and issues
Das Schwarze Korps magazine, various issues
Illustrierte Beobachter, various issues
SS-Storm magazine, various issues
Stuttgart Jllustrierte magazine, various issues

Secondary Sources

Books

Dutch Volunteers

Afiero, M. *I volontari stranieri di Hitler*. Ritter Editrice, Milano.

Afiero, M. *Nordland: i volontari europei sul fronte dell'est*. Marvia Editrice.

Duprat, F. *Les campagnes de la Waffen-SS*. Les Sept Couleurs.

Estes, K.W. *A European Anabasis: Western European Volunteers in the German Army and SS, 1940–1945*. Columbia University Press.

Hausser, P. *Waffen-SS im Einsatz*. Plesse Verlag, Göttingen, 1953.

Kraetschmer, E.G., *Die Rittenlreuztraeger der Waffen-SS*. Preussisch Oldendorf.

Landemer, H. *La Waffen-SS*. Balland, 1972.

Littlejohn, D. *Foreign Legions of the Third Reich, volume 2*. James Bender Publishing.

Lumsden, R. *La vera storia delle SS*. Newton & Compton Editors.

Michaelis, R. *Die Panzergrenadier-Divisionen der Waffen-SS*. Michaelis Verlag.

Michaelis, R. *Die 11.SS-Freiwilligen panzergrenadier division Nordland*. Michaelis Verlag.

Moore, J.P. *Führerliste der Waffen-SS*. J.P. Moore Publishing, 2004.

Neulen, H.W. *An deutscher Seite, Internationale Freiwillige von Wehrmacht und Waffen-SS*. Universitas, 1985.

Stein, G.H. *The Waffen-SS: Hitler's Elite Guard at War, 1939–1945*. Cornell University Press.

Tessin, G. *Verbande und Truppen der deutschen Wehrmacht und Waffen-SS*. Biblio Verlag

Teike, W. *Das Ende zwischen Oder und Elbe: Der Kampf um Berlin 1945*. Motorbuch-Verlag, 1981.

Werner, H. *Verbande und truppen der deutschen Wehrmacht und Waffen-SS*. Biblio Verlag.

Williamson, G. *Storia Illustrata delle SS*. Newton & Compton Editors.

Yerger, M. *Waffen-SS Commanders, Volumes 1 and 2*. Schiffer, 1999.

World War II

Carruthers, B., and Erickson, J. *The Russian Front: 1941–1945*. Cassel & Co.

Clark, A. *Operazione Barbarossa*. Garzanti Editore.

Haupt, W. *Das war Kurland*. Podzun-Pallas.

Le Tissier, Tony. *Slaughter at Halbe, Hitler's Ninth Army in the Spreewald Pocket, April 1945*.

Natkiel, Young. *Atlante della Seconda guerra mondiale*. Mondadori Editore.

Overy, R. *Russia in guerra, 1941–1945*. Il Saggiatore.

Periodicals

Der Freiwillige magazine, various issues.

Siegrunen magazine, a periodical published by Richard Landwehr; several issues.

Ritterkreuz magazine, a bimonthly publication dedicated to Waffen-SS formations; several issues.

Internet sites dedicated to the Dutch volunteers

Nederlanders in de Waffen-SS:http://www.waffen-ss.nl/main.php

Robert Janssen site dedicated to the Dutch Legion: http://www.vrijwillgerslegioen.nl/index2.htm

Internet sites dedicated to the German Armed Forces during World War II

http://www.axishistory.com
http://www.feldgrau.com
http://www.lexikon-der-wehrmacht.de
http://www.maxafiero.it

Note on Photographs

The photographs used in this book come mainly from wartime publications and propaganda material printed during the Second World War. Other photographs are from the author's personal collection and other parties and members of the Associazione Culturale Ritterkreuz. The author declares himself to be fully responsible for any applicable costs in the event of any photographs determined to be from public archives or private collections.

Endnotes

Chapter 2 Notes

1. In countries with Germanic origins (Denmark, Flanders, Norway and Holland), the organization of volunteer units was managed by the SS high command, while in other countries (Wallonia, France, Croatia, Spain), by the *Wehrmacht*. These "Germanic" legions were, however, not actually integrated into the Waffen-SS, but were defined as "affiliated." As witness to this difference, one has only to note that the foreign volunteers had to precede their rank with the title Legion, and not SS: for example, a German SS captain bore the rank of *SS-Hauptsturmführer*, while a Dutch or Danish volunteer became a *Legion-Hauptsturmführer*.
2. *Ritterkreuz* 12/04/1941, as *Oberst* and commander of *Infanterie-Regiment 90*.
3. The division was designated at the outset as the *Polizei* Division and it was not until February 1942 that it became the *SS-Polizei-Division*. As a consequence the rank designations were those used in the army. The men wore the German Army *feldgrau* uniform, police collar flashes, and *Schutzpolizei* national insignia on their helmets and caps. Only the presence of the Nazi eagle on the left sleeve of the uniform indicated that the unit belonged to the Waffen-SS.
4. The 2nd SS Brigade was formed as a security unit on May 1, 1941, based on the 4th, 5th and 14th *Totenkopfstandarten*. On May 7, it was decided to reorganize it as a combat unit, transforming the *Totenkopfstandarten* into SS infantry regiments at the beginning of Operation Barbarossa. Placed under the authority of the *Kommandosstab*

Reichsführer-SS, the unit, transformed into a motorized brigade, was employed in the northern sector of the Eastern Front as a rear area security force attached to Lindermann's 18th Army. The requirements of the front, however, led to its use as a front line unit. In August 1941, *SS-Inf.Rgt. 5 (mot)* was removed from the brigade. In October of the same year, *Flak Bataillon Ost* and *Begleit Bataillon* RFSS (the escort battalion for the *Reichsführer*) were attached to the brigade. In December 1941, after having lost the 4th SS Infantry Regiment, which was transferred to the SS Reich Division, the brigade was temporarily disbanded. In June 1942, it was reorganized by integrating the Dutch, Norwegian and Flemish Legions and several Latvian volunteer battalions.

5. Josef Fitzthum was born on September 14, 1896, at Loiersdorf in Austria. After having attended a course for officers at the *Technischen Militärakademie* at Mödling, in Augist 1916 he entered the Austrian Army as a *Leutnant* in the *3.Regiment/Tiroler Kaiserjäger*. Between 1916 and 1918 he served on the Italian front, first as a *Zugführer* and later as a *Kompanieführer*. In August 1917, he was promoted to *Oberleutnant*. In May 1918, he began aviation training at the Weiner Neustadt Fliegerschule, and beginning in September of the same year he served as *Führer der k.u.k. Flieger-(Beobachter)-Kompanie 17*, again on the Italian front. When the war was over, he left the army in February 1919. After having joined the Austrian branch of the NSDAP in 1930, in April 1932, he entered the SS, in the *11.Standarte* in Vienna, quickly earning the rank of *Sturmbannführer* In September of that same year, he became commander of the *Standarte*, attaining the rank of *Obersturmbannführer* a few months later. Because of problems with Austrian law, in 1934 he fled to Germany. Between May and October 1936, promoted to *Standartenführer*, he was involved in training the *II.Sturmbann* of the *SS. Standarte Germania*. In January 1937, he was called upon to command the *58.SS-Standarte* in Cologne, where he remained in October until he was transferred to the *SD-Hauptamt* (Central Office of the Security Service). Between 1938 and 1940, he was vice commander of the Vienna Police. In March 1940, he was relieved of his police duties because he had appropriated public funds, and then was transferred to the Waffen-SS as a reserve officer with a reduced rank. In May 1940, he took command of the *III. Sturmbann* of the *15. SS-Totenkopfstandarte* with the rank of *SS-Hauptsturmführer* After having commanded various units within *Totenkopf*, and also having temporarily led the Flemish volunteer legion, in June 1942, he assumed command of the *SS-Freiwilligen-Legion "Niederlande."*
6. There were three types of ammunition for the anti-tank guns, depending on the type of target. For direct fire against medium tanks there were the *Panzergranaten*. For heavy tanks there were the *Hohlraumgranaten* that were lighter in weight but which had a greater coefficient of penetration. Finally there were the Sprenggranate, which were shrapnel type rounds, ideal for use against infantry and light armored vehicles.

Chapter 3 Notes

1. Felix Martin Julius Steiner was born on May 23, 1896, at Ebensrode in East Prussia to a family of Austrian origin. In May 1914, after having received his diploma, young Steiner was assigned to the 41st Infantry Regiment as an officer cadet, participating in the battles along the East Prussian border at Tannenberg and in Lithuania. In 1916, while commanding an assault company, he took part in the Battle of Kurland, earning the Iron Cross First Class. Transferred to the Western Front, he took part in the fighting in Flanders and in France. At the end of the First World War he bore the rank of *Leutnant*, and in January 1919, he joined the East Prussian Volunteer Corps at Memel, assuming command of a company. Three years later, in 1921, he was integrated into active service in the Reichswehr, serving with the 1st Infantry Regiment at Königsberg. In 1927, he was promoted to captain; in 1933 he left the Reichswehr with the rank of *Major*. In 1934, he joined the *SS-Verfügungstruppe*, which would become Himmler's Waffen-SS. On July 1, 1936, he assumed command of the *SS-Standarte Deutschland* with the rank of *SS-Standartenführer*. With *Deutschland*, he participated in the campaigns in Poland and France. On August 22, 1940, he was awarded the Knight's Cross. Steiner soon became one of Himmler's favored officers; his innovative ideas about *blitzkrieg* pleased the *Reichsführer* very much, and it was not long before they were being taught to all Waffen-SS units. While he commanded the *Deutschland Regiment*, Steiner had already put his combat techniques into practice, organizing his men into small mobile units capable of intervening quickly at any point along the front. To increase the firepower of his units he modified the individual weapons issue, replacing rifles with submachine guns, and increasing the number of light and heavy machineguns in the units. Another great innovation, later followed by all of the armies of the world, was the use of camouflage uniforms to better conceal the men during combat actions. To better train his men, Steiner added intensive sports activities to the usual exercises and usual marches; his soldiers had to be able to cover 3-4 kilometers in twenty minutes, be able to climb hills and cliffs, and run as fast as possible under live gunfire. On November 9, 1940, Steiner was promoted to the rank of *SS-Brigadeführer und General Major der Waffen-SS*. On December 1, 1940, Steiner official assumed command of the new *Germania Division* that was formed with European volunteers: Danes, Norwegians, Finns, Dutch, Flemings and Swedes. In January 1941, the Division was renamed the Wiking. While commanding that division, Steiner took part in the Russsian campaign with Army Group South, fighting in the Ukraine. In 1942, he led his men in the conquest in the Caucasus as far as Grozny. In late 1942, General Steiner left command of the Wiking Division to assume command of *III.SS.Panzer Korps* that was then being formed. At that time he was awarded the Oak Leaves to his Knight's Cross.
2. Jürgen Wagner was born on September 9, 1901, at Strasburg, in Alsace (which at the time was German), son of Ernst Wagner, an infantry general. After graduating in 1925, he joined the Reichswehr, which he left in 1929 to study mechanical engineering. He soon found a job as an assistant engineer, first a Hoechst and then at Nassau. In March 1931 he joined the SS. On April 20, 1933, he was promoted to the rank of *SS-Sturmführer*, and in July of the same year he was assigned to the *SS-Sonderkommando Jüterborg*, a training and replacement unit for the *Leibstandarte Adolf Hitler*. Initially, he was assigned to the *3.Lehrsturm*, then after being promoted to *SS-Sturmbannführer* (October 1, 1933) he assumed command of *II Bataillon* of the *Leibstandarte*, which he commanded until 1939. He was then assigned to the *Germania Regiment* of the *SS-Verfügungstruppe* and then to *SS-Regiment 11* of the Reich Division. On May 16, 1940, he was awarded the Iron Cross Second Class. In September 1941, he was promoted to *SS-Standartenführer*. In May 1942, he assumed command of the *Germania Regiment* of *Wiking*. In July 1942, he was awarded the Iron Cross First Class and on December 11, 1942, was awarded the German Cross in Gold. In November of the same year, he was promoted to *SS-Oberführer*. On July 24, 1943, he was awarded the Knight's Cross. In November 1943, he was assigned to command the new *SS Nederland Brigade*.
3. Following the Italo-German military occupation, Yugoslavia had ceased to exist as a nation. Its territory, which had been inhabited by peoples who differed in their history, religion and race became practically dismembered. Germany took over northern Slovenia, Styria and Carinthia, and the administration of the Eastern Banat. Serbia, confined to its 1914 borders, became a German protectorate. Italy obtained part of Dalmatia and the province of Cattaro. Southern Slovenia, including Ljubljana, was annexed as part of Italian territory. Some of the territory of Macedonia and Kosovo was incorporated as part of Italian Albania. Montenegro was declared independent, as an Italian protectorate. Croatia, along with Slavonia, Bosnia–Herzegovina and part of Dalmatia formed the Independent State of Croatia, placed under the dual influence of Italy (the west) and Germany (the east). Other "bits" of Yugoslav territory went to Bulgaria (a large portion of Slavic Macedonia) and to Hungary (half of the Voivodina and other

areas). The armed insurrection against the occupiers began almost immediately, partly because of the hasty transfer of troops to the east in anticipation of the invasion of Russia. Entire units of the Yugoslav Army were able to hide in the forests and mountains of Serbia and quickly began conducting guerrilla warfare against the occupiers. Two distinct resistance movements operated in Yugoslavia: the Yugoslav National Army under Draza Mihailovic and the People's Liberation Army under Tito. Colonel Mihailovic did not obey the surrender order of April 1941, and along with other dispersed soldiers and officers, reached Ravna Gora, a wild and forested plateau in western Serbia. The men under Mihailovic, called "Chetniks," named after the Serb patriots who had fought against the Turkish and Austro–Hungarian oppressors, by May 1941, had already engaged in sabotage and guerrilla warfare against the German forces. During the month of July the Chetniks, in cooperation with Tito's communist partisans, organized a widespread insurrection in Serbia, putting in crisis the German forces that lost control of the region for a long while. In September, the Chetniks and Tito's forces ceased their cooperation, although they continued to fight against the common enemy. Their differences were purely ideological in nature. Mihailovic, who was loyal to the King and to the government in exile in London, dreamt of the resurrection of a pre-war Yugoslavia, tied to the western Allies. Tito, a Croat communist, dreamt instead of a communist republic of Yugoslavia tied to the USSR. This led to bitter combat between the communists and the Chetniks; Tito's forces ultimately prevailed, having gained the support of the Allies, to the detriment of the Chetniks, who were accused of having collaborated with the Axis forces.

4. Hans Joachim Rühle von Lilienstern was born on January 9, 1915, at Fritzlar (SS Number 151 372). In January 1942, he commanded the *Kriegsberichter-Zug* of the *SS-Totenkopf Division*.
5. Helmut Breymann was born on February 9, 1911, in Trieste, which at the time was a Hapsburg possession. After having been in the SA and held various political positions, in August 1935 he joined the SS in the *SS-Sturmbann Burgenland*. On October 3, 1939, he was called upon to command the *Ersatzbataillon* of the *SS-Regiment "Der Führer"* of the *SS-Verfügungstruppe*. On August 1, 1940, after his assumption into the Waffen-SS, Breymann was designated as an *SS-Untersturmführer der Reserve*. From April 10 to November 9, 1941, he served as a *Reserveführer* in the *SS-Freiwilligen-Standarte "Nordwest."* He later took command of a company of the *Flämische Legion*. On April 20, 1943, he was promoted to the rank of *SS-Sturmbannführer* and was assigned to command the II Battalion of the *General Seyffardt Regiment*.
6. Son of a career officer who bore the same name, Hans Collani was born in Stettin on December 13, 1908. His father retired as an infantry *Oberst* (colonel). His brother also pursued a military career and would die in combat in 1943, in France, as a Luftwaffe *Oberst*. After having failed to be accepted into university in Berlin, Collani was employed by a commercial company in 1928. From the autumn of 1931, he joined a maritime transportation company, traveling extensively in northern Europe. Thanks to his sailor's passport he had the opportunity to visit cities such as Leningrad and Murmansk and to witness firsthand the effects of Stalin's "Great Terror." Hans Collani joined the NSDAP in 1932 (card number 261271) and soon after joined the SA. When the SS was formed in Schleswig-Holstein, Collani joined on November 24, 1932, (SS card number 6909) and was taken on as a *Truppenführer*. He served in the *50.SS-Standarte* as *Sturmbannadjutant*. He was transferred to the LSSAH, as part of the first group of 117 men who formed the 1st Company, in essence the nucleus from which the future development of the Waffen-SS began. He was promoted to *SS-Hauptsturmführer* in the LSSAH on October 1, 1933. From February 1935 until November 1939, Hans Collani was adjutant to the regimental commander, who at the time was *SS-Gruppenführer* Sepp Dietrich. During the Polish campaign, Collani was awarded the Iron Cross Second Class on September 25, 1939. During the campaign in France in 1940, he was transferred to the 1st Infantry Regiment of the *SS Totenkopf Division*, primarily as an aide. Following a long period of illness, Collani was assigned to the *SS Wiking Division* on February 8, 1941. Initially, he served in II Battalion of the *Nordland Regiment*, then on the divisional staff, and finally was assigned as commander of the *Finnisches Freiwilligen Bataillon der Waffen-SS*, subsequently renamed *IV(finn)Nordland*, and still later definitively as *III(finn) Nordland*. Hans Collani was promoted to *SS-Sturmbannführer* on April 20, 1942, and to *SS-Obersturmbannführer* on April 20, 1943, continuing to lead the Finnish battalion of the *Wiking* until it was disbanded in July 1943. On October 18, 1942, he received the Iron Cross First Class following fighting at "Hill 711" near Grozny. After *III(finn)Nordland* was disbanded, Collani was put in command of the *SS-Freiwilligen Panzer Grenadier Regiment 49 "de Ruyter."*
7. Karl Diebitsch was born on January 3, 1899, in Hannover. During the First World War he served in the *Kriegsmarine*. After the war, he enrolled in the *Freikorps* to fight against the Bolsheviks. In 1934 he joined the SS (Number 141 990). With the rank of *SS-Untersturmführer* he was designated as a Cultural Consultant and Head of Artistic Affairs for the SS, later becoming manager of the SS porcelain factory at Allach. Diebitsch was one of the principal designers of uniforms and insignia for the SS. In 1940, with the rank of *SS-Standsartenführer* he was assigned command of *II./SS-Totenkopf-Standarte 11*. In January 1942, he was transferred to Wiking, where for a few days he commanded the *Westland Regiment*, before assuming command of *SS-Flak-Abteilung 5*. At the end of 1942, he sustained a serious head wound during combat. Following a long convalescence he was assigned to the staff of *III.SS-Panzer-Korps* in 1943. Between March and June 1944, he commanded the Italian *SS Kampfgruppe* on the Anzio front.
8. Kurt Brasack was born on April 6, 1892, at Schönebeck am Elbe. In 1913, he joined the army as a volunteer and was assigned to the *Fuss-Artillerie-Regiment "Encke" Nr. 4*, where he remained during the First World War until January 1916 when he was transferred as an aide to *Feld-Artillerie-Regiment 21*. He ended the war as adjutant of *Fuss-Artillerie-Regiment "von Heindersin" Nr. 2*. From 1921 to 1930, he belonged to the paramilitary *Stahlhelm* (steel helmet) organization. He entered the SS on March 1, 1931, (SS Number 8 216), assigned to *II./21.SS-Standarte*. Between March 1932 and April 1934, he commanded that unit. Between 1936 and 1938, he was involved in training several artillery units at the *Artillerieschule* at Jüterborg. From December 1, 1939 to April 1, 1941, he commanded the *SS-Totenkopf-Artillerie-Regiment*. Soon thereafter, he took command of *I.Abteilung/SS-Artillerie/Regiment/SS Division "Wiking,"* until May of the same year before being transferred to command of *IV.Abteilung* of the same regiment. On January 10, 1942, he took command of the *Artillerie-Regiment/SS-Division "Das Reich,"* a position he held until March 18, 1943, when he was temporarily assigned to lead the *SS-Panzer-Grenadier-Division "Das Reich."* In reserve until June 1943, after having held the position of *Führer Nachschub-Kommando Russland Nord*, from June 29 to November 10, 1943, he took command of the artillery regiment of the *SS Nederland Brigade*.
9. Erich Kuhne, born September 23, 1911, in Berlin, SS Number 463 730. In July 1943, with the rank of *SS-Untersturmführer*, he was initially designated as adjutant of *I./Pz.Gr.Rgt.48*.

Chapter 4 Notes

1. Knud Henrik Ernst Schock, born on May 31, 1899, was a former officer of the Danish Army. He was a member of the *Friekorps Danmark* as *Leg.Hstuf.* and commander of *4.Kompanie*. In 1943, following his promotion to the rank of *Sturmbannführer*, he was initially assigned to command of *SS-Stu.Abt.5*, the new assault gun unit for *Wiking*. Because the unit was slow to be formed, with the only *StuG* battery available, the nucleus of *SS-Panzerjäger Abt. 54* for *Nederland* was formed.
2. Wolfgang Roman Christian Theodor Jörchel was born on August 19, 1907, at Zaborze. After having served in the SA from 1934 to 1935, he was assigned to the SS-VT where, in October 1935, he was promoted

to the rank of *Obersturmbannführer*. He was a machine gun instructor at the *SS-Junkerschule* at Bad Tölz in 1937, and the following year he was assigned first to the *SS-Standarte Deutschland* and later to the *SS-Standarte "Germania."* From December 1, 1940, he commanded the *II./SS-Regiment "Germania."* In March 1942, he was awarded the German Cross in Gold. When formation of the *Nordland Division* was begun in 1943, he was given command of *SS-Panzer-Grenadier Regiment 23 "Norge."*

3. Rudolf Saalbach was born on March 18, 1911, at Grossenhain in Saxony. He joined the SS in 1934, initially assigned to the *SS-Soncerkommando Sachsen* and then in 1935 in the *SS-Totenkopfverband Elbe*, where he remained until 1937. In 1938, after having attended a training course for officers at the *SS-Junkerschule* at Braunschweig, Saalbach was assigned to the *SS-Totenkopfverband Oberbayern*. In August 1940, with the rank of *SS-Obersturmbannführer*, he held the position of *Chef of 1. (Krad) Kompanie der SS-Aufklärungs-Abteilung 3*. In March 1943, as *SS-Hauptsturmführer*, he assumed command of *SS-Aufklärungs-Abteilung 5*.
4. Kaspar Antoine Sporck was born on August 10, 1922, at Heerlen, in the province of Limburg, Holland. On October 23, 1944, he was awarded the Knight's Cross as *SS-Unterscharführer* and *Geschützführer in 5.(schwere)Kp./SS-Aufkl.-Abt.11* of *11.SS-Frw.Panzer-Grenadier-Division "Nordland,"* based on a citation dated 09/03/1944 and signed by the *Abt.Kdr.* Rudolf Saalbach, and endorsed on 10/05/1944 by *Div. Kdr.* Joachim Ziegler and approved on 10/08/1944 by the *Korps Kom. Gen.* Felix Steiner. Towards the end of the war, after having been seriously wounded in combat, he died at the military hospital of Bayreuth on April 8, 1945.
5. Karl-Heinz Ertel was born on November 26, 1919, at Brumbauer, in the district of Dortmund. After having served in the RAD (the mandatory labor service), on November 1, 1938, he enlisted as a volunteer in the *SS-Standarte "Germania" (1.Sturm)* and with this unit participated in the Polish campaign. On November 1, 1939, he entered the *SS-Junkerschule* of Bad Tölz. In March 1940, he was assigned to the *Ersatz-Bataillon "Germania"* in Hamburg, and the following month to the *3.Kompanie* of the same regiment. During the campaign in France, he served as assistant aide in the *I.Bataillon* and was later assigned as *Zugführer* (platoon leader) of *10.Kompanie*. On June 13, 1941, he was promoted to the rank of *SS-Untersturmführer der Reserve*. Two days later, he was assigned to *2.Kompanie* of *SS-Freiwilligen-Bataillon "Nordost,"* which was the Finnish volunteer battalion, as a *Zugführer*. In January 1942, along with this battalion, he reached the front at Mius and was assigned to the *SS-Division "Wiking."* Until March 1942, he continued to serve with *2.Kompanie* under *SS-Obersturmführer* Ladau, until he became battalion aide during the Caucasus campaign. In October 1942, he was assigned to command *9.Kompanie*. On January 30, 1943, he was promoted to the rank of *SS-Obersturmführer*. In April 1943, when the Finnish battalion was disbanded, Ertel followed Collani in the *Nederland Brigade*.

Chapter 5 Notes

1. Report as of March 1, 1944.
2. Most of the battalion's tanks had experienced mechanical problems and many of the vehicles had been dug in and used as fixed artillery positions. Initially the battalion's tank crews were thus used as simple infantrymen.
3. Helmut Scholz, born on July 1, 1920, at Grottkau, in Upper Silesia, SS Number 423 819.
4. Karl Heinz Frühauf, born on February 14, 1914, in Hamburg, SS Number 61 349. Until March 1944, he was the commander of the 5th Company of *de Ruyter*.
5. Richard Benner was born on November 15, 1911, at Fliessbach. From November 9, 1933, until April 1934, he served in the SA, before joining the Reichswehr, where he served initially with Inf.Rgt. 15 and then with *Inf.Rgt. 57*. From November 1, 1937 until April 30, 1938, he was in Spain with the Condor Legion, soon thereafter retiring from the army with the rank of *Leutnant der Reserve*. On May 1, 1939, he joined the SS (SS Number 340 798). From August 17 until October 9 of that year, he served as a *Zugführer* in *"Heimwehr Danzig,"* then to be transferred with that unit to the 3rd Regiment of the *Totenkopf Division*. On October 1, 1939, he was promoted to the rank of *SS-Obersturmführer* and in April 1940 to *SS-Hauptsturmführer*. In June 1944, he was designated *Divisionsadjutant* (IIa) of the *Totenkopf Division*. In March 1944, he was assigned to *SS-Infanterie-Regiment 6*, the future unit of the *Kampfgruppe* and later of the *Nord Division*. From March 19, 1941, until July 26, 1941, he was the commander of *6.Kompanie* of *SS-Infanterie-Rgt. 6* of *SS-Kampfgruppe Nord*, and from July 1941, he commanded the II Battalion of that same regiment. On April 2, 1942, he was awarded the German Cross in Gold. From May 1942, he assumed command of *SS-Schützen-Bataillon 6*. On June 21, 1942, he was promoted to the rank of *Sturmbannführer*. Between September 1943 and March 1944, he commanded the *SS-Skijäger-Bataillon "Norge,"* before being transferred to command of the *SS-Gebirgsjäger-Regiment 11 Reinhard Heydrich* of the *SS Nord Division*. On January 21, 1944, he was also promoted to *Obersturmbannführer*. On June 13, 1944, he took command of *SS-Pz. Gren.Rgt. 48* of *Nederland*, but he did not arrive there until July.
6. Wilhelm Schlüter, born October 19, 1915, at Elmshorn in Holstein, SS Number 405 865.
7. Testimony published on November 30, 1944, in the newspaper *Das Schwarze Korps*, the official Waffen-SS newspaper.
8. The platoon to which soldiers who had committed infractions against the military code were assigned, for example for having disobeyed an order, and which was often used in dangerous missions or doing heavy labor in the rear area.
9. Derek Elsko Bruins was born on March 20, 1923, at Vlagtwedde in the province of Groningen in the Netherlands. In 1941, he enlisted as a volunteer in the Waffen-SS.

Chapter 6 Notes

1. The *6.SS Freiwilligen Sturmbrigade Langemarck* was constituted in May 1943, with veterans of the Flemish Legion, new volunteers from Flanders, a few Finnish volunteers, and Flemish veterans of the *Wiking* and *Das Reich* divisions. The unit, with a strength of about 1,700 men, was placed under the command of *SS-Obersturmbannführer* Konrad Schellong, former commander of the Flemish Legion. After having been deployed to the Ukraine, first to the east of Berdichev (December 1943) and in the area around Zhitomir and Jampol (January 1944), in April 1944 the *Langemarck* was transferred to Bohemia to be reorganized. During its stay in Bohemia, in early July 1944, an independent combat group was formed with Flemish volunteers, the *Kampfgrupe Rehmann*, to be employed on the Baltic front. The combat group was organized with four companies and placed under command of *SS-Hauptsturmführer* Rehmann. When it reached Estonia it was subordinated to *III.(Germanic) SS Corps*.
2. Lothar Hofer, born on September 18, 1914, at Rade, near Rensburg. Awarded the German Cross in Gold with the *SS Polizei Division*.
3. Fritz Bunse, born on July 4, 1911, at Hagen in Westphalia. He attended the *SS-Junkerschule* at Braunschweig in 1936, and in April 1937, was assigned to the engineer battalion of the SS-VT with the rank of *Untersturmführer*. In June 1941, he was promoted to *Hauptsturmführer* and was designated commander of *16./Pz.GR.9 "Germania"* of the *Wiking Division*. In January 1944, with the rank of *Sturmbannführer*, he assumed command of the *Nordland* engineer battalion. On January 30, 1944, he was awarded the Knight's Cross for his successful actions during the fighting in the Oranienbaum area.

Chapter 7 Notes

1. Léon Degrelle is undoubtedly the most famous of the foreign volunteers of the Waffen-SS, the only individual who beginning as a simple soldier who was then able to earn field promotions to all of the successive ranks in the military hierarchy until he became one of the most highly decorated volunteers in the entire German Army. Degrelle was born in 1906 at Bouillon, a small town in the Belgian Ardennes, to a family of French origin. After having studied at the University of Louvain he obtained a doctorate in law. After having joined the Belgian Catholic Action, he soon became its leader. His books and his newspaper soon earned much favorable public opinion, and in 1936 his party won thirty-four seats in the Senate. That victory enabled him to meet personalities such as Hitler, Mussolini and Churchill, while at the same time being subjected to the influence of the French nationalists led by Charles Maurrras, of Italian Fascism, and of German National Socialism. At the beginning of the war in 1939, Degrelle was arrested because of his sympathy for Hitler's National Socialism, and was held in prison for several weeks until he was freed by the Germans. In 1941, following the formation of a volunteer Wallonian unit for the Eastern Front, Degrelle, who was thirty-five years old, married, and had two children, joined up as a volunteer, encouraging another thousand Walloons to follow his example. In February 1942, Degrelle participated along with his Walloons in a hard-fought battle against the Soviets at Gromovaya–Balka, during which the Wallonian unit suffered heavy losses. For valor demonstrated in battle, Degrelle was promoted to lieutenant. During the following summer and autumn, the Walloons were engaged in the campaign in the Caucasus, earning the esteem of the German commanders and of Himmler himself, who began thinking of transferring the Walloons to his Waffen-SS, which did indeed occur in the summer of 1943. With the *5.SS-Freiwilligen-Sturmbrigade "Wallonien,"* Degrelle and his men were sent, in January 1944, to the Cherkassy sector, subordinate to the *SS Wiking Division*. During the hard fighting against Soviet forces, the Walloons again showed all of their valor following the death in combat of *SS-Sturmbannführer* Lucien Lippert, the brigade commander. Degrelle was called upon to replace Lippert as the brigade commander. Miraculously emerging alive from the Cherkassy pocket, Degrelle was personally presented with the Knight's Cross by Hitler himself.
2. Max Schäfer was born on January 17, 1907. From the outset he was an SS engineer; in June 1935, he was in fact assigned to *2.Kompanie* of the SS-VT engineer battalion. In 1941, he was assigned to the *Wiking Division*, first as a company commander and then as commander of the division's engineer battalion. On February 12, 1943, he was awarded the Knight's Cross as *SS-Ostubaf.* and as commander of the *SS-Pionier Bataillon 5* of *Wiking*. On January 25, 1945, he received the Oak Leaves as commander of the engineers (*Kps.Pi.Fhr.*) of *III. (germ.) SS-PzKorps*.

Chapter 8 Notes

1. Hanns Heinrich Lohmann, born on April 24, 1911, at Guetersloh. In January 1935 he joined the SS and was assigned to *IV.Bataillon* of the *SS-Standarte "Deutschland."* In May 1935, he was promoted to SS-*Untersturmführer* and was assigned to command a platoon of the SS-VT. On April 1, 1936, after a long convalescence following an accident, he was promoted to *SS-Obersturmführer* and assigned as supervisor at the *SS-Junkerschule* at Bad Tölz, where he also attended a course for officers. In February 1937, he was designated as adjutant to the school commander. Becoming a company commander in the *SS-Regiment Deutschland*, he was promoted to *SS-Hauptsturmführer* on November 9, 1938. After having served in Army ranks from 1939 until March 1940, he returned again to the *SS-Junkerschule* at Bad Tölz. On June 15, 1941, Lohmann assumed command of *2.Kompanie* of the *SS-Infanterie-Regiments (mot.) "Westland,"* with which he participated in the campaign in Russia subordinate to the *SS-Division "Wiking,"* which was deployed in the southern sector of the eastern front. Stricken by an attack of malaria, he was repatriated and did not return to the front until October 1942, when he assumed command of *I.Bataillon* of the *Nordland Regiment* of the *Wiking*, fighting in the Caucasus until Christmas of 1942. With the same regiment he was involved in covering the withdrawal of *Heeresgruppe A* from the Caucasus. In February 1943, he was awarded the German Cross in Gold and promoted to *Sturmbannführer*. In May 1943, the *Nordland* was detached from the *Wiking* and was upgraded to a division, where Lohmann assumed command of *III.Bataillon* of the new *"Norge" Regiment*. From August 1943, Lohmann was an instructor of tactics and strategy in Paris, and then returned to his *Norge Regiment*, with which he served in early 1944 on the Oranienbaum front. On February 2, 1944, while fighting in the area of Leningrad, he was seriously wounded during an air bombardment. On March 2, 1944, while still recuperating, he was awarded the Knight's Cross. Following his hospitalization at Bad Tölz, in the summer of 1944, he attended a course for regimental commanders and for two weeks assumed command of the *Wachtbataillon* of *Leibstandarte SS "Adolf Hitler."* At the end of October 1944, he returned to the front line to take command of *SS-Freiwilligen-Panzer-Grenadier-Regiment 49 "de Ruyter."*
2. Dirk Ayel Kooiman, "Montyn," 1982, pages 121, 125.
3. Klemens Behler, born on December 16, 1921, initially an artilleryman in the Leibstandarte and later in the *SS Polizei Division* (*III./SS-Art. Rgt.4*).

Chapter 9 Notes

1. Rudolf (Rudi) Klotz was born on October 2, 1913, at Ichenheim. He joined the SS in April 1933 (SS Number 112 350) in the *62.SS-Standarte*. In 1936, he attended the *Führerschule* at Braunschweig. On September 11, 1938, he was promoted to the rank of *Obersturmführer*, and on August 1, 1939, to the rank of *Hauptsturmführer*. During the Polish campaign, he was assigned to the *2.SS-Totenkopfstandarte* and on October 23, 1939, assumed command of *5./II./SS-Totenkopfstandarte*. In the following months he was assigned first to *12.SS-Totenkopfstandarte*, where he became commader of *4.Kompanie*. In 1941, he was assigned to the *Wiking Division* as commander of *8.Kompanie* of the *Nordland Regiment*. On June 21, 1943, he was promoted to the rank of *Sturmbannführer*. On November 14, 1944, he was awarded the German Cross in Gold as commander of *Kampfgruppe "Schill,"* formed with personnel from the *SS-Panzer-Grenadier-Schule "Kienschlag"* and the *SS-Panzer-Grenadier-Ausbildungs-und Ersatz Bataillon 10* at Brünn, during October 1944, to be employed in the repression of the revolt in Slovakia. Klotz replaced Hanns-Heinrich Lohmann as commander of the *SS-Freiwilligen-Panzer-Grenadier-Regiment 49 "de Ruyter"* during the month of March and early April when Lohmannn was wounded. He was then assigned in April to the *Danmark Regiment*, falling in combat at Strausberg on April 20, 1945.
2. Siegfried Scheibe was born on May 24, 1916, at Leipzig. At the beginning of the war he served in the *Wiking Division* where, until February 1942, he commanded the 11th Company of the *Germania Regiment*, before taking command of *I.Abteilung* of *Panzer Regiment 5* of the same division, until November of 1943. On June 14, 1942, he was awarded the German Cross in Gold. In the *Nordland Division* he commanded *II./Norge*. After being wounded in combat he was assigned as an instructor at the Hammerstein training area.
3. Heinz Hämel was born on October 25, 1914, at Obervellmar, SS Number 276 603. Awarded the Knight's Cross on June 16, 1944, as commander of *II./Danmark* of the *Nordland Division*. As happened with Scheibe, he was assigned as an instructor at the Hammerstein training area after having been wounded in combat.
4. Paul Massell was born on May 30, 1910, at Stolp in Pomerania, SS Number 261 914. Promoted to *Untersturmführer* on March 10, 1935, and to *Obersturmführer* on April 20, 1936. During the campaign in Poland in 1939 he commanded *7./Deutschland*. On January 30, 1942, he was promoted to *Sturmbannführer* and in March of that year

assumed command of the *Begleit Bataillon "RF-SS."* In November 1942, he assumed command of *I./Inf.Rgt.8.* On November 9, 1943, he was promoted to *Obersturmbannführer*. That same month he assumed command of *Stug. Abt. 5 (Wiking)*, and later to command of *Flak Abteilung 5 (Wiking)*. In 1944, he assumed command of *SS-Pz. Gren.Rgt. 10 (Westland)*.

5. R. Michaelis, *Die Panzergrenadier-Divisionen der Waffen-SS*, pages 196-197.
6. These were personnel of the *Offizierlehrgruppe Scheibe* and *Unterführer-Ausbildungs-Bataillon Hämel.*
7. P. Pierik, *From Leningrad to Berlin: Dutch Volunteers in the Service of the German Waffen-SS 1941–1945*, page 264.

Chapter 10 Notes

1. Werner Rehder was born on February 14, 1906, SS Number 10 424. In 1936, he served with *III./Deutschland.* In the summer of 1941, he was assigned to the supply unit (*Nachschub*) of the *Wiking*, and in November of that year was assigned to command *4./Aufklärungsabteilung* of *Totenkopf.* Around mid-1942, he returned to command of another supply unit, this time of *Heeresgruppe Nord.*
2. Tieke, *Ende zwischen Oder und Elbe*, pages 28-29.
3. Tieke, *Ende zwischen Oder und Elbe*, pages 28-29.
4. The division had been formed in October 1944, based on the earlier *547.Grenadier-Division*. The unit was completely destroyed in East Prussia in February 1945. It was then re-formed in March 1945 with units of the *Schatten-Division Hannover*.

Chapter 11 Notes

1. National Archive II, College Park, Maryland, Rg. 338 R-79, pages 37-38.
2. Konev, *Year of Victory*, Moscow, 1984, page 182.
3. In order to make their victory appear more impressive, the Soviets reported that Busse's forces in the Halbe Pocket numbered 200,000 men, with 300 tanks and 2,000 artillery pieces (Konev, op. cit., page 181).
4. Tieke, *Das Ende zwischen Oder und Elbe*, page 323.